A
SOCIAL GEOGRAPHY
OF EUROPE

by

J. M. HOUSTON, B.SC., M.A., D.PHIL.
University Lecturer in Geography, Oxford

GERALD DUCKWORTH & CO. LTD.
3 HENRIETTA STREET, LONDON, W.C.2

First published in 1953
All rights reserved

A6145

Printed in Great Britain by
The Camelot Press Ltd., London and Southampton

Date Due

A SOCIAL GEOGRAPHY OF EUROPE

I. Celtic Fields, Fyfield Down, Wilts.

II. Open Fields, Laxton, Notts.

To

MY PARENTS

CONTENTS

Part III

URBAN GEOGRAPHY

Part IV

POPULATION STUDIES

ILLUSTRATIONS

MAPS, PLANS AND DIAGRAMS

PREFACE

IT is significant that more public interest is now being taken in Human Geography. It is a subject in which all are concerned since it considers the use made of the world and of man's adaptations to it. At the same time, if human geography has become a specialised discipline, it is so because of the extreme complexity of its subject matter. Much of its content still remains perhaps a tangled undergrowth of knowledge. French geographers have been outstanding in their pioneer works to blaze the trail, but their studies have been often too systematised and hampered by strict allegiance to scientific analogy. Academic caution probably explains the lack of British textbooks on this difficult subject, but there seems some justification for a publication to be made in this field of work. This book is an attempt to summarise selectively the content of social geography as one branch of the more general subject of human geography.

Social geography is defined as the study of rural and urban settlements, together with population studies. Some geographers might wish to include other topics but lack of space has prohibited treatment of more material here. Economic and political geography are distinct disciplines within the general scope of human geography and have not been included in this work. The writer felt that the main contribution which can be made in social geography is not in seeking principles to be enunciated broadly, but by describing its specific features within a definite regional context. It is the opinion of the writer that social geography must be more associated with historical methods than with the enforced analogies of scientific laws. Present trends of thought among geographers seem to suggest this is likely to become more emphasised.

This book is the product of several years' research and teaching. It has been written primarily to serve the needs of students. Much modern literature exists which no student can be expected to cover completely in the short course of his training. This work is therefore an attempt to summarise the broad aspects of social geography, within the general framework of Europe. Perhaps no other continent has such a variety of forms of human occupance. Consequently, the material is admittedly introductory in character and selective of regional examples. More attention has been paid to those countries of Western Europe with which the author is personally familiar. Each chapter is sufficiently self-contained for specific study of any one topic.

In the production of this work, the writer has been indebted to many friends. The maps and diagrams have been drawn by Miss M. E. Potter, to whom the writer is deeply indebted. He acknowledges the kindness of the publishers and authors to reproduce maps mentioned in the text, especially to Professor Smith for Fig. 7, Mr. M. Wise for Figs. 38 and 39, Professor Gilbert for Fig. 40, and the Council of the Institute of British Geographers for Figs. 36 and 37. The photographic illustrations have been printed by kind permission of the owners mentioned below each photograph, but special thanks is due to the following persons who lent photographs: Mr. J. Bradford for Illustrations III and VI*b*, Mr. E. A. Gutkind for Illustrations VI*a* and X*b*, and to Miss D. Warriner for Illustrations VII*a*, *b*, *c*. The writer also wishes to record his gratitude for the kind and helpful criticisms made by his colleagues, Professor Evans-Pritchard, Dr. R. P. Beckinsale, and Messrs. J. N. L. Baker, A. F. Martin, E. Paget and C. G. Smith, who read some of the chapters. He is also much indebted to his old teacher Professor A. G. Ogilvie, his colleague Professor E. W. Gilbert, and his friend Mr. R. Aitken, who read most of the proofs and gave both encouragement and suggestions. To his wife, the writer owes his chief debt, in giving so much of her time in reading the proofs and in the preparation of the index.

JAMES M. HOUSTON.

OXFORD,
1953.

Part I

THE DEVELOPMENT AND SCOPE OF HUMAN GEOGRAPHY

CHAPTER ONE

THE DEVELOPMENT OF HUMAN GEOGRAPHY

IT is difficult, if not impossible, to understand the nature of geography without some knowledge of its development. Like other subjects, geography has developed only by the limitation of its content. As one of the oldest sciences, it claimed to be the study of all terrestrial phenomena; but such a sweeping assertion could only diminish its value as a discipline. The vast accumulation of knowledge gained by discovery and exploration of other lands, especially during the sixteenth and seventeenth centuries, provided more material than any one branch of science could adequately digest. Even at the end of the sixteenth century Richard Hakluyt, 'the father of English geography,' had found it an immense task to collate into three volumes his history of *The Principle Navigations, Voyages, Traffics and Discoveries of the English Nation.*

The Changing Outlook of Geographical Thought

By the end of the eighteenth century, other factors were responsible for the recasting of much of its encyclopaedic data. The vigorous development of new subjects, such as meteorology and geology, established a basis for more detailed investigation of the earth, including the atmosphere. The *Traité de Météorologie* of Louis Cotte (1774) and the *Meteorological Observations and Essays* of John Galton (1793) laid the foundations for systematic observation in this field of study. James Hutton's *Theory of the Earth* (1785) and the subsequent work of Playfair and others established a framework for physical geography. Also, the refinement of cartographical methods and the completion of the first national topographical survey (that of France in 1793) provided a suitably accurate basis for detailed regional investigation. Meanwhile, the first contoured chart, of the English Channel, had been made by Philip Buache (1737) and the first contoured map of France was published by Dupain Triel (1791). All these achievements of the eighteenth century contributed to the subsequent birth of modern geography in the nineteenth century.

The identification of geography with the natural and the social sciences was the beginning of its modern development. If the late eighteenth century saw the rapid establishment of systematic studies in the physical sciences, it was also the Age of Humanism. Hence the role of man in a created universe lent new dignity to the subject matter of geography. This emphasis of man in a physical universe was not a new conception. In the seventeenth century, Varenius (1620-80) had considered this to underlie the unity of geography,[1] but it was left to geographers at the end of the eighteenth and early nineteenth centuries to develop this theme. Geography came into its own, therefore, as a 'bridge science,' inspired by the current philosophical theories of Kant and other philosophers and based on the scientific discoveries of the eighteenth century. As the 'go-between' of the natural and social sciences, the special position of geography has made it more sensitive to methodological discussion.

During the changing outlooks of the last century and a half, geography has gone through several phases of varying emphasis. Indeed, it is difficult to outline these phases both historically and systematically. At the end of the eighteenth century, although natural theology was still a popular explanation of this planet, Hume had prepared the way for its dismissal. Empiricism now took the place of metaphysics and the need for a systematic classification of the observable phenomena of the earth was appreciated, in order to consolidate the findings of science. Moreover, the role of man in a created world, of a cosmos as opposed to a chaos of chance, implied a teleological view of final causes. In varying degrees geographers upheld these requirements, to provide the subject with both a scientific basis and a philosophical outlook.

The year 1859 may be taken to mark conveniently the beginning of a new era in geography, since in that year Darwin published his *Origin of Species*. Although ideas of evolution had been expressed previously by thinkers such as Kant, Lamarck and Buffon, Darwinian evolution marks a break with the past. The doctrines of progress which followed have been so influential that we sometimes fail to realise how they have coloured even objective thought. Their influence on geography was soon felt. As W. M. Davis pointed out, 'since the establishment of the philosophy of evolution, the explanatory treatment of geographical problems has been steadily gaining ground; and now the conviction is widespread that the real meaning of geographic facts can be appreciated only when complicated enchainments of cause and effect, of controlling environment and responding mechanism is accounted for. It is in large measure this conviction that has given so much prominence to physical geography in recent years.'[2] Although this idea of progress provided a stimulus to physical geography, it tended to vitiate human geography with a false bias of crude determinism. Since then, attempts have been made to make determinism more 'scientific' and less open to factual criticism, but it is still dangerous to confuse the biological theory of evolution with a doctrine of progress in society. Insofar as the geographer considers man in relation to environment, he must join issue with this philosophy. Reactions against such views make it clear that deductions based on *a priori* principles tend to be suspect.

Humboldt and Ritter

The changing views of geographical thought are best appreciated by an understanding of the personal achievements of pioneer geographers. Alexander von Humboldt (1769-1859) and Carl Ritter (1779-1859) are generally recognised to be the founders of modern geography. They represent what might be called the first phase of systematic geography, or the classical period. Humboldt, in his travels through Europe, Asia, and the Americas, was motivated by 'the earnest endeavour to comprehend the phenomena of physical objects in their general connection, and to represent nature as one great whole, moved by internal forces.'[3] His use of comparative methods and the study of physical correlations provided the basis for his summary of geography in *Cosmos; a Sketch of the Physical Description of the Universe* (1844) published in three volumes. This task of correlation, rather than the mere compilation of data, was an exhausting one which was only possible because of his accomplishments in mineralogy, geophysics, botany and related subjects. Whether he studied geology, meteorology or biology, he accepted their disciplines to take up the further task of their correlation. By his example, he showed that geographical analysis was no short-cut to Science. Nor did he let philosophical speculations confuse his view of the nature and purpose of geography. As he maintained, 'I limit myself to the domain of empirical ideas. Facts remain ever the same when the hastily erected edifice of theory has long fallen into ruins. I have always kept my facts distinct from my conjectures. This method of dealing with the phenomenon of nature appears to me to be the one best grounded and most likely to succeed.'[4]

While Humboldt elaborated the physical basis of systematic geography and elucidated the regional method of empirical analysis, his contemporary and friend Ritter approached the subject with an interest in history. Ritter concerned himself with 'the delineation of comparative geography, drawn in its full extent, and in all its relations with the history of man.' His first concern had been to understand the details of the earth in order to appreciate more clearly the drama of its human history. Subsequently, he became absorbed in geography rather than history. By his immense work on the continents, the *Erdkunde* (Africa 1817, Asia 1818), he established himself as the master of academic geography. He combined a rigid scientific outlook for accuracy with a philosophical view of the purpose and unique position of man, on a unique planet. He defined geography as 'the department of science that deals with the globe in all its features, phenomena and relations, as an independent unit, and shows the connections of this unified whole with man and man's Creator.'[5] Much has been said about the mystical views of natural theology scattered throughout his works, but it is only fair to realise that he expressed such views on problems that the science of his day could not answer. They were no less objective than those of many evolutionists in a subsequent period.

Although writers emphasised the difference in outlook between Humboldt and Ritter—even comparing the rather pantheistic views of the former with the theological beliefs of the latter—their similarities of thought are much more apparent. Both emphasised the totality of the earth's phenomena, the individuality of each continent and the uniqueness of each region. Both were interested in human geography and considered 'the highest goal of all observation of nature is the knowledge of our own nature: and therefore we conclude our description with a consideration of the races of men.'[6]

Geography in the Mid-nineteenth Century

In the period that followed the deaths of these two men, more emphasis was given to physical geography. In Germany, this was partly a reaction against Ritter's mystical interpretation of the earth as the nursery of mankind. More important, the findings of geology were beginning to provide rich gains for physical geography. Ferdinand von Richthofen (1833-1905) integrated the work of previous geologists in China and became the founder of geomorphology. In this country the work of Lyell, Ramsay and Geikie made physical geography a subject of educational prestige. As we have noted above, the theory of organic evolution was a further stimulus to the rapid expansion of physical geography. William Morris Davis seized on the evolutionary analogy in his concept of the erosion cycle. As he explained, 'the evolution of the earth and the evolution of organic forms are doctrines that have reinforced each other; the full meaning of both is gained only when one is seen to furnish the inorganic environment and the other to exemplify the organic response.'[7]

The older school of geographers had marvelled at the adaptations of the earth to man; after the mid-nineteenth century, the evolutionists concentrated on the way in which man had adapted himself to the earth. In these views the lead came from the sociologists, such as Pierre F. G. Leplay (1806-82) and his two disciples Henri de Tourville and Edmond Demolins. Leplay is best known for his work *Les Ouvriers Européens* (6 vols., 1855), in which he defined the primary constituents of society in terms of 'Place, Folk and Work.' His theory of *place* determining the *work*, and the work shaping the social organisation, the *folk*, provided a useful basis for civic and rural surveys. He created a systematic method of analysis of social data which could be applied for practical improvements, and this aspect of Leplay's influence is still useful in the researches of town and country planning.[8] But the dogmatic assertions made by some of his disciples in the understanding of past societies have not been taken so seriously. In his work, *Comment la route crée le type social* (2 vols., 1907), Demolins asserted, 'it is the route which creates both the race and the social type.' Indeed, if history repeated itself, he argued, it would invariably follow the same dictates of the environment. By such views, Demolins and other determinists ignored the factors of heredity and race. Their sociological views were over-simplified by taking the family unit as the basis of study and ignoring the other more complicated elements of social organisation.

While such sociologists impinged on the field of geography, the subject of human geography was itself suffering various setbacks, especially the unfortunate division of geographical knowledge into 'physical geography' and 'academic' or 'classical geography.' This divorce and the vigorous growth of sociology might have caused the elimination of human geography in the latter half of the nineteenth century. It is to the credit of Friedrich Ratzel (1844-1904) that he sought to systematise the subject on a scientific basis. He antagonised many social scientists, however, both by the wide scope he gave to the subject of human geography and by the materialistic explanations in his studies. Ratzel set out to prove that man was a product of the earth's surface, determined by physical laws which could be enunciated. His great work, *Anthropogeographie oder Grundzüge der Anwendung der Erdkunde auf die Geschichte* (1882), attempted to systematise such views. He was concerned not with the anthropological features of man, as the title of his book might suggest, but with the works of man. The first volume outlined the physical conditions in relation to human culture, with the sub-title, *Fundamentals of the application of geography to history*. In 1891, the second volume reversed the treatment with the sub-title, *The geographical distribution of man*. His training had been in zoology and allied sciences and in his studies he attempted to establish human geography on a scientific basis. A development of his views was published in a subsequent work, *Politische Geographie* (1897), a treatise on the natural laws determining the growth, organisation and decline of political units.

The analogy of the state as an organism occupying a definable area or *raum* was to be the basis for the propaganda views of the later German school of geopolitics with its demands for *Lebensraum*. Ellen Churchill Semple eliminated these evolutionary concepts of political organisation in her work, although she accepted the general views of environmental determinism. Her two books, *Influences of Geographic Environment on the Basis of Ratzel's system of Anthropogeography* (1911) and *American History and Its Geographic Conditions* (1913) were a more cautious summary of Ratzel's treatises. Although these works were scholarly, their *a priori* reasoning led them into a false position which discredited the validity of their observations. Too often the principle of geographic influence was, to quote one critic, 'glibly enunciated, superficially exploited and compelled to support conclusions without adequate inductive material and in disregard of other types of causation.'[9] However, it is only fair that full recognition be paid to Ratzel. He re-emphasised the importance of man as a worthy object of geographical study and he attempted to systematise the content of human geography.

Development of Geography in the Twentieth Century

As we have seen, the end of the nineteenth century was marked by confusion in geographical thought. The disparity of development between physical and human geography was such that in Germany, for example, the latter was scarcely taught until Ratzel made his outstanding contribution to human geography. The crude determinism and the mechanical interpretations of the subject were other weaknesses. Determinism, as propounded by Ratzel and his followers, was not wholly accepted, however, by their contemporaries. O. Schlüter in particular denied such an emphasis in his work, *Die Ziele der Geographie des Menschen* (1906). Schlüter emphasised the cultural features of the landscape and he is best known for his studies in rural settlement.

At the beginning of this century it was difficult to find much unity in national schools of geography apart from the work of physical geographers. In Germany and France, however, two outstanding leaders gathered a wide following, Alfred Hettner (1859-1942) and Paul Vidal de la Blache (1854-1918). The methodological papers published by Hettner and his work *Die Geographie—ihre Geschichte, ihr Wesen, und ihre Methoden* (1927) sought to keep the balance between the study of man and of his environment by the emphasis on regional geography. Hettner insisted that the delimitation and description of regions was the primary object of geographical research. It was on this basis that some of the most outstanding contributions have been made by German geographers, such as the regional writings of Alfred Philippson on the Mediterranean and Siegfried Passarge on the Kalahari. Hettner's influence is also apparent in the work of geographers outside Germany such as Chisholm and Herbertson in Britain, Michotte in Belgium, Cvijic in the Balkans and Marinelli and Almagia in Italy—all of whom have contributed much to human geography within a regional framework.

While Hettner has thus influenced much regional study by his methodological writings, Vidal de la Blache founded a French school of geographers by his own regional studies. Like Hettner, he believed in the essential unity of geography and affirmed 'human geography does not stand in contrast to a geography from which the human element is excluded; the latter has not existed except in the minds of a few exclusive specialists.'[10] On the sound basis of regional differentiation, he sought a balanced view of the value of physical studies, not as an explanation of history but as the complex influence always to be kept in mind in the study of history. He considered it essential for the geographer to have a thorough grounding in geology and from that basis to make detailed regional studies. He inspired, in this way, a series of brilliant regional monographs of France made by his disciples. His own *Tableau de la Géographie de la France* (1903) is the classic exposition of regional description. He also considered a knowledge of history essential to the geographer and compiled an *Atlas of Historical Geography* (1894). After his death his lectures were published under the title, *Principles de Géographie Humaine* (1921), a study which is a model of balanced reasoning and deduction. To Vidal de la Blache, man in his regional environment is the central object of geography, the voluntary agent who chooses one of a series of possibilities offered him by his environment. The social and historical factors thus play the decisive role in the complex interactions of physical and human conditions.

One of the most brilliant of Vidal de la Blache's disciples, Jean Brunhes (1869-1930), occupied the first chair to be established in human geography in France. In following the French 'possibilist' school, he narrowed the scope of this subject in his work, *La Géographie Humaine* (1911). He enumerated what he called 'the essential facts,' the evidences of human action on the earth's surface, including man's social, economic and political activities. He reacted against vague metaphysical views of human geography, and divided the subject into a study of three groups of 'essential facts':

(1) Facts of unproductive occupation of the land, such as settlements and communications.

(2) Facts of vegetable and animal conquest, viz. cultivation and stock-raising.

(3) Facts of destructive economies, such as mining, deforestation, etc.

In assembling these data, much of his work was based on personal field studies. In his travels through Spain, North Africa, Palestine and the Caucasus, Brunhes had been struck particularly by the variety of types of settlements and houses. The influences of the environment on such features of human occupation are clearly more apparent in some regions than in others. Thus Brunhes stressed the relativity of geographical controls,[11] which he expressed in the following dictum: 'Between the facts of the physical order there are sometimes relations of causality; between facts of human geography (geographical conditions and social phenomena) there are usually only relations of connection.'[12] He thus argued that it was essential to distinguish between relations of causality and relations of connection. In his book *L'Irrigation dans la Peninsule Ibérique et dans l'Afrique du Nord* (1902), he distinguishes therefore between the causal relations of aridity and steppe on the one hand, and the complicated systems of irrigation that comprise relationships of connection on the other hand.

The emphasis given by Brunhes and Passarge on the analysis of the cultural elements of the landscape has tended to insist that geography is the science of the land and not of man. This view developed by Carl O. Sauer[13] in America has done much to narrow the subject matter of such geographers and so make it a more respected discipline. In contrast, a second and less consolidated group of geographers have emphasised man's regional activities and relationships with his environment. More emphasis is given to man himself, and consequently their field impinges closely on the other social sciences. Such is the work of Barrows in his study of human ecology,[14] a concept first developed by Haeckel in 1863 as an adaptation of evolutionary philosophy. Barrows attempted to solve the dualism of geography by the virtual elimination of physical geography, since to him geography was essentially human geography. Ellsworth Huntington (1876-1950) elaborated the climatic relationships of man, influencing his efficiency of production, his mental powers and the history of civilisation, in his works, *World Power and Evolution, The Character of Races* and *Civilisation and Climate*. To him, 'the pinnacle of geography is reached when we are able to explain why certain types of human character, certain manifestations of genius, and hence certain lines of progress and stages of civilisation are localised in various parts of the world.'[15] The principles of selection and correlation of climatic data in support of evolutionary philosophy provide the basis for his thesis. Huntington's correlations, though stimulating, have not been widely accepted, since his deductions cannot be a simple process of direct causation. Correlations of civilisation and climate cannot belong to a simple A and B relation, but a broad generalisation between A and Z. Consequently there are many 'missing links' in the evidence.

Between these two approaches to human geography, the one emphasising the analysis of the cultural activities of man as they affect the earth's surface, and the other the human relations with the environment, there have developed the more cautious views of other geographers, notably Albert Demangeon (1872-1940). Like Vidal de la Blache, he stressed that human geography must be based on physical regional units, and he demonstrated in his monograph on Picardy how this could be done. He also emphasised the importance of historical enquiry about what directly affects the present features of a region. In his detailed studies of the distribution and types of rural settlements he shows himself as familiar with the local archives as with the landscape. He also followed Vidal de la Blache in his emphasis on the modes of life within each environment. On this basis he studied human geography under four headings: the modes of life in the broad climatic zones of the world; the techniques employed, such as hunting, fishing, agriculture and commerce; the distribution, density and limits of population and their migration; and the types of rural and urban settlement. His collected essays published post-humously under the title *Problèmes de Géographie Humaine* illustrate all four aspects.

Descriptive studies of the modes of life received added interest in the work of Isaiah Bowman (1879-1950). He developed the concept of the *Pioneer Fringe* and assessed the limits of colonisation and settlement. 'It is on the edge of the inhabited lands,' he argued, 'that we have long seen most clearly the challenge of mankind to nature.'[16] This he elaborated in his study *The Pioneer Fringe* and paralleled in his editorship of *Pioneer Settlement*. Bowman was aware that such regions of the world would change from the local sphere of individual effort to that of national policy, so that a geographic analysis of such regions could give guidance to the statesman. The practical application of geography to high-level policy is amply demonstrated in his own activities within national and international councils. His work, *The New World*, is an excellent example of how sound political geography should be written, and what contribution geographers can make to the study of international affairs.

Development of Specialisms in Human Geography

This outline of personalities in human geography and their contribution to the making of the subject would be incomplete without a summary of the development of some of its branches. In a paper published in 1930, Professor Roxby divided human geography into four aspects: racial, social, economic and political.[17] The first is very much the field of anthropology and few geographers now consider it to lie within their province, although Professors H. J. Fleure and R. Biasutti have made notable contributions to this marginal subject. Social Geography is accepted by all, although the definition and scope of the subject is still a controversial issue. Economic and Political Geography have become more distinctly recognised, though as yet neither can be said to have differentiated itself as a separate discipline. It is often difficult to distinguish those geographical phenomena which may be of social, economic or political significance to man; consequently no hard-and-fast division can be made.

The term 'Social Geography' was first used by Camille Vallaux in his work, *Géographie Sociale: La Mer* (1908), as an alternative title to 'Human Geography.' The term is still used in this sense by many geographers. But the growth of the content of the subject makes it desirable to distinguish it more exactly from the general content of human geography. Recently, it has been suggested that the term should be confined to the following topics: the distribution and limits of population, migration and change; the study of rural settlements and field systems; and urban geography.[18]

In the study of the distribution of population, the work of Vidal de la Blache was one of the earliest. He demonstrated that the study of the distribution of man was essentially a geographical study and without it we could have no adequate basis for the relations of man to his habitat.[19] In this country, pioneer work in this field was done by Sir Charles Close and Professor C. B. Fawcett. Regional studies of population distribution, inspired by such research as that of Sten de Geer in Sweden, have now assumed great importance. The studies of the limits of settlement, the estimates of optimum population for given resources and the displacements of population since the war have all increased the significance of this aspect of study.

Two related but distinct subjects are rural and urban geography. A commission set up by the International Geographical Union to deal with rural settlement problems published its first report in 1928. A considerable literature now exists on the origin, structure and patterns of rural settlement, inspired notably by the work of A. Demangeon, M. A. Lefèvre and R. Dion, among others. In recent years, attention has been paid to the character and origin of field patterns, especially in the Low Countries and Germany. In urban geography, R. Blanchard led the way in his systematic study of Grenoble, followed subsequently by H. J. Fleure, J. B. Leighley, R. E. Dickinson and a number of others, particularly German geographers. Each of these topics has become a specialism in itself although closely associated with other social sciences.

Compared with social geography, economic geography has apparently a more unified field of study. It has been the most voluble of the branches of geography, although much that passes under this name has not always contributed to its discipline. The ubiquity of its material has caused considerable confusion so that 'at its best economic geography approaches the quintessence of social understanding, at its worst it is shallow and dangerous pedantry.'[20] Since it was first defined in 1882, geographers such as G. G. Chisholm and J. Russell Smith were aware of the need to relate this subject closely with economic theory. In more recent years Lord Stamp has urged the same thing. But the abstractions of economic theory and the immaturity of economic geography have kept them apart and economists have not been much impressed with the contribution of the latter subject.[21] Recently, however, economists have become more conscious of the need to understand their principles within a regional setting and so a *rapprochement* with geographic treatment appears possible.[22] Two recent economists have shown the way in notable works: H. H. McCarty's *The Geographic Basis of American Economic Life*, and Colin Clarke's *The Conditions of Economic Progress*. The wide scope of the field covered by economic geography has caused a branching out into various topics. For a time, 'commercial geography' was much in vogue, reflecting the expansion of the now outdated free trade policy. Production and transport continued to be important topics of the subject, with an emphasis on the regional problems of economic units. The principles of the location of industry are still incompletely formulated, and much remains to be learnt on this subject.

Political geography has been called 'the wayward child of the geographical family,' and in view of the explosive character of its material, this is not surprising. In origin, the term dates from Ratzel's *Politische Geographie*, already mentioned. The idea, however, goes back to the Greeks and to the views expressed by Bodin and Montesquieu. But it is only since politics ceased to be dynastic and developed into nationalistic expression that the political sciences could be established. The publication of Mahan's sensational *Influence of Sea-Power on History, 1660–1783* did much to focus attention on strategy and thus on geography at the end of the nineteenth century. However, a perverted view of political geography has been gradually developed by the German school of geopolitics, led by Karl Haushofer.[23] These geographers abused their academic position by unscholarly propaganda. They left the field of objective investigation and expanded into the realm of political metaphysics. The highest ideal of political geography to-day is as a training in world citizenship and the highest patriotism must be to insist on objective judgements.

To think objectively must be the chief aim of political geography. As such, the subject has been developed in three ways. The most numerous publications consist of studies of frontiers and boundary changes. In the existing tensions of boundary demarcations this topic is of great importance. The recent studies on this subject indicate the practical contributions which geographers can make on boundary commissions. A second approach in political geography is by the regional understanding of the country concerned, in its historical setting. This has been ably developed in works such as Ancel's *Manuel Géographie de Politique Européen*. Thirdly, the study of the resources and strategy of states is another approach to political geography. Bowman, in his comprehensive study *The New World*, after the First World War, Fitzgerald in his more recent book *The New Europe*, and East in his study of the Mediterranean exemplify this approach. The dualism of the state, its internal resources and its international relations, can be defined only in terms of its strategy. This is further complicated by the bewildering change of the subject matter, so that such surveys soon become historical documents in themselves.

This brief outline indicates the great strides which have been made in the study of geography since the early days of the nineteenth century. But the purpose of geography remains the same, though it may have assumed a more respectable academic position. It seeks to correlate and integrate the relationship of man and his world. In doing so, it is going against the tide of modern thought which tends to divide knowledge into ever smaller departments of specialism. In the resultant detail of analytic thought, geography can assume for itself a very important role in education. Provided its discipline is scientific, it is needless to ask whether it is an art or a science, since it is a co-ordinator of both.

SELECTED REFERENCES

Brunhes, Jean. *La géographie humaine*. Paris 1910; translated as *Human Geography* —latest edition. London, 1947.
Clozier, R. *Les Étapes de la Géographie*. Paris, 1949, chs. VII, VIII.
Crone, G. R. *Modern Geographers*. London, 1952.

Hartshorne, Richard. *The Nature of Geography*. Lancaster (Pa.), 1939; 2nd printing 1948.

Hettner, A. *Die Geographie—ihre Geschichte, ihr Wesen, und ihre Methoden*. Breslau, 1927.

Howarth, O., and Dickinson, R. E. *The Making of Geography*. Oxford, 1933.

Roxby, P. M. 'The Scope and Aims of Human Geography,' S.G.M., 46, 1930, pp. 276-89.

Sauer, Carl. 'Cultural Geography,' article in *Encyclopaedia of Social Sciences*, 6, 1931, pp. 621-23.

Taylor, Griffith. (Edit.). *Geography in the Twentieth Century*. London, 1951, especially Chapter Two.

Vidal de la Blache, P. *Principles de géographie humaine*. Edit. by Emm. de Martonne. Paris 1921. Translated by M. T. Bingham as *Principles of Human Geography*, 1926.

Wooldridge, S. W., and East, W. G. *The Spirit and Purpose of Geography*. London, 1951.

CHAPTER TWO

GEOGRAPHY AND THE SOCIAL SCIENCES

GEOGRAPHY is essentially a correlative science and it could not properly come into its own until the need for the integration of the physical and social sciences was more fully recognised. In the nineteenth century some geographers, such as Gerland, sought to remove all human elements from the content of their subject. More recently Barrows took the opposite viewpoint and attempted to create a subject in which the 'geo' was virtually absent.[1] Both extremes are false, since the basis of geography is the bridging of the physical and social sciences into one discipline. To maintain the old distinction of physical and human geography is to support a false dichotomy and to destroy the very *raison d'être* of the subject. In view of this the question may be asked what then is human geography? It differs only in emphasis rather than in kind from physical geography.

The teleological outlook of most of the great geographers in the last century made modern geography possible, but the present need for the integration of knowledge makes geography an educational necessity. The role of co-ordinator is not a distinctive feature of geography alone, although the subject attempts to fulfil this function more consciously than many others. Geography has not a field of facts exclusive to its use, neither has it the monopoly of certain principles, such as that of areal differentiation. Its distinctive contribution is that it seeks to correlate the findings of the sciences of the earth's surface with the needs and activities of man. Geography is concerned therefore with a plane of thought which is tangential to the physical and social sciences. As Brunhes has asked, 'in what measure is spiritual co-ordination a function of material co-ordination and in what measure has the material control of the spiritual?'[2] In attempting to answer this fundamental problem, geography suffers from a number of tensions not apparent to the same extent in other subjects. In the first place, too much emphasis on one branch of its subject matter destroys its object. If the physical aspects of geography are considered exclusively, it is splintered into a series of subjects such as geomorphology, climatology and plant geography; but these must be servants not masters of geographic thought. Alternatively, with undue emphasis on the social aspects, to the detriment of a sound appreciation of the physical habitat, the subject degenerates into a shallow superficiality of unproved generalisations. It is tempting to seek repose in the emphasis of one or other of these alternatives.

It is the welding together of the physical and social aspects of the earth's surface in a chorographical setting that gives geography its intrinsic value. But it is in this essential unity of geography that another tension arises, for there is a disparity in the development and status of its branches. The analytical method, so successfully adopted by the physical sciences for the last three hundred years, is responsible for the rich gains made by them. In the social sciences, however, systematic analysis is less practicable and the progress made has been much slower, in view of the greater complexities and multiple planes of reality with which they deal. Thus it is a mark of our age that the progress of the physical sciences has far outstripped that of the social sciences. The peculiar position of geography in this respect makes it thus most sensitive to this disparity. Moreover, the variety of tools used and the approaches taken in each branch of geography are so different that few persons to-day can be considered complete geographers.

Apart from these internal tensions, the geographer has also to contend with external difficulties. In studying the 'existence together' of phenomena which other sciences isolate and study separately, the geographer goes against the drift of modern thought. In view of this, geography has often been called a 'robber science.' But those who libel the subject in this manner forget that few subjects have an exclusive field of facts. Among social sciences the distinguishing feature is not the material with which each science may deal—for man is the subject of them all—but their distinct point of view. In geography, man is not only a subject of study but, as an agent of the habitat, the most powerful factor in the changing landscape. For man, in making history on the earth, has also made a great deal of geography. Thus the geographer seeks to integrate on the horizontal plane or spatial scale what the historian does on the vertical plane or time scale.

However, just as all history cannot be interpreted in terms of economic history, so we are reminded, 'it is not *Homo oeconomicus* who has transformed the earth in order to live; it is man in his entirety, with his desire of better well-being, but also with all he has within him of the social and religious.'[3] These two aspects of study, man as an agent of the habitat, and the nature of his agency, indicate that the geographer studies man from a different point of view than the social scientist, and yet approaches closely to his subject material. Ethnology and sociology make closest contact with the field of geography and so their subject matter and distinctive aims will be treated now in more detail.

Geography and Ethnology

Of the social sciences, ethnology comes nearest to the point of view of geography, and so it is important to distinguish the aims of these two. Attempts have been made to combine studies of both subjects, notably in the recent periodical *Revue de Géographie Humaine et d'Ethnologie*, because of their comparable interests. Ethnology has not the same interest in Europe that it once had, when regionalist movements were fostered and their adjunct study of folklore stimulated more general interest. Also, social anthropologists have stolen much of the thunder in their study of primitive societies. Some may think that for these reasons the future of ethnology lies more with geography than with anthropology, but to fix the margins of ethnology and geography will do neither subject any good, creating both uncertainty of method and confusion of aim.

In the nineteenth century, the terms 'ethnology' and 'anthropology' were used almost interchangeably. They diverged when the emphasis on the former became comparative technology, and on the latter comparative sociology. To-day, they study the same field of facts but they have parted company and their theories have only limited significance to each other. The task of the ethnologist is to classify people on the basis of their racial and cultural characteristics, to explain their features historically by the study of the movements of peoples and by the diffusion of cultures, and to supplement by circumstantial evidence the many missing links of proto-history, or the unrecorded past. The task of the anthropologist, on the other hand, is quite different. He studies social behaviour in institutionalised forms and the relations between such institutions.[4] Since the geographer is not interested in man *per se* but as the agent of his environment, his interest will come much closer to that of the ethnologist than to that of the anthropologist. Because the ethnologist has so little historical material provided in recorded form, he seeks to supplement much of his missing data by the circumstantial evidence

c

of the environment. But in so doing, he begins with presuppositions on the problem of resemblances which are so varied that they have rent the subject into many rival schools of thought. One diverse group of ethnologists has emphasised the uninventiveness of man and the facility with which ideas have spread from certain cultural regions; Elliot-Smith went so far as to see culture having all its origins in Egypt.[5] Some geographers have taken the view which Vidal de la Blache expressed in his own belief: 'Man is a being of habit more than of initiative.'[6] Other ethnological schools have emphasised multiple inventions, rising spontaneously and independently from the inevitability of evolutionary progress. Criticism of the validity of such evolutionary theories in society is no longer required. As it has been pointed out, 'People do not live at economic stages. They possess economies; and again, we do not find simple and exclusive economies but combinations of them. Development is not in one direction along a single line and some economies have played almost no part in the historical growth of particular cultures.'[7]

The view of history, which the ethnologist and the geographer would take, appears at first sight comparable. Both obtain most of their data of the past, not from documentary evidence, although this is valuable when it can be secured, but from indirect observation and deduction. But while the ethnologist sees in the present all the past, the geographer in studying the present finds much to illustrate his understanding of it from the heritage of the past. As a science of the present, geography is not therefore occupied with evolutionary obscurities nor with speculations of origins. Both these topics obsessed many thinkers after the publication of Darwin's *Origin of Species* and this still accounts in part for the ethnologist's interest in them, as the historian of primitive peoples.

The viewpoint of the geographer differs in a second way from that of the ethnologist. The preoccupation of the ethnologist with cultures and techniques means that his study is essentially analytical, whether in tracing, for example, the evolution of the plough or the cart. The geographer is not interested primarily in the instruments of human effort in themselves, but examines the results of the human agency, the yield of crops per acre, the density of stock or the production of minerals.[8] Also in his study of the region, the geographer perceives wholes and the relationship between them. Thus he studies the *araire* or *charrue* and their relation to the field patterns, the systems of land use and the nucleation or dissemination of settlement. He sees in a map of house-types, not only the variations of architectural forms in themselves, but the coincidence of certain limits with physical barriers or other regional features.

Finally, the geographer differs in his attitude to the explanation of phenomena. The intellectual attitude of the ethnologist is to explain phenomena by reference to man himself, that of the geographer by environment. Most geographers are agreed that it is landscape and not man that must be the central object of their study.[9] The subjects can best help each other not by trespassing on their neighbour's property but by remaining on neighbourly terms. Since ethnology rests uneasily between an uncertain history or proto-history and geography, its indebtedness to geography will lie chiefly in three directions.

A clear analysis of regional features, and an appraisal of the most significant factor within a region, will provide the ethnologist with a sure foundation on which to construct his historical speculations. For example, the implications of the Mediterranean drought in summer, or the length of the growing season in Finland, provide such material consideration to the ethnologist. Secondly, an understanding of the natural routeways of the world and their precise distribution, whether the sea currents and winds of the Mediterranean, or the passes of the Alps and Carpathians, or the routeways across Central Asia, provides basic data for any study of the migration of peoples, cultures or ideas. Thirdly, the delimitation of boundaries and the evaluation of their conflicts is also fundamental. Thus in the western Pyrenean foothills, ethnologists have outlined the limits of the Basque language, the types of houses and other cultural features which the geographer can correlate more accurately in terms of contour lines and isohyets (Fig. 18). In such ways, the geographer can contribute to ethnology without obscuring the vision of his own field of research. What Daryll Forde said in 1925 still remains true: 'Detailed investigation of processes, accuracy in definition and terminology, and comparative work on a world-wide scale will do much to harmonise the results of the human geographer with those of the ethnologist, and both will gain in knowledge and mutual respect.'[10]

Geography and Sociology

It is in the province of sociology that the relations of geography are much more confused and uncertain. This is because sociology professes to belong as much to natural science as to philosophy and history, and to embrace anthropology, economics, history, human geography, jurisprudence, philology, political science, psychology and comparative theology. If ever the geographer feels depressed by the scope of his own subject, he need only compare the tiny plot of his material with the prairie lands of sociology to gain reassurance.

Sociology was the child of the Age of Enlightenment, contributed by French thinkers such as Bodin, Montesquieu and Rousseau and by Scots empiricists such as Hume and Adam Smith. It began as a social ferment, and Auguste Comte, the positivist philosopher who sought to systematise the subject, did so in the grand manner. He and later social thinkers attempted to compress all social reality into the Procrustean bed of natural science. A recent sociologist maintains that 'A science of society can only be achieved by modelling its methods upon the procedures of the physical sciences. . . . It is, I fear, a case of social science or no social knowledge at all.'[11] Thus the theories of many sociologists are still based on analogies drawn from physics and biology: from physics so that the environmental influences may be analysed in terms of cause and effect; and from biology so that the behaviour of societies might be studied as organisms involved in an evolutionary progression. It is therefore considered possible to enunciate a series of laws in terms of order and progress. On a pyramidal structure has been built a three-tiered system of human ecology (the study of relations in environment—function—human organisms), of demography (the study of quantitative averages by social groups) and of biology (the influence of race and the physical traits of man). Crowning all is a 'social morphology' which comprises a whole series of subjects dealing with social behaviour, institutions and the activities of man in town and country.

Human Ecology

Disciplines, whether in the sciences or humanities, have progressed because they realised their limitations, making no pretensions to an attainment of absolute reality; but much confusion has arisen in sociology and its relations to allied subjects, because it has assumed itself to be more than a partial understanding of social phenomena. Thus Bews in his outline of human ecology concludes his subject to be a science with its own special technique, a philosophy and an art.[12] Such efforts after holism may be worthy aspirations but they do not advance very far and the subject has not achieved much academic distinction. It has been suggested that the popularity of human ecology in America may itself be nothing more than the influence of an urban environment in a constant ferment of change.[13] One may attribute similar reasons for the views some New World geographers hold on determinism. It may be that as historiography tends to reflect historical trends in the study of history, so certain environmental views express in themselves environmental subtleties, influencing the outlook of the geographer. But human ecology is also a product of nineteenth-century thought. Professor Fleure has said: 'To describe Darwinian studies the name "Ecology" has been coined, and Human Evolution is a province of study that we also designate by the title "Human Ecology." It sees man and environments continuously interacting and producing cumulative results, so that we need to follow the accumulation of these results—i.e. to study the evolution of the present—if we are to have any understanding of the present itself.'[14] He then goes on to suggest that studies of the evolution of man need to be interwoven with those of the evolution of environments. Such views not only deny the duality of man and nature but assume the false implication that cultural patterns can be explained satisfactorily from biological analogies. Thus human ecology is more a school of sociological philosophy than a field of study.

Demography

In the subject of demography, geography has a more objective relationship. Both are concerned with the study of averages and cover the same field of material; but they have a difference of method and a difference of emphasis. Demography may be considered as that branch of statistics concerned with population data. Though its results are mutually of interest to the geographer and the sociologist, and its findings are applied to social and political theories, it lies rather within the realm of mathematics as an objective study. Just as economic geography can learn a great deal from economic theory, as Lord Stamp has pointed out, so more recently M. Chevalier has urged that social geographers should keep abreast with the new methods of demographic research.[15] But the emphasis of the geographer, whether in economic or in social studies, is different from that of the economist or the demographer. As the geographer is concerned with the particularism of the environment, he cannot afford to be abstract. To him the human reality of the world is not stable both because of its historical and its spatial content. Statistics of population data only express for him general laws of averages in terms of population distribution and density, migration and the social structure of mankind.

Thus the geographer finds it impossible to understand and explain the density and migration of population, without a linked study of the modes of life, the land utilisation and what has been called 'the elemental distribution of population,' i.e. the types and character of rural and urban settlement.[16] Such is the content of social geography, which by its emphasis and method differs distinctly from the field of demography. It is in the detailed and thorough analysis of the population distribution map that the geographer demonstrates his contribution to be quite distinct from that of the sociologist's studies of social and biological compositions. However, both are necessary for a complete understanding of the human pattern.

Racial Studies

The third aspect of sociological study, the biological traits and racial features of man, few geographers would admit to be relevant to their detailed consideration. 'Racial geography' cannot claim to belong to geographical study since its methods have no distinct difference from those used by physical anthropologists.[17] It so happens that some geographers have pioneered in studies of physical anthropology, but that is all. To draw maps and chart deductions or theories of man's physical features is no specifically geographical role any more than quoting dates is necessarily history. The culminating study of sociology, that of social structures, is also outside the field of geographical concern. Indeed, to the anthropologists who are concerned with the social structure of primitive societies, their relation to geography is negative. Social anthropologists discern what have been environmental influences on their society and eliminate them from the further consideration of their problems.

SELECTED REFERENCES

Bowman, Isaiah. *Geography in Relation to the Social Sciences.* 1934.
Daryll Forde, C. *Habitat, Society and Economy—a Geographical Introduction to Ethnology.* London, 1942.
Le Lannou, Maurice. *La Géographie Humaine.* Paris, 1949.
Sorre, Max. *Les Fondements de la Géographie Humaine.* Tome I: *Les Fondements Biologiques, Essai d'une écologie de l'homme,* 2nd edit. Paris, 1947. Tome II: *Les Fondements Techniques,* part one, 1948.
Vallaux, C. *Les Sciences Géographiques.* Paris, 1925.
Wooldridge, S. W., and East, W. G. *The Spirit and Purpose of Geography.* London, 1951.

CHAPTER THREE

THE RELATION OF GEOGRAPHY TO HISTORY

THE lag of human geography behind physical geography is not just historical, that it has taken longer to develop. It appears rather that the reason lies inherent in the nature of the subject. Attempts have been made to prove that geography is a science, but it cannot be included within the systematic sciences. The reason also lies in the human element of its subject matter. Geography has been variously termed a science of the earth, a science of correlations and the science of chorography. It is all these things and yet no one of them adequately comprises all its scope of study. It is therefore perhaps a false emphasis to consider the scientific role of geography; history probably helps to illuminate the nature and scope of the subject more clearly. Hettner[1] and more recently Hartshorne[2] have suggested that the relations of geography and history are more fruitful for comparison than they have been realised generally.

The Use of Scientific Analogies in Humane Studies

In the past, both history and the social sciences followed too closely the analogies of physical science. At the beginning of this century Bury insisted in his famous dictum, 'history is a science, no more and no less.' Indeed the Buckles, Guizots and Taines belonged to the same generation as the Ratzels and Semples, when the vain attempt was made to hitch the waggon of humanistic studies to the bright star of natural science. It was a natural inference that if science could establish an evolutionary linkage between the physical environment and organic life, it was not stretching imagination too far to project such concepts into humane studies. Croce, the Italian historian, who revived interest in history as an art, thus observed at the beginning of this century: 'modern sociologists are rather to be blamed not so much for the illusion in which they are involved when they talk of an impossible science of sociology, as for the infecundity which almost always accompanies their illusion.'[3] Similar criticism was made by Lucien Febvre in his highly critical book against the human geography of the determinist school, whose writings he judged merely to be 'syllogistic deductions or purely literary dissertations.'[4] In using scientific analogies for a systematic outline of principles in human geography we can learn from the adverse effects of this in historical writings. Thus Trevelyan has insisted, "The idea that the facts of history are of value as part of an exact science, confirmed by specialists, is due to a misapplication of the analogy of physical sciences.... The analogy of physical science has misled many historians during the last thirty years right away from the truth about their profession.'[5] It is significant that, in addition to modern historical thought, many workers in other humane studies now recognise clearly and more soberly the validity of the historical method as an analogy to be followed in their own subjects. Social anthropologists, such as Kroeber[6] and Evans-Pritchard,[7] believe that it is essential to re-consider their subject in terms of the historical method. The human-ities are not concerned with natural processes which can be perceived and analysed, but with human affairs which need to be understood from the inside. The passion to discover the origin of things ('la hautise des origines,' as Marc Bloch has called it) has made the study and explanations of many social scientists such as the function-alist school of anthropology too mechanistic in their interpretations.[8]

The analogy of geography and history is not new. Immanuel Kant described logically the position of geography and history when he said 'History is a narrative, geography a description,' the former related to time and the latter to space.[9] Similarly, Humboldt and Ritter worked out their relations clearly. It appears that it was only during the nineteenth century when geography became closely identified with the systematic science of geology that its position became obscured. The development of history as an academic subject with its own mental discipline has made the position of geography, partly a non-systematic science, no longer disconcerting. It is interest-ing therefore to compare the scientific and historical methods.

The Methods of Science and History

Science is concerned with the analysis of the universal and abstract, whereas history is concerned with the particular and the concrete, framed in a time-scale. In a sense it is true that all state-ments must be generalisations, otherwise language would be meaning-less; but the degree of abstraction is the important thing to determine. The scientific method has to consider the particular, but it does so on the basis of timeless and placeless laws, whereas the historical method has the reverse emphasis.

A second difference results from this first distinction. Whereas science can within bounds claim prediction as its prerogative, the concern of history is retrodiction, that is the establishment on the basis of present evidence what the past must have been like. Prediction is a possibility for the scientist because he deals with timeless and placeless laws. It is the particularism of time and the nature of man, which alone make it possible for the historian to retrodict.

These two distinctions help to clarify the methods and role of geographical research. The human element in geography makes it impossible to establish universal laws from which predictions can be made. Also the individuality of place from place makes it difficult for the geographer to generalise too broadly. On the evidence of past changes in a region the geographer can only retrodict to give him a more accurate understanding of a present and particular landscape. In this sense he is concerned with the historical method. The geographer differs from the historian however in that he requires also a scientific training in the systematic sciences. Before the geographer can fully understand the content of the landscape, he has to base his observations more fully on the systematic branches of his subject, such as geomorphology and climatology. This distinction between systematic or general geography and regional geography has long been recognised. In systematic geography the basis is the scientific method, but it builds on this foundation a greater super-structure of regional studies by the adoption of the historical method. Both in history and in geography, the collection and analysis of material might be considered 'scientific,' but their presentation and systematic description is an art.

If geography can clarify its own objectives by the analogy of history, so its methods can be more clearly understood by knowing what are the essential features of the historical method. History cannot provide a plane of knowledge completely different in kind from science. It must be based on the scientific discipline of collecting and assorting significant facts. In discerning what are the significant facts, it should be objective. Geography, as has been noted above, has this same basis in a more emphatic manner. History, however, is also an art, both by its literary description and its poetic feel for the narrative. The regional monographs of French geographers indicate the same quality of the artistic in their subject matter. However, whereas the artist states what he sees, the geographer would do more; he assures himself that what he sees is understandable and significant for explanatory description. Nor is he concerned with the possible or the probable, but with what the evidence obliges him to assert is true. The thesis and antithesis of determinism and possibilism has distracted the geographer from the proper study of his subject, the art of explanatory description within the regional context. The disassociation of the causal from the casual can be an interesting pastime in geography, as in history, but it is not necessarily the chief object of his study.[10]

The explanatory account of any geographical phenomenon depends on generic analysis and so adopts more emphatically than history the 'scientific' methods. If, however, the emphasis is on the analysis rather than on its synthesis, on the search for causation rather than on its description, the research worker soon leaves the orbit of geography. Indeed, in physical geography, geomorphology belongs properly to the field of geology.[11] and climatology tends more and more to belong to the field of physics. On the other hand, the explanatory description of regional geography, though based on these analytic branches of science, is more properly in the realm of historical study. This is especially true of the human aspects of regional geography, where man as an agent of the environment adds to the particularism of the regional concept. As it has been recently stated, 'so far as concerns the *elements* of geography, it is futile to assert that "human" or "social" geography can be seen in terms of formal categories and universal principles and processes, as can physical geography. This imputes to it no inferiority; it is rather to admit that it is infinitely more complex, subtler, more flexible and manifold.'[12]

The Historical and Geographical Context

The modern tendency in geographical thought is to decry the traditional division of the subject into systematic and regional geography. Few to-day would hold out much hope for the holistic regional geography, and more emphasis is being given to what Ackerman has called 'monistic' geography.[13] Like the historian to-day, the geographer has to become more and more a systematist. Does this remove the emphasis so long given to the regional concept in geographical literature? In a recent article, 'The Inadequacy of the Regional Concept,'[14] Kimble would remove with the bath water of presumptive geography the baby of valid geography. We all appreciate to-day the inadequacy of an inadequate regional concept. Regions, as neatly tabulated units of the earth, which are empirically observable, do not exist, but regional contexts do exist and are the binding forces of geographical study.

If the comparison of geography and history helps to clarify the position of geography as a branch of knowledge, it also gives a balanced assessment of the regional concept. The province is to the geographer what the century is to the historian. This does not mean that the geographer or historian find any mystical attributes about his province or century. These are units of space and time, which are not observed empirically, but defined conceptually, confined by a relative and not by a predestined framework. Both are the means whereby the fluidity of space or time may be examined statically, yet recognising that neither is stable in itself. Thus to ignore the relationships and linkage between one region and another, or one century and another, is to freeze the unitary concept into something far removed from actuality. Both have also a hierarchy of measurement, and the more detailed the unit, the more accurate is the description and the less liable to be conditioned by subjectivism on the part of the observer. The province, the region, the tract and the stow are such unitary measurements for the geographer, as the century, the generation, the decade and the year are for the historian.

Spatial units have more importance perhaps for the geographer than time units have for the historian. The latter does not worry himself about the meaning of time but concentrates his attention on the drama enacted on its stage. So the geographer need not suffer any inferiority complex if he cannot define his regions; his task is to get on with the art of recognising and describing both the measurable and the qualitative features within their context. As S. B. Jones has said, 'If geography could make no other contribution to knowledge than this concept of total possible relevance within a regional context, it would have justified its existence.'[15]

Geography and Time

Apart from the analogies of the historical method mentioned above, geography shares with history the use of the time context. It is true, as Hettner has pointed out, that in geography time steps into the background.[16] Geography is not concerned with the course of time as such. The subject needs a generic conception of the problems it meets and studies, but this must not become history. It is equally false to consider geography as the study of the present since in the study of man every period of time brings changes. Consequently the use of a temporal average has only limited validity. Nor can one speak of an evolutionary method in historical geography. Over a period of time there is not one but many historical geographies, each of which needs separate treatment by sometimes different methods, as so many photographic plates which are developed after distinct exposures. Geographers in integrating areas recognise there are separate geographies for each period of time, just as historians recognise more or less separate histories for each major area of the world. The essays, edited by Professor Darby in *An Historical Geography of England*, are excellent examples of this approach.[17]

A second aspect which the geographer considers is the element of time in his generic studies. For example, the rural landscape reveals the legacy of time as a succession of heritages which have been superimposed on each other. Each has to be recognised and described. This outlook is of particular importance in Europe which has been called the most humanised area of the world. A view of the diverse rural landscapes of Europe is comparable to the geological map with its distribution of rock outcrops which have survived the ravages of time to present to-day a palimpsest of the past. Whatever the changes they never succeed in sweeping all the past away. Cities grow by using old sites and building on new sites beside them. The relics of former town plans and the modern inconveniences of location that we may suffer are tributes to the past. The changes we may make are in fact such compromises with the past.

Time can also be viewed as a factor in geography.[18] The rhythm of life varying with the seasonal changes of climate is important wherever man lives close to the soil. The construction and analysis of 'sociographs' or 'ergographs,' depicting such changes in relation to land utilisation and population density, can reveal much of practical value. The factor of time in the mapping of synchronous features is also important in studies of urban geography. The time factor has to be considered therefore as objectively as the spatial factor, to appreciate more fully the dynamic content of geography.

Conclusion

It is clear that the subject of human geography should not be considered as being, but in its becoming. Many of the problems which are considered by the geographer can best be resolved by viewing them in their historical context. Human geography has suffered much by presuppositions which are no longer tenable. In the following chapters, certain views therefore underlie the treatment of this subject which perhaps run contrary to beliefs once widely in vogue. In the first place, there can be no natural separation of studies in the humanities. Human geography cannot be said to have a completely different discipline, since its distinctiveness is rather its point of view and emphasis. As Professor Fleure has stated: 'I know that, in human geography, French thinkers have attempted to set forth a subject with foundations or principles. Vidal de la Blache, the greatest master in our field in modern times, Jean Brunhes and Maximillien Sorre have all tried. I cannot think any of them has made a real success in this particular line, and I do not think it is a line to be followed.'[19] Attempts to systematise the content of human geography and establish formal laws and principles are no longer accepted. In this respect the subject must view its material very much as history considers its data, in a specific context.

In the second place, it appears that the evolutionary philosophy which underlies so much of the earlier writings on geography is no longer tenable. The term 'evolution' has had the hypnotic influence of a blessed word, but it is a view of man and his world which philosophers would no longer accept.[20] In being so accommodating it has become too abstract to remain very convincing, and the ambiguity of the term makes it innocuous and empty. It has also been discounted by historians, such as Sir Charles Oman, who has declared: 'I entered my protest in many a page against the evolutionary theory of national and intellectual development.'[21] Similarly in historical geography, E. W. Gilbert has stated: 'The historical geographer should also avoid any desire to present his reconstructions as an example of evolution. The dangers of applying the scientific doctrine of evolution to historical geography are considerable.'[22] Attempts to enforce by procrustean methods the analogies of science in the humanities, whether through evolutionary philosophy or other viewpoints are unsound. The concept of evolution can only be legitimately used in geography in the original meaning of the word, as the spreading out before the mental vision of a sequence of changes and forms, according to a time-scale.

The third viewpoint which underlies this study of human geography is that the subject cannot be studied adequately on a holistic scale. The geographer needs to be sufficiently concrete to describe reality and yet sufficiently abstract to be able to give exact generalisations. This can only be possible within the regional context.

Some would suggest that human geography is 'macro-geography,' which 'seeks to elucidate . . . the general problem of man's relationship with his environment . . . an oecumenical geography.'[23] It appears to the writer, however, that the only satisfying way to treat human geography is with an emphasis on regional studies, viewed only from a different angle from that of physical geography.

SELECTED REFERENCES

Baulig, H. 'La Géographie, est-elle une science?' Bull. de la Soc. Geog., XVII, 1948, pp. 17-26.

Clozier, R. Les Étapes de la Géographie. Paris, 1949.

Daryll Forde, C. 'Human Geography, Sociology and History,' S.G.M., 55, 1939, pp. 217-34.

Febvre, L. La Terre et l'évolution humaine. Paris, 1924. Translated as A Geographical Introduction to History. London, 1932.

Hartshorne, R. The Nature of Geography. Lancaster (Pa.) 1939; second printing 1948.

Hettner, A. Die Geographie—ihre Geschichte, ihr Wesen, und ihre Methoden. Breslau, 1927.

Vidal de la Blache, P. 'Les conditions géographiques des faits sociaux,' A. de G., XI, 1902.

Walsh, W. H. An Introduction to Philosophy of History. London, 1951.

Wooldridge, S. W., and East, W. G. The Spirit and Purpose of Geography. London, 1951.

Part II

RURAL GEOGRAPHY

CHAPTER FOUR

THE RURAL LANDSCAPE

THE landscape may be said to reveal the social and economic history of a region. Its areal content, however, makes its analysis more properly a geographical than an historical study, though much of the material used is drawn from history. The geographer, in viewing a landscape retrospectively, appreciates that the past is modified by the present as much as the present is influenced by the past. Wherever possible the geographer should recognise the significance of physical factors, but this must not blind him to the recognition of other influences in the landscape. He must recognise and accept the historical explanations of social and economic factors which have often played the most important role in fashioning the detail of the rural landscape. The landscape reveals, in its pattern of fields, farms and villages, layer upon layer of historical accretions, sometimes clearly preserved through many centuries, at others effaced by new and deliberate changes.

In the kaleidoscopic change of time, two fundamental processes have together influenced the features of the landscape, evolution and creation. In this context by 'evolution' is meant the slow and uncertain changes inherited from the past, and by 'creation' those systematic and planned modifications associated with such changes as the parliamentary inclosures and landscape-gardening in eighteenth-century England. In view of these processes, it is impossible to assume that the elements of a rural landscape have been static through a long period of time, even though the structural elements, the villages and field patterns, may have persisted quite rigidly. Thus in most regions it is a false assumption to think of historical continuity as being static. Meitzen was mistaken therefore when he assumed by his brilliant generalisations that certain types of landscape could be delimited historically as well as geographically, a criticism which will be discussed later. In the anatomy of the rural landscape, the geographer is concerned with three aspects of its cultural features: the field systems, the types and patterns of rural settlement and the house-types. Detailed consideration will be paid in this chapter to the origin and distribution of field systems. Rural settlements and house-types will be considered in the following two chapters.

D

Effects of Inclosure on the Landscape

Apart from the physical milieu, the two most formative elements in the rural landscape have been inclosure movements and traditional field systems. In much of Western Europe, it appears that inclosure movements have been the more important factor in fashioning the present landscape. This is true particularly of south Sweden, Denmark, Scotland and Ireland, less so of England and Germany, and least of northern France. In Southern Europe, inclosure does not appear to have been an important factor in many regions, although there are exceptions. Sometimes inclosure movements have radically transformed the landscape. Thus in southern Sweden[1] and in Denmark[2] the inclosures of the nineteenth century changed the basic pattern of nucleated villages into one of dispersed farms, so that as many as 85 per cent. of the farms, formerly located in villages, were scattered among their fields. In contrast, the French landscape which Arthur Young saw at the end of the eighteenth century was still one of open fields, particularly in the Paris Basin. The explanation for the persistence of this open-field practice in France appears to have been the high density of rural population, the greatest in Western Europe during this period. The physiocrats and progressive land-owners had long realised that these archaic practices of cultivation were not satisfactory for increased production and improved systems of farming, but the divisions into strip holdings were often too fragmented to provide economic units, even when enclosed and consolidated. For example, in the commune of Seichamp in Lorraine, on an area of 330 hectares, the number of holdings was 1,451, giving an average of 0·23 hectares per unit. Figure 1 illustrates that one representative farm of 132 scattered holdings had only 48 hectares. In the Scandinavian countries there was not this problem of extreme parcellation, and the comparison between enclosure in France and in the countries of northern Europe may be explained in part therefore by higher and lower densities of population respectively.

Social and legislative contrasts suggest other variant influences, associated with inclosure in the rural landscape. An interesting example is provided by the differences of inclosure in England and Scotland. Inclosure in England had commenced in the Middle Ages, aided by acts such as the Statute of Merton (1235) and particularly in later times by the conversion of arable to pasture for the Tudor wool industry. In Leicestershire alone there are traceable the sites of over fifty villages, mostly abandoned as a consequence of enclosure.[3]

At the end of the eighteenth century, however, there was still a wide belt of open fields across the English Plain. In Oxfordshire, for example, many parishes of the Oxford Clay lowlands were not enclosed until after the mid-eighteenth century.[4] To-day, reticulated

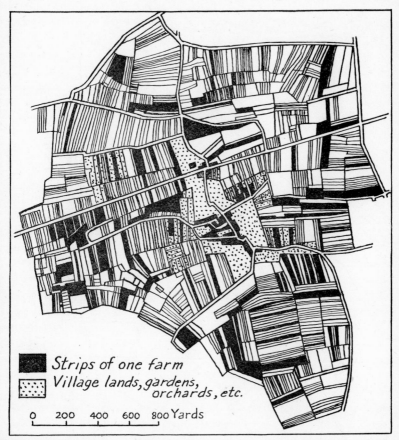

Strips of one farm
Village lands, gardens, orchards, etc.

0   200   400   600   800 Yards

Fig. 1. Field Patterns of Seichamp (Lorraine) before Redistribution (*after Demangeon*).

across many parts of England are the grassy rigs of former cultivation, and the open-field system is still recognisable in many field patterns (Ill. II). In sharp contrast the field boundaries are clearly systematised in many parts of Scotland, where the created patterns of straight, fenced lines and broad fields exist side by side with older, evolved layouts. Such patterns have been described in the Lothians

46/45

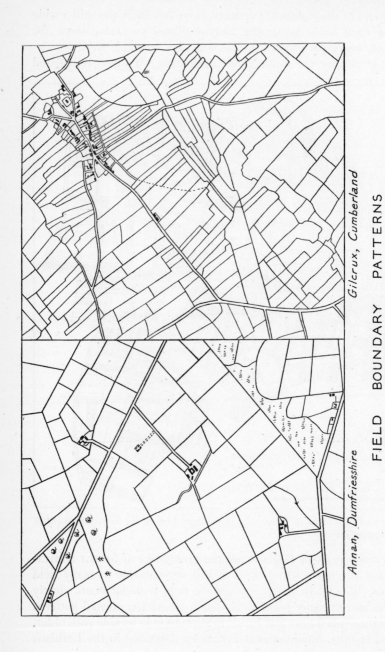

Annan, Dumfriesshire   Gilcrux, Cumberland

FIELD BOUNDARY PATTERNS

Feet 1000′   500   0   1000   2000 Feet

Fig. 2. Field Boundary Patterns (traced from the Ordnance Survey maps 1 : 25,000, by permission of the Comptroller of Her Majesty's Stationery Office).

by Geddes[5] and in Central Ayrshire by Lebon[6]. The most striking example is to be seen at the head of the Solway Firth, where the created landscape of much of Dumfriesshire, designed during the latter half of the eighteenth century, is contrasted with the evolved features of Cumberland (see Fig. 2).[7]

Differences in national legislation appear to be responsible for this latter contrast. Enclosure in England although begun early in the south east, was a piecemeal process, each parish requiring its own bill of inclosure to be authorised by act of Parliament; in the period 1774 to 1813, for example, 2,632 inclosure acts were passed by Parliament. In Scotland, the various acts passed between 1669 and 1738 had 'left nothing to be wished for on the subject of enclosures':[8] the Acts of 1669-1717 enabled march fences to be drawn straight and the Acts of 1695-1723 permitted mixed rigs to be combined into field blocks. Since the Scottish tenants had no *locus standi* on the land, and the country at the end of the eighteenth century was owned largely by some eight thousand proprietors, these radical changes were possible in the rural landscape of Scotland. Thus in the island of Arran, for example, the factor's diary notes that prior to enclosure in 1815 there were 113 *fermtoun* settlements consisting of farm groups of four to ten tenants. After that date the lands were divided into 458 farms, 53 being large units and the remainder holdings of two to forty acres each.[9] Such radical changes effected by inclosure were impossible in the English countryside. Thus in a study of a rural landscape it is essential to begin by considering the influences and changes associated with inclosure.

Distribution and Origin of Field Systems in Europe

Although enclosure has radically modified the field patterns of many parts of Europe, it is still clear that the underlying field features owe much to systems of cultivation once practised. Some historians have classified field systems into three general types: open fields with long acre strips, open fields with irregular parcels, and land completely enclosed as *bocage*. Others have interpreted these contrasting systems in relation to distinct agrarian economies. It appears, however, more satisfactory to consider the field systems in terms of extensive and intensive forms of cultivation, related both to the economic evolution of agricultural practice and to the local soil and topographical conditions. On this basis, it seems more advisable to classify the field systems into the following categories: shifting cultivation, run-rig or one-field system, the regular two- and three-field systems and the irregular, open-field practices.

Primitive Field Systems

In primitive systems of agriculture, it is apparent that shifting cultivation was a widespread necessity. Air photography has indicated in southern England that this system was practised by Neolithic and Bronze Age settlers. Two types of field patterns are found: small circular fields and square fields. The round fields, usually about one-third of an acre in size, are well preserved on Dartmoor. They cannot have been associated with plough cultivation and so it is suggested they were possibly cultivated by hoe.[10] From the end of the Bronze Age the square 'Celtic' field pattern appears, commonly between one-quarter to three-quarters of an acre in size. It is probable this field type was associated with cultivation by the use of a light two-ox plough or ard.[11] This square field type which still shadows the downlands of England, may have marked a transition from a form of shifting agriculture to a more settled practice, but the evidence is indefinite. Elsewhere however extensive practice of shifting cultivation has persisted for much longer time. According to Giraldus Cambrensis, the Welsh were still a nomadic people in the twelfth century A.D.[12] In Ireland, it appears that the hill peoples were still semi-nomadic until the eighteenth and even early nineteenth centuries.[13] The introduction of the potato did much to settle these peoples in a permanent system of cultivation. In the forests of the Ardennes, the system of *sartage*, was a primitive practice of shifting cultivation, which also continued until the beginning of the last century. In Central and Eastern Europe, similar practices have long persisted, especially among the Slavs, who lived as hunters and herders until the Middle Ages. Annual fallowing on the land was only introduced into Russia, for example, during the latter part of the fifteenth century.[14]

Run-rig Systems

The run-rig or one-field system of cultivation is an improvement on shifting agriculture, associated with the intensive cultivation of an arable open field, manured and continually cropped. This system persisted in Wales, Ireland, Scotland, and parts of Northern Germany and Scandinavia until the seventeenth and eighteenth centuries. In England it also occurred on poor sandy lands such as the brecklands of East Anglia.[15] It would be erroneous, however, to assume this system was associated generally with poor lands. Rather it was the selective use of the best lands in regions of sparse population.

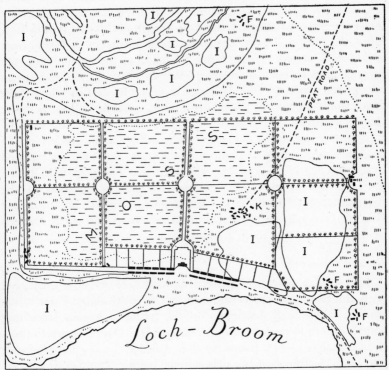

Fig. 3. A survey and a design for a village at Ullapool drawn about 1758. A detailed survey of the land use was made which illustrates the old practice of run-rig with the infield arable lands (I), the rough pasture of the outfield lands and the moss and waste land. The plan envisages the re-grouping of the 'fermtouns' (FF) and the 'kirktoun' (K) into a planned village with its bold design of new field boundaries. (Re-drawn from plan in Registry House, Edinburgh.)

The system was characterised by two features: the divisions into 'infield' and 'outfield' and the practice of 'run-rig.' The 'infield' or arable land was manured and cropped continuously within a rotation that varied according to the crops available, chiefly oats, barley and pease. The 'outfield' or low-lying waste provided pasture for the stock and part of it was enclosed for cultivation from time to time, and then abandoned when its soil fertility became exhausted. Local topography provided diverse practices in the use of the 'outfield' land.[16] The practice of 'run-rig' was the periodic redistribution of the holdings or 'rigs' among the tenants who cultivated their lands communally. Extreme parcellation of the fields has continued after inclosure in some parts of Ireland, as a result of this run-rig practice. Thus the Devon Report, speaking of the township of Glentornan in Donegal, stated: 'If the farms be made as the tenant wish, the external fences alone would cover upwards of one-fourth of the grass area of the property, and the miles travelled by cart in tilling these farms would amount to 18,860 per annum, instead of 5,120, as under the arrangement proposed by the proprietor.'[17] Yet the tenants' resistance to change in field patterns is still apparent in some of the more backward areas of Ireland. In contrast, Scotland has retained little evidence of the old 'run-rig' features. The plan of Ullapool indicates one example of the dramatic changes imposed in the reconstruction of the fields and settlements during the land planning (Fig. 3). Generally, however, the transition from 'run-rig' to modern field boundaries was more gradual.

Regular Open-field System

The regular open-field pattern of long acre strips is associated with the two- and three-field systems of cultivation. Prior to inclosure, it was well developed on the fertile loess soils stretching from northern France, across Germany and the Danube lands towards the Ukraine (Fig. 11). It was developed also in the English Midlands and found scattered on the rich, alluvial lands of south-west France, in Denmark, parts of Sweden, and even in the Mediterranean in such fertile plains as the Campidano of Sardinia.[18] The field patterns associated with this régime are still preserved intact as long, rect-angular strips, in such landscapes as Northern Burgundy, Lorraine, the Alsatian Plain, Hesbaye and many parts of Swabia, Saxony and in the Danubian lowlands. These strips commonly measure a furlong in length and one-tenth of a furlong in width, though their dimensions vary considerably according to the lie of the land, the nature of the soil, the density of the population and the subsequent amalgamation or fragmentation of holdings.[19] Where the holdings have not been consolidated since inclosure the landscape has still an open-field appearance, since the shadow cast by the hedgerows would waste a high proportion of their area.

In Denmark, where the open-field landscape is still marked, writers have shown that there have been three ways of dividing up the strips of arable in this system of cultivation, and the same probably applies to other European countries.[20] The most primitive is the *formskift*, where the strips are distributed irregularly and without planned arrangement. The German *eschflur* expresses the same pattern of irregular and scattered fields in waste land, though it was more usually associated with a one-field system, rather than a two- or three-field system. Secondly, there is the *boolskift*, where the strips of arable are divided according to the position of the dwellings in the villages, so that neighbours maintain common bounds on their lands. In Denmark this system appears prehistoric in origin. In many forest villages of Europe, this system is apparent, the holdings being laid out systematically according to the position of the houses along the main street (Fig. 6). Thirdly, there is the interesting system of *solskift*, introduced into Denmark in the thirteenth century A.D., and also found in Finland and Scandinavia. The plan of Thorsjö in Sweden illustrates the features of this practice, where the holdings are arranged systematically in the same position, according to the sun's rotation from east to west, and south to north (Fig. 4). There are indications that this system was practised in other regions of open fields. In England, for example, some documents describe the strips in the open fields as being *versus solem* and *versus umbram* where holdings in the south and east sides of the fields were preferred because of their longer insolation.[21]

Another feature of strip holdings within the arable fields is that they could be extended outwards as new land was colonised and the nucleated settlement, associated with these open fields, was expanded. There was therefore elasticity of development within a rigid, legal control of the communal land. When the bounds between the lands of one village and the next met, the disappearance of the waste meant even stricter control of the common grazing rights of the stubble, a feature which was characteristic of such landscapes as Lorraine and the English Midlands.

The origin of the two- and three-field systems is obscure. A useful summary of the varied opinions of scholars is given by Professor and Mrs. Orwin in their book, *The Open Fields*.[22] It is apparent that these systems are old in some regions, a more recent introduction in others. In France, for example, the three-field system goes back to Frankish settlement and it is clearly described in the *Polyptique d'Irminion* of the ninth century.[23] According to Bloch, it is probably of much earlier origin.[24] Air photographs of Belgic fields in England suggest that these curved rectangular strips were the beginnings of open-field cultivation

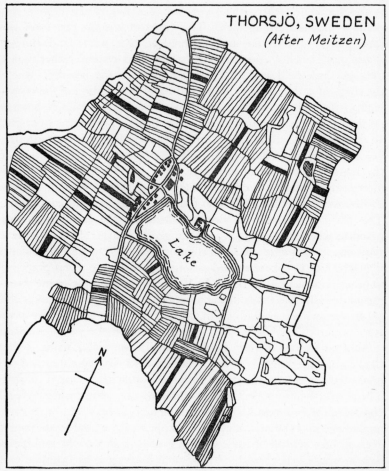

Fig. 4. Plan of Thorsjö, Sweden. The black strips are the holdings of one proprietor distributed according to the practice of *solskift*.

in the second and first centuries B.C.[25] (Frontispiece). Other authorities have suggested the system is of Roman origin, while another school of historians attributes it to the Anglo-Saxon invaders.

Whatever the date of its origin, it is apparent the system was not universal in open-field districts. The three-field system was considered an agricultural improvement in Britain, less extensive in thirteenth-century England than the two-field rotation. In Russia, the three-field system, or *Trehk-Polynaya*, was not introduced until the second half of the sixteenth century.[26] This indicates that the system was the expression of more systematised and extensive husbandry, wherever the soil was sufficiently fertile and adequately level land was available. The existence of this practice, or *gewannflur* as the Germans call it, on the loess soils of Central and Western Europe is an indication of this physical need.

The three-field system consisted of a three-year rotation of winter wheat, spring sown oats or barley, and fallow, distributed in three large fields. Fleta notes that under this practice 90 'acres' were desirable for the size of fields, in order to provide the workable unit or *carucate* for the economic returns of ploughing the land, whereas the two-field rotation needed only 60 'acres' for each field.[27] The actual size of the fields, however, would depend on the nature of the soil and the relief, with a larger unit on light, easily worked lands, a smaller one on the heavier clay lands. It has been pointed out from the remarks of a medieval writer, Walter of Henley, that the three-field system was more economical of labour returns in relation to crop yields than the two-field system.[28] Consequently, wherever the climatic conditions, the soil fertility and the relief permitted, the three-field system tended to predominate, but wherever physical factors upset the necessary requirements the three-field rotation gave place to the two-field cultivation. Thus, even in Lorraine, where the three-field system was most typical, the two-field system was developed on the dissected slopes of the plateau.[29]

In England, wherever the rainfall was too high for successful wheat cultivation, that is over 30 inches, the three-field system was absent. In western England therefore, it is only in select areas such as the Carlisle Plain of Cumberland and possibly in eastern Somerset where the three-field system was introduced. Drought equally dictated the absence of the normal three-field year rotation in much of southern Europe, as in Spain, where the system of *año y vez*, i.e. the rotation of one year's cropping followed by two years of fallow, divided the land into three fields but practising a two-field rotation.[30] Soil conditions also seem to have played their role: on the Chalk and on the brashy soils of the Oolites in England, the two-field system was commonest, whereas the three-field system was best developed on the clay lands.[31]

These examples of physical controls would suggest that the two-field system was inferior to the three-field rotation, usually related to restricting, physical factors. However, this was not always so; in some instances a two-field system was a more intensive form of improved agricultural practice. In the Alsatian Plain, for example, the three-field system which had been developed on the fertile loess lands at least since the ninth century A.D. was changed for a two-field system during the eighteenth century in the plain north of Strasbourg.[32] The introduction of 'froment' or improved wheat and of crops such as potatoes (1725) and trefoil (1750) made the system more intensive, not less. It is further associated with a complex sequence of economic and social factors facilitating the change. This example indicates how difficult it is to generalise on the merits of field systems or even on the factors involved in their individual development.

Irregular Open-field Systems of Southern Europe

In Southern Europe, open-field practice belongs generally to the fourth category, that of irregular parcels. The contrast between this type and the regular rectangular strips of the *gewannflur* has been recognised to be in part the product of two fundamentally distinct types of plough, the heavy plough (Latin *caruca*) and the light plough (*aratrum*). It is apparent that the heavy plough of the regular three- or two-field systems was most economical on a long furrow, whereas the light instrument, adopted to provide a surface tilth for dry-farming, could be lifted and manipulated for small and irregularly shaped fields. Some writers have made the further comparison of different food needs and climatic conditions. Dion argued that in the regular open-field system of Western Europe the emphasis has been on bread grains, whereas in Southern Europe arboriculture has also been important, providing the Mediterranean triad of bread, oil and wine.[33] It is even true that bread grains in the Mediterranean can be substituted by chestnut flour, as in the Cevennes and in Corsica. But this comparison of the two contrasted economies in the north and south of Europe is subject to several criticisms and does not adequately account for contrasts in the field systems.

Two criticisms of the above generalisation can be made. In the first place, as it has been pointed out, it is unreal to make such a broad comparison of two contrasted economies.[34] Despite the unity of their food cultures, the Mediterranean lands exhibit a great diversity of regions, even within this triad of crops, such as the wheat lands of Sicily and Old Castile, the vineyards of Tuscany and New Castile, and the olive groves of Attica and Andalusia. Indeed the range of economies between the forms of pastoralism in the mountains and the systems of intensive horticulture in the irrigated plains is greater in the Mediterranean than anywhere else in Europe. Therefore no southern economy can be associated solely with one particular field system. Secondly, it has been demonstrated, in studies of field patterns in Languedoc, that the significance of arboriculture cannot be used to explain the irregular features of open-field patterns in the Mediterranean.[35] For one reason, much of the wooded landscape of olives, citrus crops or vineyards, is the result of extensive planting since the eighteenth century. Also, the field patterns associated with such tree crops are often quite regular in shape.

The true causes of the irregular field patterns in many parts of Southern Europe are the result of the accidented relief and the social character of its peoples. The Mediterranean cultivator has had to scratch the thin soil cover of hill slopes, wherever terraces could be constructed and, on the plains, faced with problems of drainage, he has created quite different field patterns. Also, the individualistic activities of Mediterranean society contrast with the strongly marked communal organisations found further north. Dion himself has contrasted the legal contract, so binding in the communal cultivation associated with the three-field system of Western Europe, with the voluntary communal relations of Southern Europe. All these factors complicated by the indirect relations with each other together account for the comparisons between regular and irregular field systems.[36]

The origin of the irregular two-field system, prevalent in the Mediterranean, is very ancient. Professor Ridgeway has described the system in Greece during pre-classical times.[37] Jardé thinks the biennial rotation of cereals and fallow has continued in the Aegean from classical to modern times with little change.[38] It has been suggested that the reason for its continuity lies in the unchanging conditions of the physical milieu,[39] in a series of landscapes, especially in the poorer hill lands, where the rhythm of history has continued with measured gait. Even to-day the system of open-field cultivation with communal pastures or *baldíos* continues under a two-field rotation in some parts of Portugal. The system of *año y vez* in Spain, mentioned earlier, with strips of cultivated land (*sembrado*), land periodically taken into cultivation (*barbecho*) and fallow (*rastrojo*) is still common. Variations of a biennial or triennial rotation occurred throughout the Mediterranean according to the nature of the soil, intensity of drought, and whether the emphasis was laid on stock-raising or cereal cultivation. The difference in the size of holdings is equally complex to explain. Where the land has been ploughed by mule the strips have tended to be larger than those worked by oxen. Again, the irregularity of the terrain, the historic processes of amal-

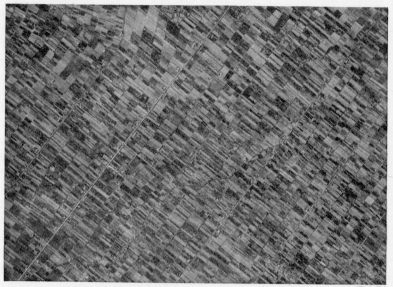

(R.A.F.)

III. Roman Centuriation, near Treviso, Italy.

gamation and reclamation, the character of the land tenure, etc., all need to be considered to explain such variations. The stone walls that petrify the small, irregular fields along the rocky coasts of Dalmatia, Greece, and South Italy, or the cyclopean terraces on islands such as the Balearics and Santorin can be understood only in their physical setting. Again, the created landscape of the Roman surveyor can be understood only in terms of the Latin legacy of centuriation. Air photography has revealed this imprint on the land-scape in parts of North Africa, Dalmatia and even in Andalusia, while in Italy there are extensive areas where the centuriated pattern still marks the landscape.[40] The region around Milan is in essentials much what it has been in its field layout ever since the Romans occupied Cisalpine Gaul and similar buried landscapes lie not far beneath the surface in the basin of the Arno and in the plain of Tavolière (see Ill. III).

It is thus apparent from this brief survey that in the study of field systems, the particularisms of time and place are too stubborn to be coerced into systems of facile generalisations. One cannot speak of Celtic or Germanic traditions as Meitzen did, without committing indiscretions in one's assertions, a criticism we shall consider in more detail in the following chapter. Sir Paul Vinogradoff once stated, speaking of Scandinavian types of settlement, 'there is no such thing as a Scandinavian custom; the *gaard* of Norway and the *by* of Sweden follow very different practices'; the former associated with dispersed farmsteads, the latter with the communal practice of nucleated villages. Similarly we cannot speak of any broad comparison between a three-field system in Western Europe and an irregular open-field system in the Mediterranean lands, associated with nucleated and dispersed types of settlement respectively. There are too many exceptions to make such generalisations valid. In the previous chapter, we saw that as in history so in geography, generalisations not kept concrete by specific examples leave the orbit of reality and truth. In view of this, the second half of this chapter is concerned with specific examples of rural landscapes in Britain.

The Rural Landscape of England and Wales

To understand the features of the rural landscape it is necessary to view it in time as well as in space. At first sight, the landscape of Britain appears submerged by urban sprawl and unified by modernism. If Neolithic man in Britain was lost in forest, we are near to getting ourselves lost to-day in conurbations.[41] But beneath this urban strata of the Industrial Revolution, there lies the ordered dignity of eighteenth-century Britain, with its planned estates and refashioned enclosures. Still further buried, beneath the irregular chessboard of the Agricultural Revolution lies the bewildering confusion of spider's web field patterns, associated with the medieval arrangement of open-field practice. Nor is the examination yet complete for, beneath it all, are still earlier patterns, the ill-arranged groupings of square and circular fields, dimly traceable across the grassy downlands. The whole landscape is thus like the crabbed scrawl of a palimpsest overlaid by the neater penmanship of a well-written manuscript. In some places the ancient forms approach close to the surface as in the landscapes of Wales and south-west England

(*Aerofilms Ltd.*)

IV*a*. Enclosed Landscape, Chew Valley, near Bristol.

(*Aerofilms Ltd.*)

IV*b*. Open Field Landscape, Lincolnshire.

(Ill. IV*a*); elsewhere the middle layers of open-field practice can be traced in field rig and manor plan as in the landscape of the Midlands (Ill. IV*b*). But in some landscapes, the creative impression of eighteenth-century planners, such as Lancelot Brown, has proved only too capable of transforming the scene *tabula rasa*. There are very few areas, however, where it is not possible to retrace by the bends of the roads, the lay of the fields, and the setting of the villages, features fossilised by time.

In retracing the successive features in the formation of the rural landscape there are four elements of particular importance. The first two are physical conditions: the physique of the country, and the distribution of prehistoric forest and marsh; the second two are human elements: the evolution of the field systems since the early Middle Ages, and the enclosure movements from Tudor to modern times. Only by considering these four aspects can we appreciate the regional diversity and the heritage of each rural landscape.

The Physique of England

The generalised division of Britain into Lowland and Highland zones, which Sir Cyril Fox has described in his book *The Personality of Britain*, provides a broad comparison.[42] To the north and west, the broken relief, the high altitude and poor soils, have been the chief physical factors in maintaining the Highland zone as the dividing line between Celtic settlement within it, and early English colonisation to the south and east. The stone dykes and rocky talus slopes of the Highland zone, its sparser population and its pastoral economy, have in the past sharply differentiated it from the Lowland zone with its hedgerows, clay plains and nucleated villages. The settlement of Lowland Britain has been directly related to the lithological character of its soils and their vegetation cover. Professor Wooldridge has shown the importance of the 'loam-terrains' of south-east England as areas of denser settlement, between the heavy clay soils of the lowland tracts and the sandy, infertile tracts of some of the upland areas.[43]

However, this intermediate category includes many variable pedological types, such as the lighter boulder clay soils of East Anglia and Essex, the terraces of the lower Thames, the soils associated with the Chalk and Jurassic limestones, and the Tertiary and post-Tertiary belts along the southern and eastern coastal strips. In contrast, the heavy clay lands with their difficulties for primitive

E

agriculture, the marshes and fens with their obstacles to communication, and the barren tracts of sandy heath unsuited to cereal cultivation, all provided the framework of areas negative to primary settlement (Fig. 5). These lands include the outcrop of the London, Weald, Wadhurst, Kimmeridge, Gault, Oxford and Liassic clays and the residual clay-with-flint of the Chiltern Hills. Other negative lands included the poor sands and gravel tracts of New Forest, Bagshot, Weald, Beaconsfield, Blackheath, the Suffolk Sandlings, Breckland and the Triassic plateaux of the Midlands. The silts and alluvial deposits of the Fens and the coastal estuaries complete the list of negative areas.

Settlement has moved downwards as the economies practised have changed or developed. It was on the higher land such as the Pennines above 2,000 feet and Dartmoor at about 1,000 feet that the best high-level grazing grounds attracted prehistoric man. At a later date, the concentration of 'Celtic' settlements with their field systems on the English downlands, in Hampshire and Sussex for example, accounts for the different needs of permanent agriculture practised in rectangular fields (Frontispiece). The light soils of these lands explain for example, such a concentration on the Sussex Downs between the valleys of the Adur and Ouse. There, air photography has revealed that out of a total of 65 square miles, at least 23 per cent., i.e. 14·5 square miles, were under cultivation in Celtic times.[44] Anglo-Saxon settlement with an attack on the damp oak forests of the heavy clay lowlands and the use of a heavy plough suggests a third change in location, associated with the typically developed open-field practice. This has been called the 'valley-ward movement,' but it implies more a change in economy with more developed communal cultivation and more intensive exploitation of the land, than a topographical shift of location. With this development the changes in field pattern have been completed and the landscape colonised systematically.

The Forests and Marshes of England

The second element of importance, the distribution of forest, is also related closely to field and settlement patterns. Professor Tansley thinks that in 'Atlantic' times the whole of Britain below 2,000 feet was probably forested. He suggests that in the subsequent Sub-Boreal period when the climate was drier, much of the chalk and oolitic plateaux of the country would be bare of trees and would have become pasture with a little arable.[45] By Roman times there was

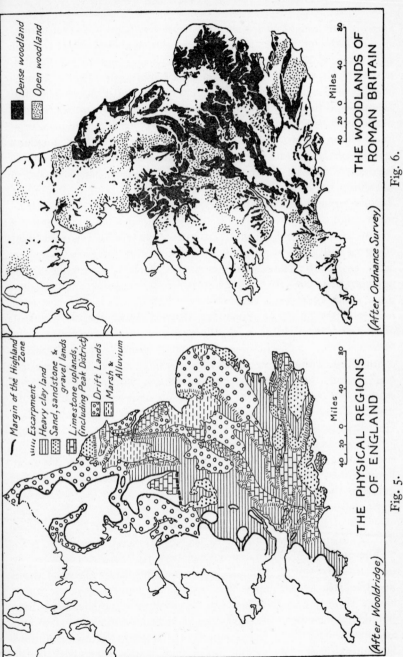

Margin of the Highland Zone
Escarpment
Heavy clay land
Sand, sandstone & gravel lands
Limestone uplands, (including Peak District)
Drift Lands
Marsh & Alluvium

Dense woodland
Open woodland

THE PHYSICAL REGIONS
OF ENGLAND

Miles

40 20 0   40   80

(After Wooldridge)

Fig. 5.

THE WOODLANDS OF
ROMAN BRITAIN

Miles

40 20 0   40   80

(After Ordnance Survey)

Fig. 6.

possibly still a good deal more forest and woodland than that shown on the Ordnance Survey map (Fig. 6). This map however is a useful indication of the extent of forest which has been cleared subsequently. It provides also a clear correlation with the lithological features of Lowland Britain (Fig. 5). The process of clearance of the forest has influenced the expansion of the isolated groups of Anglo-Saxon settlers from nuclear areas of more favourable primary settlement. Thus the wooded hills of the Chilterns formed the northern frontier of the Middle Saxons, and the forests of Essex were similar barriers to the East Saxons. The Weald of Andred, heavily wooded, stretching 120 miles long and 30 miles broad, also isolated the South Saxons, while the forests of the Midlands provided barriers to settlement there.

The contrasts in field and settlement patterns in many English counties still preserve the medieval distribution of forest and open land. In Hertfordshire, for example, the open downland of the northern districts with the three-field system and nucleated villages must have contrasted with the two-field practice and scattered hamlets throughout the remaining districts of the county. Maps of place-name distribution in Middlesex explain the sharp comparison between many coherent open-field patterns and villages of Saxon colonisation along the river terraces to the south, and the irregular field systems, the scattered communities and the stretches of woodland in the north, the latter preserved in more than a memory by Enfield Chase.[46] In the Midlands the Liassic clay lowlands with their open-field practice in nucleated villages, and the Triassic Sandstone forests of Sherwood and Arden, likewise explain the contrasts in the rural landscape still seen in the counties of Nottingham and Warwick. Place-names suggest that extensive areas of forest were cleared between the fifth and tenth centuries A.D., a process accelerated throughout the later Middle Ages. For example, the Domesday Surveys of East Anglia and Essex indicate reduction of woodland in 112 villages between 1066 and 1086.[47]

The drainage of the marsh has not been so straightforward as the task of deforestation. Consequently marshes have played a more negative role in settlement and landscape changes than the forest cover. Modern research, however, has indicated that such areas may not always have been the inhospitable waste and uninhabited swamp associated with them. For example, in the Fens the many finds of Romano-British colonisation and 'Celtic' fields, particularly in the silt areas and on certain islands, have suggested that deterioration started only in the third century A.D. and that abandonment was completed by the fifth century.[48] The transformation of the marshes of the Fens is chiefly the epic story of drainage techniques employed since the seventeenth century, and elsewhere since the eighteenth century, the field patterns suggesting changes in the techniques adopted.

Field Systems of England and Wales

The third element in the changing landscape has been the evolution of field systems. The aspect of late Medieval England must still have been one of woodland with some important forest areas, but the activities of man were infusing more and more cultural elements into the landscape, notably in the lay-out of the field systems. Professor Grey has revealed the geographical distribution of these field systems during the twelfth and thirteenth centuries,[49] and they may be classified as follows:

1. Regular Open-field System of the Midlands.
2. Irregular Open-field Systems—(a) East Anglia, (b) Kent and (c) Northern and Western England.
3. Composite Field Systems of South-west England.
4. Wales.

As Figure 7 indicates, the regular open-field system comprised the English Plain, bounded by the Jurassic and Cretaceous escarpments to the west and east respectively, by the Wash, and by the forests and moorlands to the south-west and north. The map showing the distribution of open fields indicates that the system did occur also in parts of Dorset, south Sussex and even in south Durham[50] (Fig. 7). The development of the three-field practice within this region was closely associated with the agricultural opportunity afforded as noted earlier in this chapter. In the more dissected terrain of the dip-slopes and escarpments it is frequent to find evidence of the two-field system, whereas the three-field system is more dominant a feature of the clay vales. Sometimes the subsequent expansion of the arable land by the clearance of the forest added another field, changing the rotations from two to three fields. Thus at Haddon Rudley (Yorkshire) there was the north field, south field and northbrocks (*broc* meaning *assart*) which suggests this expansion from an original two-field system.[51] Irregularities such as the distribution of river valleys, royal forests and moorlands broke up the regular three-field system so that it would be

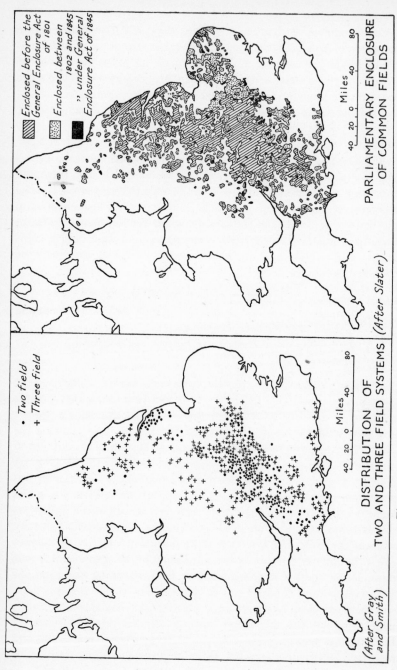

DISTRIBUTION OF TWO AND THREE FIELD SYSTEMS (After Gray and Smith)

• Two field
+ Three field

Miles
40   20   0   40   80

Fig. 7.

PARLIAMENTARY ENCLOSURE OF COMMON FIELDS (After Slater)

Enclosed before the General Enclosure Act of 1801

Enclosed between 1802 and 1845

,, under General Enclosure Act of 1845

Miles
40   20   0   40   80

Fig. 8.

wrong to conceive the whole of the Midlands as framed by the occurrence of regular open fields. Apart from these topographical features, the enclosures from Tudor times onward, and innovations in field systems with a view to the improvement of agriculture, would also provide many individual features.

In East Anglia, the open-field system has been a much more hybrid growth, related to the changes of Saxon and Danish colonisations, the emphasis given to sheep-rearing and to the distinctive manorial structure of the region.[52] The practice of sheep folding and the general arrangement of a tenant's land in one field, following a three-crop rotation were features of the East Anglian system. Also, whereas the manor, nucleated village and the parish, tended to be units in the Midlands, more often there were two or more manors in the large villages of East Anglia.

In Kent and parts of east Sussex, physical, social and economic factors account for regional features. The pattern of land use characterised by extensive areas of weald or forest land held in common, the scattered patches of arable land and distribution of communal marshes along the coasts, provided distinctive administrative features of the parishes and manors.[53] The practice of *gavelkind* during the Middle Ages tended towards the fragmentation of holdings and the scattering of manorial lands over a wide area.[54] Other factors which developed the fragmentation and irregular patterns of fields were the early enclosures, associated with a money economy brought over from the Continent at an earlier period than elsewhere in England,[55] and the absence of a three-course rotation.

In the west of England, especially in Shropshire and south Cheshire, the extent of forest land gave rise to irregular field practice, early enclosure and the characteristic pattern of hamlets and small villages. Further north in Lancashire, Cumberland and Northumberland, the irregular distribution of open fields, the prevalence in some districts of run-rig cultivation and social differences of tenancy account for other variations. In Northumberland and Cumberland, the manorial units often comprised several townships within one or more parishes so that the parish often consists of several small villages or hamlets.[56]

The south-west of England has physical and cultural affinities with Brittany as part of 'Atlantic Europe.' The wet, mild climate, the broken terrain of talus slopes and rock-strewn waste and the extensive moorlands, are not suited to an arable economy. The appearance of the south-west is therefore of *bocage* on the lowlands (Ill. IV*a*) and dry stone inclosures on the moorlands. During the Civil War, Cromwell was well aware of the strategic advantages of engagement with the royalist forces in the open-field landscape and kept clear of the south-west, 'lest we should engage our body of horse too far into that enclosed country,' he wrote.[57] As Figure 9 indicates, open fields or *gweals* (like the Breton *mejou*) were introduced into the south-west around the towns and in ecclesiastical lands. They were probably introduced by the Normans, but they appear as extraneous features in a landscape which has consisted predominantly of small enclosed fields. Around the edges of the granite uplands another marked pattern consists of the regular fields associated with mining colonisation (Fig. 9).[58] Flatrès has shown from records of the thirteenth and fourteenth centuries that enclosure was then in progress so that since the late Middle Ages enclosed fields of three to four acres and hamlets of five to ten households have been the prevalent features of this region.[59]

In Wales, the 'Celtic' features of land ownership and field patterns intermingle with open-field cultivation. Unlike the south-west, however, where the place-names indicate a predominantly English settlement,[60] the Welsh remain ethnically distinct in their forms of settlement, with a marked absence of manorial features. In the Englishry, Anglo-Norman influences have added their features to pre-existing conditions of tribal organisation. Thus despite its distinctive cultural unity, the field patterns and settlements of Wales suggest a rich variety of historical types with open fields, run-rig practice, ancient megalithic settlement and squatter colonisation all adding to the historical legacies inherited in the present landscape.[61] Small circular placed fields centred on an ancient settlement, some probably of megalithic origin, square 'Celtic' fields and numerous regular and irregular fields of squatter colonisation in more recent times suggest this variety of origin. The substitution of primogeniture for *gavelkind* with the Union with England in 1536 ended the minute subdivision of holdings and from this period onwards are to be dated the squatter settlements built beyond the original tribal areas and often associated with larger field units.[62]

The Inclosure Movements

Undoubtedly the most important factor in the formation of the actual rural landscape has been the inclosure movements. Regional

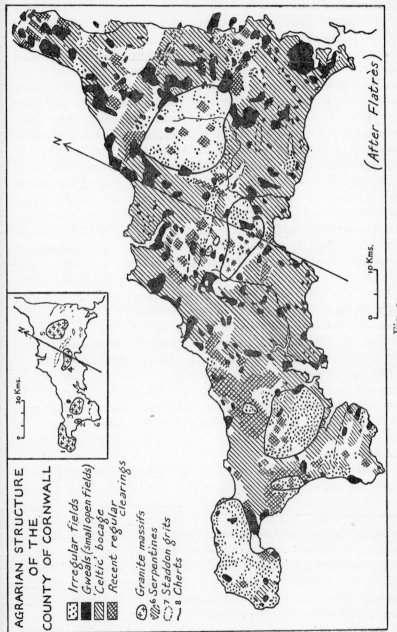

AGRARIAN STRUCTURE
OF THE
COUNTY OF CORNWALL

Irregular fields
Gweals (small open fields)
'Celtic' bocage
Recent regular
      clearings

5 Granite massifs
6 Serpentines
7 Staddon grits
8 Cherts

30 Kms.

N

0   10 Kms.

Fig. 9.

(After Flatrès)

distinctions discerned in the field systems appear also in the progress and character of the inclosure movements which were in part at least influenced by the terrain. A comparison of Figures 7 and 8 illustrates this. As Dr. Slater recognised, the distinction between the landscapes associated with Parliamentary inclosures and those related to earlier and voluntary enclosures is fundamental.[63] Across the grassy shires and oolitic escarpments of the west enclosure started in the reign of Henry IV and continued in a piecemeal process throughout successive centuries, associated with evolved and more irregular features in the landscape than the subsequent Parliamentary inclosure. There were, however, some drastic changes associated with these medieval enclosures, such as the disappearance of 72 settlements in Warwickshire before 1485.[64] Consequently, as Beresford has indicated, there were probably more villages in existence before 1320 than at any other time before the Industrial Revolution.[65] In the rural landscape, however, the contrast between the old and Parliamentary inclosures has left a marked difference. As Slater has pointed out, 'In the country of old inclosure we find narrow winding lanes; in the "belt of Parliamentary inclosure," broad straight roads with margins of grass on either side occasionally with nothing but grass and cart-ruts. You find here almost all the houses of a parish clustered together in compact villages; while in the country of early inclosure they may be so scattered that if it were not for the church which seems to attract to its neighbourhood the inn and the smithy, there would scarcely be a recognisable village at all.'[66] The contrasts between the landscape of Parliamentary inclosure and that of voluntary enclosure, is further developed in the differences between the South-East with its Continental relations and the South-West with its isolation and traditional features.

To-day, the pattern and shape of the fields over the English landscape still expresses the varying types of enclosure, related to the environmental features. In the lowlands of England the fields, especially since Parliamentary inclosure, have been divided by 'quickset' hedges, and in the south-west by wide earth-banks faced with stone, while in the hills of upland Britain dry walls of stone have been erected. The arable enclosures frequently occur in long, narrow fields, with parallel and slightly curving hedges, indicating the distribution of former open fields (frontispiece). The former common lands divided for the extension of arable cultivation are represented usually by large square or rectangular field blocks, whereas the land enclosed from waste by an individual cultivator can often be distinguished by its irregular boundaries. The age of the inclosures of waste can be discernible at times, the older inclosures with irregular field boundaries contrasting with the parallel straight line fences of the more modern fields. Inclosures from the forest tend to be either oval or circular in shape, suggesting clearances such as some of the fields of Delamere Forest in Cheshire,[67] or else irregular fields enclosed piecemeal fashion. Extremely irregular boundaries sometimes suggest inclosure for pasture, as in the Tudor plan of Whatborough (1586) in Leicestershire which Tawney reproduced in his study.[68] In contrast, the reclamation of marsh is usually associated with a herring-bone pattern of strip holdings as in many field patterns of the Fens, Isle of Axholme and West Somerset. Finally, in upland moors the large fields are often polygonal, square, or circular in shape, centred on isolated farmsteads from which reclamation has expanded outwards.

Regional Examples of British Field Patterns

The complexity of factors and elements which together account for the landscape mosaics can best be summarised by the analysis of specific examples, illustrated in Figure 10. Laxton, in Nottinghamshire, is the only place in England where the open-field system is still practised in all its essentials. The distribution of its three fields, the West Field, Mill Field and South Field, together with the demesne land, is still traceable (Fig. 10). There were 3,853 acres divided into 3,333 parcels of land among the lord of the manor and about twenty-five freeholders, according to a survey of 1625.[69] Since then, the chief changes have been in the increased size of holding and consolidation of strips owned by fewer small landholders, reclamation of waste, exchange and inclosure. The area of open-field farming has been reduced gradually until it is now only about 500 acres.[70] But the process of consolidation and exchange of holdings carried out during 1904 in Laxton is a living example of the process and evolution of field patterns common to many open-field districts of England during the eighteenth and early nineteenth centuries.

The field patterns of Littleport, near the banks of the Little Ouse in the South Level district of the Fens, illustrate the features of a marsh-land landscape (Fig. 12). A Domesday vill, the settlement was sited on an island, surrounded by fenland, which is still distinguishable in the field patterns. On the island site of 1,000 acres, the three-field system

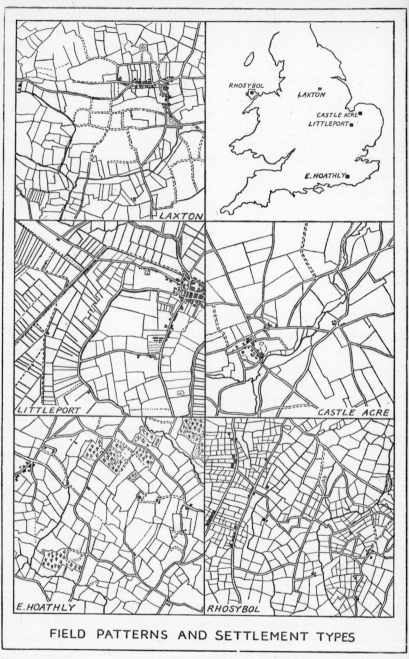

FIELD PATTERNS AND SETTLEMENT TYPES

Fig. 10. Field Patterns and Settlement Types in England and Wales (traced from the Ordnance Survey Maps 1 : 25,000, by permission of the Comptroller of Her Majesty's Stationery Office.)

was practised, surrounded by 16,000 acres of fen noted for its fishing and sedges.[71] In 1277 there is reference to some reclamation here and in the sixteenth century enclosures were made for the conversion of arable to pasture land for sheep-raising; 547 acres were enclosed in 1549 for this purpose.[72] Vermuyden's scheme of 1638-42, to reclaim the Ouse drainage, included Littleport, and active enclosure must have taken place with the resultant pattern of dyked, strip fields. However, as late as 1794, pumping the fenlands by 75 windmills was extremely precarious and only the more modern pumping methods—the steam engine introduced after 1830 and the diesel engine from 1913—have made possible efficient cultivation in the fen holdings.[73]

Castle Acre illustrates the features typical of the settlements and field systems of East Anglia (Fig. 10). Situated on the ancient trackway of Peddar's Way, Castle Acre occupies a Romano-British site, and the Saxon finds which have been excavated suggest long continuity of occupation. The village is still framed by the Romano-British earthworks, while one of the gateways of the Norman castle spans the village street. A Cluniac Priory established here also suggests its medieval importance. The present field patterns reflect three features characteristic of East Anglia. Before inclosure, the arable was divided into three fields, West, Middle and East, divided by highways and approximately the same size. According to a Tudor survey, there was no subdivision of the holdings by 'fields' in the Midland sense. Thus nearly three-fourths of the acres of the first holding enumerated lay in the West field, while another proprietor had 80 per cent. in Middle field, etc.[74] Such arrangements suggest the system practised was inconsistent with the Midland usage, though a three-course rotation might be individually worked on the different strips within the same field. Another distinctive feature was the periodic cultivation and subsequent inclosure of the 'brecks,' suggested by the rectangular fields. The consolidation of farm properties to-day into large units is also apparent from the map.

A striking contrast is presented by the small irregular fields of East Hoathly in Sussex (Fig. 10). Situated on the Hastings Beds, the water supply in the district is good and numerous springs are found along the valleys. The district was heavily forested as many of the local place-names indicate. East Hoathly is not mentioned as a vill in the Domesday Survey and it is apparent the settlement was not made until the clearance of the forest associated with the development of the iron-smelting industry in the latter Middle Ages. Piecemeal enclosure of small fields in the woodland with small settlements loosely scattered from the manor is characteristic of this type of country.[75] It provides a contrast with the field patterns of Ripe, some four miles to the south-south-west, where there is clear evidence of Roman centuriation near the coastal plain. Between the villages of Ripe and Chalvington have been traced the Roman fields or *centuriae*, consisting of 210 and 240 *jugera*, which must have belonged to a freehold land settlement of Roman soldiers.[76] The subsequent fragmentation of manor lands and the mosaic of individual holdings has not appreciably altered this planned division of the land. It is possible similar centuriated patterns of fields are yet to be discovered in south-east England, such as in south Essex. The typical features of the Kent and Sussex landscape however are the scattered hamlets, the archipelago of manorial lands isolated by forested tracts, and the concentration of more markedly nucleated settlements along the south coastal plain.

The final example, Rhosybol in Anglesey, illustrates a distinct rural landscape (Fig. 10). Two features help to explain the variety of field patterns in Anglesey. In the first place it has not so many mixed and hybrid forms of settlement as occur in other coastal districts of Wales,[77] such as Glamorgan. There was no Anglo-Saxon invasion of Anglesey, and the first English influences date only from the bastides of Edward I. Consequently nucleated villages are not characteristic of the island, and are only of recent origin. Secondly, its society emerged more recently from tribal bonds than in the Englishry.[78] Stages of development from nomadic or semi-nomadic occupance of the land are attested by characteristic patterns of settlement.[79] Together these two distinguishing features imply that the variety of field and settlement types are more associated with stages of development and occupance than with intrusions of different societies. Thus four major types can be discerned on the map.[80] Firstly, there is the hill-top settlement of Pen-y-graig-wen in the south-east, a hamlet with a radial pattern of small square fields, possibly the original settlement of the district. Secondly, there are the isolated squatter homesteads and small fields of later colonisation, which may date from Tudor times or later. Thirdly, there are the series of mining homesteads in the north-west, associated with the quarrying industry developed during the eighteenth and nineteenth centuries. In the centre and north-east is the fourth type of field pattern, associated with the large fields and farms of most recent origin, often occupying the poorer lands which were drained and reclaimed only in the nineteenth century.

This outline of some English examples illustrates how difficult it is to generalise about field systems and field patterns. Physical and economic conditions may account for certain features of settlement, but they are usually only permissive controls. The positive forces are the colonists themselves, and it is apparent that two different peoples may use an identical environment in markedly contrasted ways. The ethnic factor is continually apparent in the landscape but it is not an unknown influence, as Meitzen conceived in his studies; it is the central figure on the stage. As a legacy of many centuries of man-kind, the rural landscape in all its complex features reminds us however, that it is not *Homo oeconomicus* which has transformed it, but man with all his social as well as economic needs.

SELECTED REFERENCES

Aufrère, L. 'Les systèmes agraires dans les Iles britanniques,' A. de G., 1935, pp. 385-409.

Bloch, M. *Les Caractères Originaux de l'Historie Rurale Française*. Oslo, 1931.

Curwen, E. C. *Air-Photography and Economic History*. London, 1938.

Darby, H. C. (Edit.) *An Historical Geography of England and Wales*. Cambridge, 1936. Especially chapters 3 and 5.

Dion, R. *Essai sur la Formation du Paysage Rural Française*. Tours, 1934.

Gray, H. L. *English Field Systems*. Cambridge, Mass., 1915.

Le Lannou, M. 'Sur les origines de l'openfield,' in *Livre Jubilaire offert à Maurice Zimmermann*. Lyons, 1949.

Orwin, C. S. and C. S. *The Open Fields*. Oxford, 1938.

Sion, J. 'Sur la civilisation agraire Méditerranéenne,' Bull. Soc. Lang. Géog., vol. X, 1939, pp. 16-41.

Slater, G. 'The Inclosure of Common Fields Geographically Considered,' G.J., vol. XXIX, 1907, pp. 35-55.

CHAPTER FIVE

RURAL SETTLEMENT IN EUROPE

ONE of the fundamental tasks of human geography is the systematic study of the structure of settlement. The delimitation of settlement patterns and the explanation of their origin is the chief task of the student of rural settlement. There are several aspects of this subject which will be considered in this and the following two chapters: the general pattern and distribution of settlement types; the more detailed description of regional studies; the relation of settlements to field systems; and the origin and classification of house-types. Since 1928, when the first *Report of the Commission on Types of Rural Settlement* was published by the International Geographical Union, much interest has been aroused among geographers in this branch of study. Such is the complexity of the subject matter, however, that no general laws can yet be formulated, and indeed it is questionable if they should be sought. Hitherto, all attempts to do so have been mere sophistry, leading to generalisations disproved by too many exceptions.

Patterns of Rural Settlement

Even a superficial glance at a series of topographic maps will indicate that there are wide variations in the patterns of settlement. Broadly, these may be grouped into two types, the nucleated and the dispersed. In England and Wales the wide range of types indicates that there are many variations from these two main patterns. The scattered hamlets of Kent and east Sussex, the nucleated villages of the Midlands, the forest hamlets of Shropshire, the fen villages of west Somerset and south Lincolnshire, and the farms and hamlets of upland Wales, are all distinct patterns.

In Europe, the nucleated settlement predominates in the north and east of France, in southern Belgium, in Denmark, south Sweden, central Poland, across the plains of north Germany, east of the river Weser, in Bohemia, lower Bavaria, the Swiss Jura and across the Danubian plains (Fig. 16). In Hungary and in the Mediterranean regions of Castile, Sicily, southern Italy and Greece, the large nucleated village is the prevailing type. The term 'village,' however, has the widest connotation, ranging from centres of 20,000 to 30,000 in the Hungarian steppe to small units of 200 to 500 inhabitants in parts of Western Europe.

In areas of dispersed settlement, the houses are scattered among the fields, or grouped in hamlets. Most of Scotland, Ireland and Wales are associated with dispersed settlement. Two-thirds of France has dispersed forms, ranging from the dissemination of west Brittany, south-west Aquitaine and north Flanders, to the hamlet patterns of Limousin and other areas of the Central Massif. Dispersion is also prevalent in northern Belgium, the lower Rhine plain, most of the Netherlands, the high plateaux of central Germany and throughout the mountainous belts of the Carpathians, Alps, Pyrenees, Cantabrian ranges, Apennines and the Balkans (Fig. 16). In Italy, the dissemination of farmsteads in Tuscany contrasts sharply with the large agglomerated villages of the south, and in Spain, comparable contrasts occur in Catalonia and Aragon respectively.

Such generalised comparisons of the nucleated and dispersed settlements do not bring into focus, however, the wide range of intermediate types. It is better therefore to distinguish three units of settlement, the nucleated village, the hamlet and the isolated dwelling. Intermediate types such as patterns of agglomerated dispersion and agglomeration with dispersion can also be discerned. Difficulties arise in some cases in distinguishing hamlet patterns from dispersed types. The farmhouses of Beauce and Hesbaye, the *corte* of the Po valley, the *caserio* of the Basque lands and the *mas* and *masía* of Valencia, Catalonia and southern France, are all forms of dispersed settlement but they vary widely in their detailed pattern. Similarly, the *catuni* of Roumania, the *kolibé* of Bulgaria, the *kopanice* of Slovakia and the *hoefe* of the Alps have all minor differences. Moreover, if the word 'village' has such a wide range of definition, the term 'hamlet' is also loosely defined. In Italy a hamlet is a settlement with as many as 500 inhabitants, whereas in Flanders one-fiftieth of this number would qualify it for this term. Consequently definition can only be made in relation to the regional pattern observed, each region being considered on its own merits.

Cartographic Representation of Settlement Patterns

Problems of nomenclature and of statistical definition have necessitated the use of cartographic methods whereby the patterns of settlement can be measured and delimited. This too is fraught with difficulties, and no general agreement has been reached on one

F

particular formula to express nucleation, agglomeration and dispersion. One difficulty is the lack of uniform statistical data in the different national censuses. The detailed data given for each commune in the French census are not available in the Belgian census. Few censuses give in detail the number of buildings per commune which is available in the Spanish and Italian statistics. The British census has not much detailed data from which to construct formulae of nucleation or dispersion. Moreover, regional diversity is such that no one formula has yet been discovered which will adequately express all the values required.

Two types of cartographic representation have been attempted, those based on personal observation and those based on statistics. The most successful have been those based on personal study of settlement patterns from topographic maps and a detailed knowledge of their variations. Such maps of settlement types have been constructed for Belgium,[1] the Netherlands,[2] Germany,[3] Switzerland,[4] Italy,[5] the Balkans,[6] Roumania[7] and Poland.[8] However, the diverse definitions and the subjective views of the authors make it difficult to use such maps for comparative purposes for the whole of Europe. It is to avoid this difficulty that numerous formulae have been devised.

One of the earliest and most successful mathematical formulae to express nucleation and dispersion is that of Demangeon.[9] He expressed the settlement pattern as $K = \dfrac{E \times N}{T}$ where K is the coefficient required, E the population of the commune except for that of the chief nucleated settlement, N the number of settlements except for the chief centre, and T the total population of the commune. The French census provides detailed population statistics for each *écart* or settlement unit in each commune, so that the formula can be easily applied there. The difficulty in adopting this formula, however, is that it cannot be worked out from other census reports, such as those of Britain and Belgium, which do not provide the statistical data required. The method is also insufficient to bring out the detailed limits of natural regions, and it takes no account of historical influences; but these criticisms are valid for other mathematical formulae.[10] More serious criticism is that Demangeon's formula does not discriminate sufficiently between different types of dispersion. Moreover, no definition of the *écart* is made for purposes of international comparison. The formula is useful for areas of homogeneous patterns of settlement, such as Champagne or Flanders, but it is unsuited to areas of wide variations where there are sharp local contrasts and where K can be identical in value for very different characteristics of pattern.

An amendment of Demangeon's formula can be made by substituting the number of *écarts* for an areal measurement. Thus it might be $K=\dfrac{S\times N}{T-E}$ where S is the area covered and the other data the same as before. This enables a more detailed delimitation, provided there are detailed statistics for each unit of settlement. Meynier went further in devising 'curves of frequency' but his method is too elaborate and demands much work for extensive areas.[11]

Zierhoffer has devised another formula on the assumption that the degree of dispersion of settlement will increase with the corresponding increase of area per dwelling.[12] The degree of dispersion R is thus expressed by the formula $R=\dfrac{p\times s}{d}\times K$, where p is the average area per dwelling, s is the number of house groups in the commune (i.e. *écarts* and the chief settlement), and d the total number of inhabitants. K is a constant coefficient, calculated at 0·005, so that in the case of complete dispersion R equals 100 per cent. and for absolute concentration the value is 6·66 per cent. This method which is quite elaborate does not give sufficient contrast to the value of R in intermediate categories, between complete dispersion and absolute nucleation. Also the formula tends to diminish the importance of the concentration of population in large urban centres and to exaggerate the concentration in village agglomerations. A third criticism of Zierhoffer's method lies in the determination of the value p. It is difficult to determine what are the waste lands and the productive lands of any settlement. Moreover, the assumption that the degree of dispersion increases with the area of land per inhabitant is not always valid.

Several other formulae have been conceived, usually modifications of Demangeon's conception of the relation of the number of settlements per commune to the total population, or of Zierhoffer's spatial formula. Bernard's formula $K=\dfrac{S\times M}{N^2}$ is an example of the first category.[13] S is the area of the commune, M the total number of houses, and N is the number of settlement groups. This formula, however, does not discriminate closely between the settlement variations and K can be identical in value with very different patterns.

Debouverie's formula is one of the most successful attempts yet made to relate regional variations of settlement with the standard conceptions of concentration, agglomeration and dispersion.[14] He contends that the minimum number of houses which must comprise a settlement is roughly proportional to the total number of settlements situated in the area considered. That is to say, each regional pattern will provide in itself a yardstick for the definition of nucleation or dispersion and it is necessary to evaluate this in the first place. Debouverie recognised that in each commune there is a distinction between a *lieu habité* or house unit and a *centre d'habitat* or settlement unit. To distinguish these, some arbitary definition must be made and several geographers have already provided such areal definitions. Lefèvre defined an agglomeration as a unit where the distance between each dwelling was not more than 50 to 100 m. Zierhoffer defined dispersion as arising where the dwellings were separated from each other by distances of 150 to 200 m. The actual distance will vary according to the regional conditions, and so Debouverie, thinking of Belgium, fixed the figure at 100 m., to mark the limit of the dispersed settlement pattern.

There are several stages in the Debouverie formula, $X = \dfrac{H}{L}$. The minimum number of dwellings that will comprise a *centre d'habitat* or settlement is the value X, which will vary according to each regional pattern. K is a constant value, H is the total number of dwellings, and L is the number of settlement units. It is necessary, first of all therefore, to fix the value of K. This is found by the formula $K = \dfrac{X \times L}{H}$. Where there is complete dispersion in 1 sq. km. and the houses are at least 100 m. from each other, H will equal L and X will be 1. If there is absolute concentration of population and the houses are at least 50 m. from each other the resultant value of K will be $\dfrac{1}{16}$ as follows: $K = \dfrac{X \times L}{H}$. L is 1; H is 50×50 m. divided by the 1 sq. km. of area, that is 400; and X is estimated at 25, the number of houses estimated to convert a dwelling unit into a settlement unit. Thus $K = \dfrac{25 \times 1}{400} = \dfrac{1}{16}$. Between these two extremes of complete dispersion $(K=1)$ and absolute concentration $\left(K=\dfrac{1}{16}\right)$ the average value of $K=\dfrac{1}{4}$ has been taken by Dubouverie. To take an example, where there are only two settlements in a commune, one with 200 houses and another with 50, then $H=250$, $L=2$ and $X=K\dfrac{H}{L}=\dfrac{1}{4}\times\dfrac{250}{2}=31\cdot25$. Or again, when there are 200 dwellings grouped in one settlement, 40 in a second, and 20 are scattered, then the result will be as follows: $H=260$, $L=22$ and $X=\dfrac{1}{4}\times\dfrac{260}{22}=2\cdot8$.

This formula is particularly useful in distinguishing types of nucleation and concentration, but the values of disseminated patterns are not so clearly presented. It is successful in relating the variations from region to region. However, all these mathematical formulae have their limitations. The attempt to determine statistically such highly variable factors of settlement is perhaps illusory.[15] The plan and pattern of regional types, whether one thinks of the Lorraine villages, the Slav settlements or the Mediterranean agglomerated types, are so variable in character that statistical analysis can only be generalisations partially classifiable.

Theories on the Origin of Settlement Types

The task of the student of settlement is not only to examine the map patterns of the inhabited area, but to understand their origins. Theories of origin may be broadly grouped into three categories: those based on physical determinants; those which explain all features by ethnic and racial influences; and those which attribute the types to historical causes. The generalisations of the determinists were too simple to explain settlement variations, and it is now recognised that factors such as soil types, water supply and relief cannot alone explain dispersion or nucleation. Racial or ethnic theories have been much more plausible explanations and we shall consider these in some detail.

At the end of the nineteenth century, an outstanding contribution to the study of rural settlement was made by August Meitzen in his four-volume work, *Siedelung und Agrarwesen der Westgermanen und Ostgermanen* (Berlin, 1895). Meitzen distinguished two patterns of settlement associated in Western Europe with the *haufendorf* or agglomerated village and the *einzelhof* or isolated dwelling. He thought that the type of settlement was the direct result of the agrarian régime practised. Thus he related the *dorfsystem* or *gewanndorf* to open-field and communal cultivation, while the *haufendorf* and the *hofsystem* or *einzelhof* he associated with individual cultivation and scattered settlement. Meitzen noticed that whereas the nucleated village is the chief type found in Germany, the isolated dwelling occupies most of France. He argued from this observation: 'It should not be doubted that the mode of settlement in isolated farms, which still occurs to-day in two-thirds of France, in Brabant and in the region north of the Rhine and as far as the Weser, goes back to the ancient Celtic mode of land occupation, which Caesar had found so markedly prevalent.'[16] He further argued: 'It seems demonstrable that the villages in opposition to the isolated farms of Celtic origin, must owe their existence to the Germanic conquests.'[17] The extent of the nucleated village in northern France was to Meitzen an indication of the Germanic conquest over that territory, just as the villages of the English Midlands could be explained in contrast to the Celtic traditions of Wales. Meitzen discerned a third ethnic influence in the Slavonic settlements of Central and Eastern Europe. The round village plan, the *runddorf* and the street village or *strassendorf* indicated their influence. Thus Meitzen neatly divided European settlement into the three ethnic categories of Celtic, Germanic and Slavonic.

Though historians appreciated the industry of Meitzen in his collation of much data, including an atlas of field and settlement plans, they were immediately critical of his conclusions. Jacques Flach, among others, disproved Meitzen's explanation of French settlement types.[18] It has been pointed out that the eastern boundary of the *einzelhöfe* in Germany, coinciding with the River Weser, was equally Germanic on both sides.[19] Similarly it has been shown that the settlers of Belgium were equally the same north and south of the Boulogne-Maastricht boundary between the nucleated and dispersed types of settlement.[20] Nor can field systems be identified exactly with types of settlement. In the Channel Islands, where Meitzen noted the *einzelhöfe* pattern, open fields of the *gewanndorf* system were practised until inclosure took place in the eighteenth century.[21]

It is now recognised that nucleation or dispersion is much too complex to be explained by a simple reference to 'racial' influence, which is in itself meaningless. French scholars have shown that according to the exigencies of different periods, nucleation and dispersion have been more or less marked. Thus the insecurity of the fifth and sixth centuries A.D. led to an emphasis on village life for defence needs; other anarchical periods, such as the tenth and early eleventh centuries, also led to the disappearance of many isolated dwellings. Decimation by plague and the shortage of labour after the Hundred Years' War were other reasons for the same tendencies. Again, the devaluation of money during the fifteenth and sixteenth centuries in France, and the consequent decline in value of the fixed village rents, forced landowners to encourage tenant settlers to occupy isolated holdings on their demesne.[22] Colonisation and enclosure of the waste had the same effect in increasing the extent of dispersion.

Although Meitzen's theory is now discredited, no one can deny that certain cultural influences may help to explain certain distinct types of rural settlement, such as the Welsh *tref*, the Norwegian *llan*, the Roman *villa*, the Frankish *mas* or *mansum*, and the Slavonic *zadruga*. The controversy over cultural explanations, however, arises from the question how far such cultural continuity can be traced. This problem has been considered particularly in England where so many hybrid types of settlement may be discerned, related to the succession and mixture of invasions and movements of colonisation. There are those who believe that the Roman system of land-holding and settlement was adopted by the Anglo-Saxon invaders of Britain and that there has been continuity since Roman times. Seebohm outlines this theory in his statement, 'more things went into the making of England, than were imported in the keels of the English invaders of Britain.'[23] D'Arbois de Jubainville expressed similar views in his studies of France.[24]

In opposition to the Roman school, the Teutonic school emphasises the break in continuity with the Germanic invasions. English place-names suggest considerable displacement of the Celtic peoples by Anglo-Saxon settlers, while Stubbs declares that the vestiges of Romano-British law that have filtered through local custom are infinitesimal. Air photography has recently shown that the theories of the Teutonic school are more probable, for there is a distinct break between the Neolithic and Romano-British field systems and settlement types on the one hand, and the English field system on the other.[25] The mapping of their respective settlements has indicated a change in geographical distribution, between the Neolithic and

Bronze Age settlers who tended to avoid the damp oak forest, and the later settlers of the forest associated with what has been termed the 'valley-ward movement' of settlement.

Apart from these different historical schools of thought concerning the significance of cultural influences, other controversies have

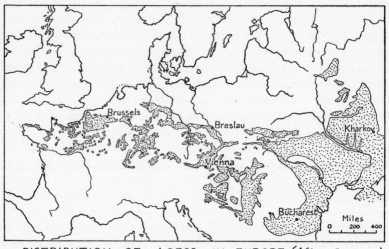

DISTRIBUTION OF LOESS IN EUROPE *(After Gradmann)*
Fig. 11.

arisen from the consideration of physical influences, notably in the theories of M. R. Gradmann.[26] Like Meitzen, Gradmann assumed that there was a fundamental relation between field systems and settlement types. He believed the evolution of man to be dependent on the rural economy practised, and so to him the history of civilisations was essentially agrarian history. There were two great civilisations in Europe, he argued, one associated with the Mediterranean Sea and the other related to the North Sea and the Baltic, with different agrarian régimes and differing factors involved in their evolution. He concerned himself in his numerous studies with Germanic settlement which, he believed, first developed on the fertile and dry loess regions of Central Europe (Fig. 11). His *steppenheide* thesis assumed that since primitive man could not have cleared the forest, he must have advanced through the loess and adjacent hill regions, when a deterioration of climate had made them forest free. A steppe-heath vegetation covered these regions, he maintained, during Sub-Boreal time, an epoch which he believed to have coincided with the advance of Neolithic man westwards through Central Europe.[27]

The findings of palaeo-botany and of modern archaeology have disproved the circular argument that because Neolithic man avoided the forest, there must have been little forest wherever Neolithic finds have been discovered. Gradmann's *steppenheide* theory is discredited because we now know that Neolithic settlement actually took place during the damp conditions of the Atlantic phase of climate (5000-2500 B.C.). It is also known now that deciduous forest was widespread over the loess regions and even over the chalk uplands of Europe. Thus Clark has concluded, 'Neolithic farmers were more concerned with the ease and fertility of loess soil than with its forest cover.'[28] Where necessary they sacrificed fertility to ease of working, with their ards and simple two-ox ploughs, as has been discovered in parts of southern England, in Schleswig-Holstein and in other parts of Europe. As Miss Garnett has said in summarising this problem, 'General considerations seem therefore to suggest that the direction of geographical emphasis may have been fundamentally wrong in assuming that Neolithic man, unable to modify a forest environment to suit his needs, made use of more open country only.'[29]

Some authorities have now come round to the opposite view, such as Nietzsch, who thinks the presence of forest would be an absolute requirement for early settlement. In fact such writers think that prehistoric and early historic economy was an economy of forest peoples in Western and Northern Europe. Thus modern research has shown that the clay belts of the English Plain, the Paris Basin, Swabia and Franconia, and other areas, canalised movement and settlement, not because they were forested but because they were too heavy to till with the primitive instruments available. Only as the heavier ploughs were introduced could these lands be cultivated and settled.

Modern views on the origin of settlements may be summarised as follows. Archaeological research has demonstrated in Denmark and elsewhere that compact villages in association with dispersed farms date at least from the Iron Age. This was possibly associated with the change from a semi-nomadic economy to permanent settlement, with the deterioration of climatic conditions.[30] The choice of land for settlement was at first determined by the ease with which it could be cultivated by the ard; later, with the introduction of suitable ploughs, there was scope to choose more fertile lands irrespective of tillage conditions. Judging from Caesar's texts, Roman Gaul had both *vici* (villages) and *aedificia* (isolated farms) though we are not entitled to transpose all regional differences of nucleation or dispersion to Roman times where the evidence is indecisive.[31] We can date the formation of the majority of villages in France from the fifth century A.D. and in England from the sixth century. Most of the Romanised village names of France, such as Savigny (Sabinus), Fleury (Flores), Lagny (Latiniacus) and Vitry (Victoriacus)—as well as the Spanish Villa Arcayo or Arcaya (Arcadius, Arcadia), Berberana (Barberanus) and Antoñana (Antonius)—date from this formative period. Place-name and cadastral evidence help to elucidate the later phases of colonisation of the waste and expansion of existing settlements. But in all the evidence, it is apparent that the correlation of historical, cultural and economic evidence must be considered in relation to the permissive factors of the physical landscape and the geographical location. It is therefore necessary to consider what have been the historical factors involved in settlement patterns, and then to examine the physical milieu.

The Historical Significance of Settlement

The historical data from which settlement studies are derived fall into three categories. There is firstly the documentary evidence contained in such surveys as the Domesday Survey of England, the *Repartimientos* of several Spanish kingdoms, the *Landnámabók* or land settlement survey of Iceland (A.D. 870-930), and numerous charters,[32] terriers and polyptics. Secondly, there is the evidence of place-names, both of field-names and settlement-names, though the latter are the more stable and reliable for evidence in early historical enquiry. Such studies as those made by Olsen, using the 50,000 farm names of Norway, indicate what contributions to the historical analysis of settlement can be made by this evidence. However, place-name studies are investigations which peel off layer after layer of data without succeeding in revealing at last the innermost kernel. Olsen has therefore suggested that 'the most promising line of study in the immediate future will be researches of a regional description, partly of a specialised historical nature, and partly aiming at a synopsis of regional geography.'[33] To do so the third series of data, the cadastral plans and topographic maps, are an essential equipment. The early cadastral plans of the sixteenth and seventeenth centuries are mostly seignorial in origin. Most terrier plans date from the eighteenth century and the great national surveys such as the English tithe plans (1834) and the French first cadastral survey (1808-50) are later.[34] There are, however, some excellent German surveys of the eighteenth century and the Schlesvig survey begun in 1768 on the scale of 1 : 4,000 is very good.[35] Some of the early topographic surveys are also useful sources of data, such as the Military Survey of Scotland (1755-67) on the scale 1 : 20,000,[36] and the map of Corsica made in 1794 on the scale 1 : 10,800.[37]

From these sources of historical data, it is apparent that settlement has been significant in Europe for at least three reasons. It has brought about the mingling and stratification of peoples from which the European nations have developed; it has influenced the establishment of frontiers; and it has also meant the more intensive use of the land and the colonisation of the waste.

The evidence of place-names suggests how complex and important for settlement studies have been the migrations of peoples. Among these the most important have been the expansion and settlement of peoples during the time of the Roman Empire, the Germanic invasions from Northern Europe, and later the invasions of Huns, Magyars, Turks and others from the east. As they came from a variety of habitats and brought with them different economies, they have produced great diversity of cultural influences. The migration of Germanic peoples has been of great significance in the development of settlement in Central Europe. The colonisation of the Vikings in Iceland and North-West Europe during the ninth and tenth centuries, and of the Normans in France and England have both been notable among the smaller waves of migration. The inroads of Arabs and Berbers into the Iberian Peninsula and Sicily have left the tide of their advance indelibly marked, especially in the southern parts of these territories, where they stayed longest. Finally, the eastward colonisation movements of Germanic peoples from the eleventh and twelfth centuries, and the settlement of Slavs, have profoundly influenced the types of settlement in Central and Eastern Europe. It would be erroneous, however, to consider this influence of cultural differences to be the dominant factor.

The second significance of settlement to bear in mind has been the establishment of frontiers, associated with physical, ethnic, folk, national and empire boundaries. The frontiers of the Salian Franks in the Low Countries, for example, were influenced by the barriers of forest and marsh. Des Marez has indicated in detail how this people in their migrations of A.D. 358-450 avoided the great forest of Silva

Carbonnière in Flanders, the marshes along the coast, and the poor hilly lands of Campine, to settle in the valleys of the Lys and Scheldt.[38] In Britain the folk frontier is well illustrated by the expansion of small social and political groups which emerged after the Anglo-Saxon conquests to form such provinces as Wessex, East Anglia and the Midlands, each with their characteristic features of settlement.[39] An ethnic boundary is well exemplified by the *Limes Sorabicus* between Slavonic and Germanic settlement in Europe which partially accounts for certain contrasted types of villages. As we have seen, however, in the critique of Meitzen's theory this explanation has to be used with caution. It is certain however that the marklands established by the Germans in the eastward conquests and by the Christians in the reconquest of the Iberian Peninsula have marked zones of settlement, whose distribution can be explained by such military frontiers.

National frontiers have not been so important for the demarcation of settlement types, since the chief migrations of peoples and their colonisation movements were completed before the concept of nationality had been much developed. Differences of national legislation, however, have provided some contrasts as in the case of the Solway Firth Plain on the borders of Scotland and England. Here the dispersed farms and estate villages of Dumfriesshire, erected during the Agricultural Revolution of the eighteenth century, contrast sharply with the small agricultural villages, traditional to Cumberland.[40] Different social traditions and the enclosure legislation enacted by the two countries account for this contrast within the physical homogeneity of this region (see Fig. 2). Empire frontiers, such as those of Charlemagne and of the Ottoman Turks in Eastern Europe have not been effective frontiers of settlement. A notable exception, however, is the Roman *limes* which has stamped indelible limits, such as the boundaries of the centuriated field patterns in Dalmatia, and the frontier outposts of settlement in the Rhine valley.

The third and most significant feature of European settlement has been the colonisation of the marsh and the forest and the more intensive use of land already settled. Each region has had its entrance phase of settlement, followed by colonisation and expansion. Such a sequence was at first selective of the most suitable terrain, but becoming less so as more and more of the land was occupied and settled, and the barriers of waste between each community were removed.

Colonisation of the marsh was first systematically carried out by

(*Aerofilms Ltd.*)

V*a*. Dutch Polders.

(*Aerofilms Ltd.*)

V*b*. Coombe Martin, Devon.

the Romans although lake-dwellings were an earlier development. The rigid framework of centuriation in Italy, as in the Po valley (Ill. III), Arno Basin, the Roman Campagna and the Tavoliere di Puglia, attest to this movement of reclamation. The same purposeful dissection of suitably level land was also carried

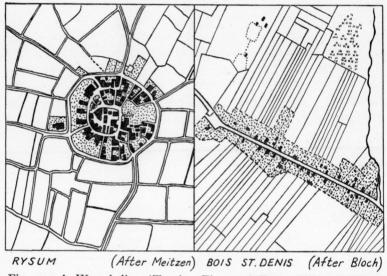

RYSUM   (After Meitzen)   BOIS ST.DENIS   (After Bloch)

Fig. 12. A Westphalian 'Terp'   Fig. 13. A Forest Village in Aisne
       Village.   (France), 1715.

out in parts of Andalusia. This formal precision in the lay-out of fields and settlements has scarcely been surpassed by the modern colonisation of the New World in the gridiron arrangement. Extensive reclamation of the marsh, however, had to wait until the period between the eleventh and fourteenth centuries. In Flanders, 95 per cent. of the settlements date from this period[41] (Ill. Va). Half of the Netherlands and one-third of Belgium arose from the salt marsh during these centuries. The *terpen* and polder settlements of the Low Countries and northern Germany arose during these attempts at land reclamation (see Fig. 12).

More important than settlement in marshlands has been the colonisation of the forests of Europe. The Romans cleared great tracts of Calabria and Apulia, and deforestation became a marked feature of other Mediterranean regions. But along the Roman *limes* of Central

Europe, the forests were cleared only in small patches, such as along the terraces of the Rhine. It appears that early deforestation was associated with deciduous rather than coniferous forest, since the brown forest soils of the oak forests are better suited to arable farming than the podsols of the resinous conifers. Gradmann has pointed out that the Roman *limes* between the rivers Neckar and upper Danube followed approximately the boundary between the coniferous and deciduous forests.[42] There is evidence from place-names of sporadic clearances during the so-called 'Dark Ages', usually of brushwood and woodland which had reverted to waste, rather than of primeval forest. The name of the Belgian province 'Brabant' indicates such a type of vegetation, cleared from hundreds of settlements about the sixth century. Such efforts, however, were only sporadic and it is estimated that by the ninth and tenth centuries very little waste had been cleared systematically. Only a very small proportion of the land in Spain and in Italy, except for Sicily, was under cultivation. Half or more of France, two-thirds of the Low Countries and Germany, and four-fifths of Britain remained uncultivated.[43]

'The Golden Age of Labour,' as the period A.D. 1050 to 1350 has been called, was the great era of colonisation. The challenge given to settlers in the great forestated belts of Europe was like that given by Joshua to the Children of Israel, 'If thou be a *great* people, then get thee up to the wood country and cut down for thyself there.'[44] East of the Rhine the numerous place-name suffixes in *rod*, *reud*, *ried*, *rath*, *brand*, *hain*, *scheid*, and *grün* indicate how extensively the Germanic peoples took up this challenge to clear the forests. The English suffixes in *den*, *falt*, *holt*, *hurst*, and *ward* indicate the same process of clearing on a smaller scale. Both ecclesiastical and lay lords were responsible for this organised movement of clearance. The three thousand two hundred Cistercian abbeys and houses, the two thousand Cluniac priories, the numerous Carthusian and Trappist monasteries and the countless hermitages, were later rallying points for thousands of colonists who settled in the forest. Figure 14 illustrates how important was the role of ecclesiastical settlement in the great forest lands of Bas-Maine in France during this period.[45]

Secular lords had also a very decisive influence on the successful clearance of forest. Sometimes the tension between the peasants who coveted waste for their own enclosure and the lords who guarded it strictly for the game preserves, meant that the forensic use of the

term 'forest' had often more significance than the botanical use of the
word. In some instances, however, whole districts were carved up by
lords eager to see colonists clear the forest, as in Normandy and in

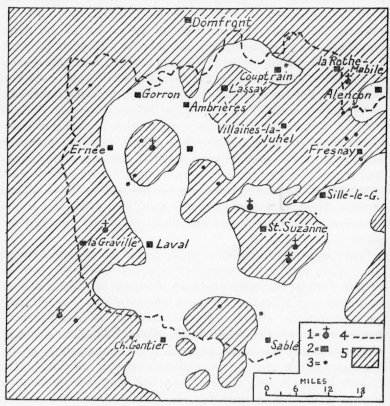

Fig. 14. Forest settlement in Bas-Maine (after Musset).
1. Settlements associated with an abbey.
2. Settlements associated with a château.
3. Chief priories.
4. Limits of Maine.
5. Forested areas.

parts of the Rhine valley. Favourable legislation, such as the Statute
of Merton (1235) in England, permitted lords of the manor to add
to their demesne such parts of the common waste as were beyond
the needs of the tenants, so that in Shropshire, Nottinghamshire
and Somersetshire and other forested areas of England, clearance

proceeded unhindered. Everywhere the balance between the cultivated and the waste was largely decided by the great lords, although
the success of colonisation depended largely on the number of *hospites*
or freemen available for such schemes.

The outcome of the colonisation movements was that by the
fourteenth century much of the present landscape of Western Europe
was recognisable and patterns of nucleated and dispersed settlement
were already apparent. This is particularly true of France which
had in 1328 about 3,300,000 householders in 32,000 parishes, that
is about ten to twelve million inhabitants.[46] This would give a
density not reached or surpassed except by some favoured districts
of Italy; some regions of France had as many rural dwellings at
this period as were counted at the end of the eighteenth century
when the maximum rural population was reached. In England, the
population could scarcely have exceeded three and a half million
during the fourteenth century, so that the rural pattern was probably
not so clearly fixed.[47] The population of Central Europe was even
sparser and the eastward colonisation movements continued. Some
countries around the Baltic, such as the Grand Duchy of Lithuania,
did not have their present settlement pattern fixed until the sixteenth
century, when they were colonised with small street villages or
reihendörfer.[48] In Russia, settled agriculture was only developed
after the eleventh century by the Slavs and during the following
centuries clearance of the forest took place along the rivers, especially
in the valleys of the Upper Volga, Moskva, and North Dvina which
were sheltered from the Tartar invasions. Forest hamlets or *derevni*
and street villages or *sloba* became the dominant types of settlement
in the great mixed coniferous forest belt of the country.[49]

Physical Factors Affecting Rural Settlement

The above summary of historical factors indicates that it is impossible to generalise and explain patterns of settlement in terms
of a few isolated factors. Similarly it is inaccurate to assess the
distribution of settlements in relation to a few physical conditions.
Fifty years ago many geographers explained the occurrence of
nucleated villages by favourable hydrological conditions. It is
certainly true that many villages are sited in relation to wells and
springs, as in Northamptonshire, where 200 out of 290 villages,
towns and hamlets are sited at the contact of two geological outcrops.
Contact springs in the Northampton sands account for the position of

G

one-third of the villages in the county.[50] But it is also true that the deep wells of Picardy and Beauce, which to-day supply the needs of large nucleated settlements, were only made in the last two or three centuries, half a millennium after the formation of these villages.[51]

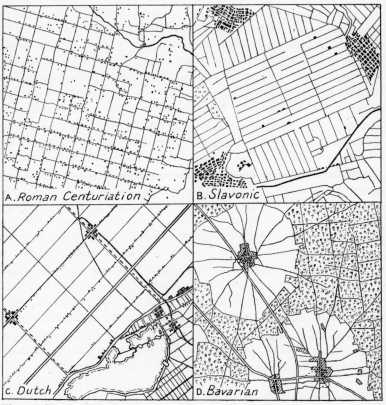

Fig. 15. Types of Colonisation in Europe: A. Roman Centuriation in the North Italian Plain, in Venezia; B. Slavonic settlement in the Danube Basin; C. Dutch polder settlement near Haarlem; D. Bavarian forest settlement near Munich.

In the Causses, where nucleated settlements around well sites might be expected, there is dispersion. In the plains of Hungary, where the water-table is near the surface for shallow wells, large nucleated villages occur. Water supply is now recognised to be a factor of only secondary importance in explaining nucleation and dispersion in Central and Western Europe.[52]

Conditions of relief have more general importance. Vidal de la Blache noted that nucleation was most apparent in areas where the area of arable was continuous enough to permit uniform agrarian practice. Dispersed settlement was more often associated with broken relief as in mountainous areas.[53] Thus the nucleated villages of the Burgundian plain give place to the hamlets and farmsteads of the Vosges. Hungarian villages are found in the Danubian lowlands and hamlets mark the limits of the Carpathian foothills. In Mediterranean regions it is apparent, however, that nucleated villages occur in both hilly and flat terrain, except where irrigation water encourages dispersion, as in the *huertas* of Spain.

Associated with relief is the influence of insolation on the distribution of settlement in mountainous areas. The *adret* and *ubac*, corresponding to the sunny and sheltered slopes of French valleys are features recognised in many districts. But it is not sufficient to identify slopes receiving strong noonday sun or possessing the advantages of a general southern aspect as the law of assimilation would suggest. For an increase in the intensity of light by a certain increment induces an increase in the intensity of assimilation which is greater the nearer the light is to the minimum. In a series of interesting studies of Alpine valleys it has been demonstrated that the duration of sunshine is of more importance in the distribution of settlements than the intensity of light.[54] Grouped settlements in the Alps are everywhere located with reference to spring insolation on high hillside positions. The oldest hamlets are placed where, in addition to spring insolation, there is a long duration of winter sunshine. In Corsica and the Cevennes the *adret* and *ubac* slopes have reverse importance. Many villages are concentrated in the shade, since the settlements are built in the zone of the chestnut forest which has been the traditional source of food supply, and the sweet chestnut does not like too much sunshine.

Soil conditions are now recognised to be one of the most important series of factors in the distribution of settlements. Distinctions have been made broadly of three types of soil: *limon* or loess and loamy soils, impermeable clay soils, and poor soils either leached of their plant material, or naturally infertile, such as certain sandy soils. Geographers have long recognised the importance of the loess soils, stretching through Northern France, Germany and Eastern Europe to the Ukraine. These soils are well suited for cereal cultivation and usually associated with the nucleated villages and the

open-field system. Their ease of working, their fertility, their ability
to maintain moisture and their extent have attracted settlement since
Neolithic times.

In contrast to such soils of primary settlement are the heavy
clay lands which have remained as forest (*silva*) or waste (*saltus*) until
the colonisation movements from the end of the Middle Ages began
to settle them. Their dispersed dwellings often indicate them to be
areas of secondary settlement. Dion has explained why these soils
have been most frequently associated with dispersion. Because of the
nature of these soils, the periods when they could be treated were
shortened, either by wet seasons when ploughing was impossible or
by drought when the soils were baked hard. It was essential therefore
for the labourer to live as near as possible to his fields to take full
advantage of favourable weather conditions. The difficulties of
communication under such conditions where transport was impeded
by mud, encouraged the same tendency towards dispersion of
dwellings. Also such conditions of cultivation did not allow for a
large community to depend on the low and uncertain returns from
such soils. It has therefore been concluded, 'it is in these conditions
set by the agricultural labourer and not by the conditions of water
supply that it is necessary to look for the true cause of dispersion of
rural settlements in clay regions.'[55] Considerable confusion, however,
may arise in the use of terms such as 'boulder clay,' where the
geological term for the subsoil is mistaken for the nature of the surface
soil. Thus a study has shown that although 87 per cent. of the
Neolithic remains of Anglesey occur on 'boulder clay,' more detailed
investigation indicates that only 17 per cent. are actually on impermeable soils and the remainder are on light or well-drained soils.[56]

The third category of soils, the infertile sands and leached soils,
has given rise to an interesting theory. Attempts to correlate leached
and senile soils with tertiary peneplane surfaces have been made in
the Paris Basin[57] and in the London Basin.[58] The sterile soils covered
with forest in High Perche, North Berry, Puisaye and Forêt d'Othe in
the Paris Basin, and the upper dip-slope of the Chilterns and North
Downs, have been associated with ancient peneplanes. But the rate of
soil formation has still to be studied in many areas and it is uncertain
in southern England, for example, how many of these soils have been
developed *in situ*. There is no doubt, however, that these belts of
poor or sterile soils have been zones of negative influence upon
settlement.

Social and Economic Factors Affecting Rural Settlement

Often features of settlement can only be explained by man himself and his needs. Among social factors, defence has played an important role, especially in areas recurrently liable to invasion. In the plain of Roussillon in the south of France, some 93 villages were left deserted in the coastal lowland by their inhabitants who founded new settlements in the hills, during the Corsair raids of the twelfth and thirteenth centuries.[59] In Provence, the perched villages explain the same need of security. Le Lannou relates that nearly all Sardinian villages date from the anarchy after Justinian's rule, when the insecurity of the period necessitated communal defence.[60] Similarly in Corsica, the *scolca* were proprietors who banded themselves together to defend their lands. Fortified village sites are still apparent in the plain of the Po between the Oglio and Adda.[61] Subsequent changes have frequently led to a new development of settlement. In Scotland, for example, many of the old *castletouns* or hamlets grouped under the shelter of baronial castles, were rebuilt by landlords seeking to improve their estates. Such are Inverary, Glamis, Fochabers, and Newcastleton.[62]

The relation of agricultural systems to settlement forms has been long recognised. It has been assumed that the Welsh with their dispersed settlements remained semi-nomadic in the twelfth century, partly because of the nature of the mountainous relief and partly as the result of the pastoral economy.[63] The dispersion of settlement in Herve (Belgium) has been associated with cattle-rearing practised there, at least since the fourteenth century.[64] The marked nucleation of settlement under the open-field system, especially the three-field system, has also been noted by many writers. The contrast between the dispersion of Tuscany and the agglomeration of south Italy has been explained by differences of tenure. The *mezzadria* system, or share-tenancy, with family unit or *podere*, and mixed subsistence farming, together encouraged the dissemination of farms in Tuscany from the Middle Ages. In contrast, the *feudatori* régime of the south with its emphasis on monoculture did not demand the constant residence of the proprietor. However, it was more convenient to the landlord that all his workers should dwell together in nucleated settlements where they could be more easily supervised.[65] In Russia, similar conditions made nucleation more desirable during the sixteenth and seventeenth centuries.[66] The system of *hamarskift* in Sweden, whereby the holdings of each settler were reallocated over a period of years, tended to encourage dispersion of settlement, wherever this ancient practice persisted.[67] Students of economic history have indicated that the character and variations of manorial structure have played some influence in the types of villages which can be distinguished in England.

The Distribution of Settlement Types in Europe

In conclusion, the interpretation of the map of settlement types helps to summarise the variety of factors recognised in this study (Fig. 16). The map is based on a number of compilations mentioned on page 256, references 1-9. In view of the lack of uniform definition on a statistical basis, the distribution of these types can only be considered in terms of broad generalisations. The map, however, reveals certain fundamental features. Firstly, it demarcates the limits between the dispersed and nucleated settlements and certain gradations between these types. Secondly, it defines a series of nucleated types of settlement conditioned by physical and economical factors. Thirdly, it illustrates the influence of cultural factors in certain distinctive types of settlement.

Broadly, the map may be divided into four great belts of settlement types across Europe. Throughout the great mountain ranges of the Carpathians, Alps and their continuations, are hamlets and scattered farms. In such areas, the economy practised and the influences of the relief, together may account for this pattern of dissemination. The degree of dispersion may depend however on other historical factors. Thus in the Basque lands there are many scattered farms to be found in tributary valleys, bearing the name *Borde*, indicating them to be daughter homesteads of farms in the villages, situated in the main valleys. Most of these secondary settlements date from the seventeenth and eighteenth centuries and can be traced to the original farmsteads, since the houses of both bear the same name. Other groups of dispersed settlement, such as those of Armorica, the Low Countries, Lower Saxony, Kent and Wales, are more difficult to explain. Some are *einzelhof* or isolated types, developed as the initial form of colonisation, such as the Jutish settlement of Kent and the Celtic settlement of Wales, and maintained by the features of the economy practised. Others are associated with scattered hamlets and irregular settlements or *eschdorf* types, more clearly related to clearance of the forest or marsh during the early Middle Ages, as in some parts of the Low Countries. Some German scholars consider this second type as a transition from the hamlet to the compact village with its communal, agricultural practice. Local and peculiar

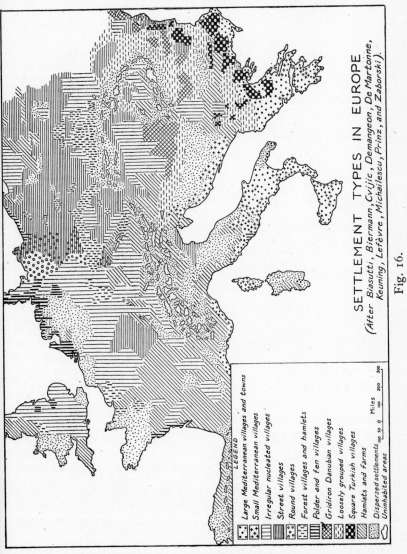

SETTLEMENT TYPES IN EUROPE
(After Biasutti, Biermann, Cvijic, Demangeon, De Martonne, Keuning, Lefèvre, Michailescu, Prinz, and Zaborski).

Fig. 16.

LEGEND

Large Mediterranean villages and towns
Small Mediterranean villages
Irregular nucleated villages
Street villages
Round villages
Forest villages and hamlets
Polder and fen villages
Gridiron Danubian villages
Loosely grouped villages
Square Turkish villages
Hamlets and farms
Dispersed settlements
Uninhabited areas

Miles
100 50 0   100   200   300

variations of soil and ground water may account, however, for either form of settlement in some areas. As we have noted, secondary infilling of settlement may occur at any historical period which may

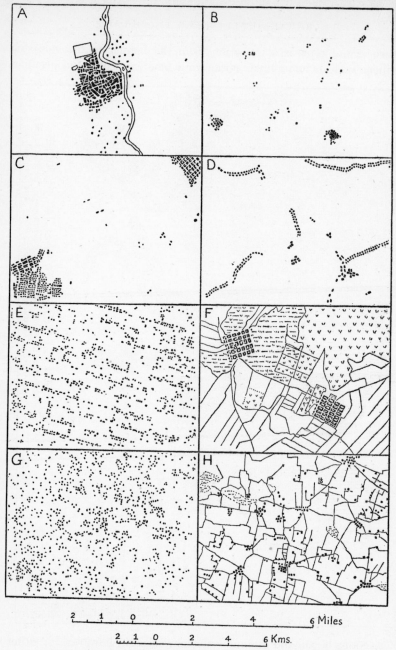

Fig. 17. Types of Rural Settlement Patterns in Europe.

A. Large Mediterranean village, Andalusia, Spain. B. Small Mediterranean villages, Peloponnesus, Greece. C. Danubian villages. D. Elongated 'street' villages, Bilo Gora (Yugoslavia). E. Dispersed corti and street villages, N. Italian plain. F. Gridiron Danubian villages, Alfold. G. Dispersed Settlements, Galicia, Spain. H. Irregular nucleated villages, E. Denmark.

favour it, such as the inclosure movements of the eighteenth and nineteenth centuries, and the squatter settlement on the waste.

Nucleated types of settlement occur in Europe in three broad belts, associated with quite different series of factors. Most noted are the irregular nucleated villages of the loess soils, extending from northern France through Germany and southern Poland into Hungary and beyond into the Ukraine. It may be significant that this type of settlement or *haufendorf* occurs roughly to the south of the limits of the Würmian glaciation. Because of their ease of working, these soils were probably the earliest to be colonised, settled by Neolithic farmers migrating westwards from the Danubian lands. Agrarian practice, throughout its changing techniques, has favoured the nucleation of settlement on these soils.

To the south, the agglomerated villages around the shores of the Mediterranean, form a second belt of nucleated settlement. Some of these villages are very ancient because the communal defence of the nucleated settlement could best survive the constant threat of pirates and other forms of anarchy. Distinction between the smaller and larger Mediterranean villages is arbitrary, though often quite appreciable. The degree of aridity often expresses a relationship with this difference, marked agglomeration being frequently associated with areas of low rainfall, as in New Castile, parts of south Italy and Greece, and Thrace. The *Čiflik* village in the Balkans illustrates the influence of cultural factors in its distinctive arrangement. It consists of a square plan, sometimes walled, within which the homesteads of the peasants are arranged more like continuous cells than houses. It is a legacy of the Ottoman rule.[68]

Across North Central Europe and with scattered areas to the south, extends the 'street' village or *strassendorf* (Ill. VI). This type of nucleated settlement is commonly associated with colonisation in the forested lands and therefore dates from the *rodungszeit* or forest clearance of the Middle Ages. In Western Europe this movement of colonisation was earlier, starting, as we have seen, in the sixth century A.D. but gaining momentum in the period 1050 to 1350. In Eastern Europe, however, this process of settlement was later. It began about the tenth century, but it was most effective after the thirteenth century. The first permanent settlement of many Slavonic peoples was associated with such 'street' villages and therefore some writers have attributed this type to Slavonic tradition. However, it is certain the German colonists also settled in many 'street' villages. Two types

VI*a*. Austrian village near Vienna.

VI*b*. Settlements near Barcs, N. Yugoslavia.

of village plan have been developed from this arrangement: the *angerdorf* or oval-shaped village, and the *strassendorf* or street plan proper. The systematic clearance of the forest behind the road settlement and the organised colonisation, supervised by 'locators,' explain the prevalence of these types in the forest lands. Another type of village which has been attributed to the Slavs is the *rundling* or 'round' village, centred on a village green. This type was copied by the German colonists in Brandenburg and Styria as a planned settlement (*rundplatzdorf*). However, rather than generalise between Slavonic and Germanic types, it is safer to compare them only with the aid of place-name identification. The suffixes *-itz*, *-ow*, *-thin* are a better guide to the extent of Slavonic colonisation than the distribution of village types.

Finally, there are the marsh villages, called by the Germans *marschufendörfer*. These are also 'street' plans, though some of the earliest are associated with the distinctive mounds, *terps* or *vliedbergen*, as these are called in the Netherlands (Fig. 12). Some one hundred and thirty-five of these *terp* settlements have been traced in the Netherlands.[69] More common are the linear settlements of the polders, drained in Flanders, Holland and the North German coast from the thirteenth century onwards (Ill. V*a*). With the early progress of peat-cutting the formation of pools confined the settlements to the ridges remaining. In the polders and fens drained during the last century or so, more effective pumping has enabled settlement to disperse.

This summary of settlement types illustrates the complexity of the subject matter and of its varied forces of causation. As has been pointed out, settlement studies should be undertaken on the basis of structure, process and stage, recognising that the processes and in consequence the forms of settlement vary from one region to another.[70] Specific data for each environment and for each historical period are required before any generalisation of types and patterns can be accepted as valid.

SELECTED REFERENCES

Aurousseau, M. 'The arrangement of rural population,' G.R., vol. X, 1920, pp. 223-40.

Brunhes, J. *Human Geography*. London, 1947 (abridged edition).

Clark, J. D. G. *Prehistoric Europe: the Economic Basis*. London, 1952.

Demangeon, A. *Problèmes de Géographie Humaine*. Paris, 1942.

Dickinson, R. E. 'Rural Settlements in the German Lands,' A.A.A.G., vol. XXXIX, 1949, pp. 239-263.

Dion, R. 'La part de la géographie et celle de l'histoire dans l'explication de l'habitat rural du Bassin Parisien,' Pub. de la Soc. de Géog., Lille, 1946, pp. 6-80.

East, W. G. *An Historical Geography of Europe*. London, 1948, chapters 1-5.

International Geographical Union, *Reports of the Commission on Types of Rural Settlement*, three volumes, 1928, 1930 and 1931.

Lefèvre, M. A. 'La Géographie des formes de l'habitat,' B.S.B.E.G., III, 1933, pp. 186-211.

Monkhouse, F. J., and Wilkinson, H. R. *Maps and Diagrams*. London, 1952, chapter six.

Sorre, M. *Les Fondements de la Géographie Humaine*. Paris, 1952, tome III.

CHAPTER SIX

RURAL HOUSE-TYPES

IN the rural landscape the traditional house is an important element. It provides evidence of the complex relations between man and his environment. Indeed, in a region such as the Basque lands the house is the symbol of its regionalism, expressing both the distinctive social organisation of its inhabitants and also their rural economy. To the geographer, the house is primarily an element of the landscape, expressive of both the physical conditions of a region and the conservatism of its inhabitants. For this reason much emphasis has been placed on the analysis of house-types in regional monographs, written on parts of Europe, such as the Alps,[1] the Garonne valley,[2] Picardy,[3] Belgium,[4] Lower Saxony,[5] Italy[6] and the Balkans.[7]

The Aim and Scope of Geographical Study

House-types are complex because there are at least two aspects of study which have to be borne in mind. Firstly, house-types illustrate the interaction of physical and human controls in the use of building materials and their influence on the architectural features. There is a close relationship between the traditional house-type of a region and the terrain from which it has been fashioned, both in the use of local building stones and of the vegetation cover. Secondly, the plan of the house and the lay-out of the farm buildings are important to study since they indicate the rural dwelling to be a functional unit which is related to the agricultural economy, the population density and the standard of living. The rural dwelling is both a shelter for man and an instrument of his agricultural activities. Often two or more house-types occur together in the same region and rarely are they separated by lines, although mountain barriers and rivers may do so.

In the modern landscape of Western Europe, radical changes usually mean that the geographer's interest in house-types lies in the past. To-day, the widespread rise of imported building materials, the uniformity of construction and the decline of agricultural population all contribute to the gradual disappearance of traditional forms in many regions, although resistance to change has varied widely. Thus in Wales there are now few examples of traditional house-types still extant. Such has been the impact of the Industrial Revolution

(a)　　　　　　　　　　(b)

(c)

VII. House-types in Eastern Europe.

　　a. Smoke house, Bosnia.
　　b. Slovakian cottage.
　　c. Village street, Transylvania.

(*Photos by D. Warriner*)

in Britain that a recent report on house-types suggested they should be studied prior to 1840.[8] Many parts of Southern and Eastern Europe still provide marked regional diversity in house-types but they also can be studied satisfactorily only by reference to the past (Ill. VII). It is thus only by the elucidation of historical types that the many hybrid forms of house-types to-day can be classified and studied.

Another aspect of study that has to be borne in mind is the social character of the dwelling. The peasant house is of the greatest geographical interest, since it reflects the most clearly the direct influences of the environment with the absence of extraneous and sophisticated features usually exhibited in the richer houses. As it has been noted: 'In peasant architecture, the fundamental issues of building are made more clearly apparent. Social, climatic and geographic conditions are combined to produce an architecture in which fashion or style play little or no part. The primitive need for shelter from the sun and the rain induces the peasant folk to build a shelter for themselves and their cattle. There are no architects. The peasant knows his wants and builds. With the meagre resources he builds as simply as possible, in the local materials available. He is able to conceive and create his work because of the simplicity of his life, simple and direct.'[9]

Climatic Factors in House-types

The axiom that houses are made to live in suggests that the early development of dwellings was primarily as shelters against cold and heat, and they were only of secondary importance for defence. Thus Tacitus describes some of the most primitive of European house-types, the pit-dwellings of Germanic tribes, in the following extract: 'they are accustomed to make artificial caves in the ground. They cover these with great heaps of dung, so as to form a shelter during the winter, and a store-house for the produce of the fields. For in such dwellings they moderate excessive cold, and if at any time any enemy should come, he ravages the parts he can see, but either discovers not such places as are invisible and subterranean, or else the delay which search would cause is a protection to the inmates.'[10] Man's need of shelter has thus been the primary factor in the early development of the house. Many climatic factors have influenced the orientation and external architecture of the dwelling, such as insolation, direction of the prevailing wind, rain and snowfall, and temperature conditions.

The influence of insolation is better illustrated in the sites of settlements than in the orientation of individual dwellings (see p. 99). Houses are often commoner on a south-facing slope in mountainous terrain, than on level sites, since trial and error has proved that radiation is greater on such a site. In northern middle latitudes on clear days, the effect of a south slope of one in ten is to increase the heating result on the ground by about 15 per cent.[11] Sometimes, however, the orientation of a house may be explained by irrational causes. In the Cotswolds, for example, the house was often so orientated, that the principal rooms faced north and east. The belief was held until the end of the eighteenth century that it was injurious to face the sun.[12]

The direction of the prevailing wind clearly influences the orientation of houses, especially along coastal areas subject to frequent gales. For example, in north-east Scotland, in fishing settlements such as Cullen, the only arrangement of the old village is the generally north-easterly arrangement of the gable ends, facing the direction of the prevailing wind. In Flanders and Brittany, the fronts of the houses always face east or south-east, never to the north-west, for the same reason. Roof adjustments are made against the same climatic element, such as the German curb-roof made to prevent the wind uplifting the roof, or the variously pitched ridge-roofs of lowland and upland areas. Sometimes the roof is built asymmetrical so that the larger slope of the roof faces the prevailing wind.

Even in modern houses the temperature controls in building construction influence both the type of material used and the thickness of the walls. In southern England, Belgium and Holland a thickness of 9 inches generally gives a sufficient insulation, 10 inches is the minimum in Western Germany, 15 inches in Central and Eastern Germany, 20 inches in Lithuania and Poland, and 28 to 30 inches in Russia. It may be estimated as a rough rule that the thickness of a house wall should be 9 inches if the mean temperature of the coldest month is 34° F. or more, and should increase by 1 inch for every degree by which the mean temperature of the coldest month falls below 34° F.[13] In windy situations the thickness needs to be increased, hence the generally thick walls of upland farmhouses.

The flat roof, common throughout the Mediterranean lands, is usually considered to be a climatic adaptation to heat (Ill. VIIIc). However, in hot weather gabled roofs with good air space below give more comfortable conditions to the rooms immediately below than do flat roofs.[14] The use of the flat roof as a verandah is one explanation for its occurrence. Within the limits of the date palm, another factor may be the length and strength of palm rafters to support the roof terrace. Other definite adaptations to high temperature conditions are the interior *patios* or courtyards of the Andalusian house and the wide verandahs, to provide air circulation, with thick stone walls to equalise the temperature of the interior.

The popularity of the troglodyte or underground dwelling is partially explained by local geological conditions, and by high temperature conditions in the summer months. Cave-dwellings help to equalise the thermal variations, warm in winter and cool in summer, while the dry air of the Mediterranean and Danubian lands excludes damp. Some cave-dwellings are ancient but many are recent excavations. The colonies of cave-dwellers at Almeria, Guadix, Granada and Valencia in eastern Spain are mainly the result of the exigencies of urban growth since the mid-nineteenth century (Ill. VIII*d*). At the beginning of the present century there were over 37,000 underground dwellings in France, Switzerland and Italy, and 32,300 of these *bordeie* in Roumania. The *burdels*, cut in the loess in Bulgaria, and the caves, excavated in limestone and travertine in Dalmatia and Istria, are still numerous.

Precipitation influences house construction in several ways. Where the rainfall is excessive for certain crops, a common feature is an open gallery on the principal façade of the house. Thus along the Basque coast, wherever the rainfall is over 1000 mm., the *caserío* and *etche* have sheltered balconies on the first floor, where the green cobs of maize can be hung to ripen. Similarly in the Swiss Jura, in the plain of Alsace and in the basin of Bresse, the gallery is useful for drying the tobacco crop. Another factor is the heavy incidence of rainfall, characteristic of the Mediterranean lands. This is probably the most satisfactory explanation for the flat roof since a steeply pitched roof would rapidly gully the drip point around the house. A flat or gently inclined roof prevents this danger.

Two other adaptations to excessive precipitation are in the steeply pitched roof and the stone base of the walls. Where the rain or snowfall is excessive the pitch of the roof may be as much as 60°, and the walls are low in relation to the area covered by the roof. Overhanging roofs to protect the walls and thick stone bases to wooden houses are other features common to rainy districts. Similar precautions are taken against damp in clay lowlands such as in the

H

VIII*a*–**VIII***d.*
House - types in Southern Europe.

(*a*) *Trulli*, Fasano, Apulia.

(*b*) *Barraca*, Valencia.

(*c*) Cypriot House.

(*d*) Cave Dwellings near Granada.

(*Italian State Tourist Dept.*)

(*a*)

(*Camera Agricola, Valencia*)

(*b*)

(M. Marshall)

(c)

(Dirección General del Turismo)

(d)

Flanders Plain. Where the snowfall is excessive the orientation of the house is so fixed that the roof slopes tend to receive an equal fall of snow, as in the high-pitched log houses of Bosnia, the Carpathians and in parts of the French Alps. In the high mountains, the peasants often prefer to fix rods or hooks on the gently pitched roofs to lodge a snow cover as an insulator against the low winter temperatures.

House-types in Navarre

An interesting example of house-types related to climatic and other influences is found in the province of Navarre, in northern Spain. The division of the province into four regions of house-types is related clearly to the environmental conditions (Fig. 18).[15] In the Pyrenean districts of Navarre there are a variety of sub-types related to the local traditions of each valley unit. They are all characterised, however, by certain common features: the pitch of the roof is steep, 45° or more, because of the heavy rainfall, and there are usually four roof surfaces to lessen the force of the wind. The Pyrenean houses are built of stone. On the lower lands of north-west Navarre the roof is pitched between 20° and 40° and it consists of two slopes aligned perpendicular to the front of the house. Climatic conditions are less rigorous, timber is more abundant, and the houses are built of wood on a stone base. The third region, central Navarre, is transitional between mountain and plain, with the roofs pitched at 10° to 20°, and the house materials are more commonly bricks baked in the sun. In the south or fourth region, which is typically Castilian, the roofs are almost flat, built on one slight slope, and the materials are adobe and brick. In the lower villages of the Ebro valley some 10 per cent. to 30 per cent. of the inhabitants live in caves. The fundamental distinction between the house-types of the plain and the mountains in Navarre is also the cultural limit of Basque and Castilian speech and customs, and as frequently happens, the boundary zone of distinct house-types has also been an important cultural divide (Fig. 18).[16] The zonation of building materials also indicates the importance of this factor in regional types of dwellings.

Building Materials of House-types

Earthen and clay dwellings framed by wattles, osiers, or reeds are survivals of the most primitive types of dwellings. They still exist in the more backward parts of Europe, although their use is both a result of the environment as well as of the standard of living. In general, two main types can be distinguished by their form: the round house and the rectangular dwelling. Examples of the round

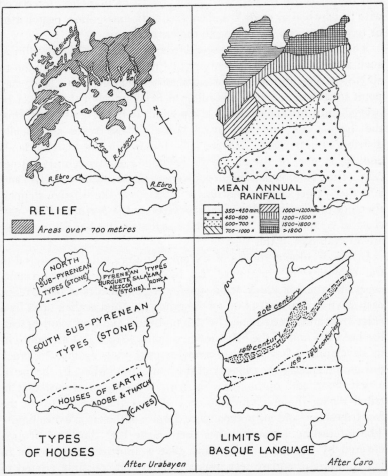

RELIEF
Areas over 700 metres

MEAN ANNUAL RAINFALL
350-450 mm.
450-600 "
600-700 "
700-1000 "
1000-1200 mm.
1200-1500 "
1500-1800 "
>1800 "

TYPES OF HOUSES
After Urabayen

LIMITS OF BASQUE LANGUAGE
After Caro

REGIONAL FEATURES OF NAVARRE
Fig. 18.

type are the *savardak* of the Dinaric Alps, the *capanna* of the Pontine marshes in Italy, the *pallaza* of Galicia in north-west Spain, the Scottish *bothan* and the Irish *clachan*. It is also found in Norway, in the Swedish provinces of Öland and Götland, and in the Lapp *riskätor*. Excavations have demonstrated its form in the Stone Age dwellings in Finland, Germany and England, and its origin is therefore very remote. The walls are usually low, built of mud or stone and the roofs are framed with poles, reeds, or branches, interlaced with brushwood or reeds,[17] and covered with moss, grass, peat, earth, or baked clay, etc., according to the environment.

The rectangular hut is the second form, found in the lake-dwellings, such as the village of Glastonbury in England, but it is common to all North-West Europe. Its strong persistence in the Celtic lands may point to its origin there, according to Seebohm, but this cannot be proved until further evidence is available. It has at least two forms, the 'long-house' and the 'Saxon house.' These types are usually distributed in lowlands and are still common in the Danube lands and the steppes of Russia. At the beginning of this century, 34 per cent. of the Roumanian dwellings were made of wattle and clay, and a further 33 per cent. of clay only.[18] The *izba* of the Russian steppes, the *kuta* of Finland, the *kálivia* of Greece, the *barraca* of the east coast of Spain (Ill. VIII*b*) and the *bourrine* of the Vendée marshes, are all examples of this type.

In the deciduous forests of Europe, a more enduring material in the evolution of the house has been the half-timbered frame, especially the oak cruck arrangement. A pair of forked oak trunks, each sawn in two and set up on the ground, united at their apex by a ridge tree, and strengthened by two tie-beams and four wind-braces, has been the unit of the half-timbered house (Fig. 19). Later steps in its development have been to straighten the walls against the cruck beams and enlarge the capacity of the house unit or bay, by the use of a first floor and outhouses (Fig. 19). It has been shown that in tribal Wales, the chieftain's house was twice the size of that of the free tribesman, and his in turn twice the size of the taeog's dwelling.[19] The interesting suggestion has been made that the 'bay' or area covered by the two cruck-beams, that is approximately 16 feet in length and 240 square feet, was a taxable unit, possibly related to the shelter which could be given to two pair of oxen.[20] This would suggest a relationship between the size of holding rented, the number of oxen used for the plough-team and the size of the house itself, that is, the number of bays it contained. This relationship of house and land was widespread in medieval Europe, occurring in Sweden, Ireland, Wales, England, France and possibly elsewhere.

The half-timbered house is characteristic of all the deciduous forest areas of Europe. It is represented in barns, wool stores, oast-houses, mills, moot and guild halls, as well as in dwellings. The commonest timbers used are oak and beech, although cherry in the

Fig. 19. Development of Roof-types. A—primitive cruck frame; B—the bergschuur of the Flemish polders; C—the development of the cruck frame; D—the transition from the cruck to the post-and-truss frame; E—the Saxon farmhouse.

Jura and chestnut in the Cevennes and Corsica are also used. Elm, poplar and even willow and ash, have also been utilised. The use of green timber in the frame, subject to subsequent warping, has accounted for the irregularity of line and surface so characteristic of the half-timbered house. The materials used for filling in the walls have varied according to local resources, ranging from wattle and daub to stone, flint and brick. Sometimes the external frame has been altered from adobe walling to tile-boarding, but the original frame has remained the same.

In the coniferous forests of Europe, the houses vary in at least two ways. Firstly, there is not the same variety of timbers and of house styles as in the deciduous forest areas; the Swedish *farbodar*, the Finnish *savupirrteja*, the Polish *chata* and other types in Central Europe do not differ very much in form. Secondly, this is because the log-cabin and chalet are usually made entirely of wood, since Norwegian pine, fir, spruce and other conifers can be more easily split for the walls of a log-cabin or sawn into planks for a chalet.

These types of wooden house occur in two distributions: latitudinally in the great coniferous forest belt of Northern Europe, and altitudinally on the slopes of the mountain ranges. In European Russia, represented by so much coniferous forest, the great majority of houses are of wood and even at the beginning of this century only 4 per cent. of the dwellings were of stone.[21] Despite the conflagrations which have destroyed repeatedly many of the towns of Northern Europe, wooden houses are still in the majority. According to the census of 1900, the chief towns of Finland had the following percentages of wooden houses: Helsingfors 64 per cent., Äbo 84, Tammerfors 84 and Viborg 90.[22] Half the dwellings of eastern Poland[23] and a third of those in Roumania are built of timber.[24]

In the great mountain systems of the Carpathians, Alps and Pyrenees, the zonation of vegetation accounts for a marked sequence of house-types according to altitude. Three broad types of dwelling are distinguishable. On the edge of the plains there are usually large, ornate houses with high façades and numerous outbuildings. Stone is often used for the lower walls, surmounted by wooden planks. On the lower mountain slopes, in the forest belt proper, the *chalet* (Ill. IXc), *landerhaus*, and *caserío* are typical, usually smaller dwellings with the family and animals under the same roof. As these types are built frequently on steep slopes with the roof at the back of the house near the ground, they lack the symmetry of construction found in the lowland types. But both these types have often ornately carved façades. In contrast, the dwellings on the higher slopes near the tree-line, are simple log-cabins or other poorer types, such as the *borde* of the Spanish Pyrenees, the *cabane* of the Alps, the *brvnara*

(E. Paget)

(a)

(Belgian Marine, Railways, Tourism)

(b)

(E. M. Houston)

(c)

IX.

(a) Farm buildings, central Sweden.
(b) Campine farmhouse, Belgium.
(c) Chalet, Austrian Alps.

of the Balkans, and the *stîna* of the Carpathians (Ill. VII). Stone becomes commoner as a building material as the dwellings reach above the tree-limit.

Stone houses are most widespread in the deforested and desiccated lands of Southern Europe. The most primitive house-types of this part of Europe are all built of stone, such as the *garritas* or *talayoti* of the Balearic Islands, the *nuraghi* of Sardinia, the *trulli* of Apulia and similar types in the Aegean islands (Ill. VIII*a*). These stony areas are associated with well-jointed, strongly compact limestone, used for the local building materials. The Nuragic house, of which there are the ruins of 8-10,000 in Sardinia, may possibly be associated with the Bronze Age migrants coming from the Ionian islands about 1000 B.C.,[25] and comparable beehive dwellings existed in the Scottish Hebrides and in Ireland.[26] The thick stone walls of the *trulli*, which help to equalise seasonal variations of temperature, probably account for their persistence to-day in modern settlements such as Albero-bello in Apulia.[27] Thus the Mediterranean world is divided into two environments, the bare stony landscapes with their stone-built houses, and the alluvial plains and deltas with their marsh vegetation, and clay and reed dwellings. In Northern Europe, the turf and stone-fronted cottage is a common type in regions poor in natural resources, such as the blackhouses of the West Highlands and Ireland, and the *tarfbaeir* of Iceland.

No sharp dividing line can be drawn between the timbered and stone dwellings, since many parts of Europe adopted stone as a material between the thirteenth and eighteenth centuries as their own local supplies of timber began to diminish, and when transport facilities were improved. Compared with wood and brick, stone has been a most costly material to transport, so that the use of stone has always been localised unless it was imported for special purposes, such as cathedrals and other luxury buildings. It has been estimated that in medieval England the cost of carrying stone for about twelve miles by overland transport was equivalent to the value of the stone itself.[28] Consequently, stone-built houses have expressed in their distinct architectural styles their own vernacular of material, following neither folk nor national boundaries, but the geological outcrops. Thus the stability of architectural form and use of material were ensured by the difficulties and cost of transport except along rivers and coastlines, where water carriage could be used more cheaply. The admixture of Cotswold stone in the buildings of Oxford has been facilitated by the river system of the Thames.[29] Along the east coast of Britain, cheap transport has accounted for such alien features in the architecture as Flemish pantiles, while along the shores of the Baltic and North Sea, brick has been the building material common to most Hanseatic towns and the Flemish influence is also apparent in the style of house construction.[30]

English House-types and Their Building Materials

The influence of geological outcrops on regional types of houses is clearly seen in England, where the great geological succession of outcrops, compressed into such a small compass, has influenced many types of dwelling. Dry-stone and mortared walls, half-timbered frames with adobe walling, and chalk, flint and gravel fillings, all express local conditions. The limestones, chalk, sandstones, volcanic, crystalline and schistose rocks, clays and marls, have all influenced such a variety of nuances in house-styles that it is impossible to generalise without considering each in its own setting. A comparison of Figs. 5 and 6 helps to explain the variety of English building materials.

The forested counties of the south-east, Kent, Sussex, Hampshire and Essex, and those of the west, Worcester, Warwick, Hereford, Shropshire and Stafford, as well as Cheshire and Lancashire, are all associated with the timber-framed cottage. But there are distinct differences between the houses of the south-eastern and the western counties. The gabled houses along the north-east coast of Kent show Dutch features, while the adoption of tile-hanging in Kent and Sussex during the eighteenth century further suggests the distinct influence of trade in this region of England.[31] There has also been a more careful use of timber in building construction than in the west, since the iron-smelting works of the Weald and the shipbuilding yards of the south coast took the best of the timber. The use of the local Horsham stone slates, which are heavy, has tended to lower the pitch of the roof to avoid drag and strain on the laths and pegs. In contrast, the heavily timbered houses of the western counties have often shown a lavish and sometimes wasteful use of wood because of the abundance of forest land and their relative isolation.[32] The timber frames are generally more massive, the overhanging is bolder, and in Cheshire and north Lancashire especially there is elaborate ornamentation or 'magpie work' on the timbered façade.

The chalk country of the south and south-east has a distinctive architecture with rubble walls infilled with chalk. The upper Cretaceous strata are usually too friable for building purposes, so that in the counties of Cambridge, Norfolk, Suffolk, Hertford, Buckingham and north Hampshire, Middle and Lower Chalk is used. Quarries in these areas, such as the famous Beerstone workings near Axminster, date back to Norman times. Flint also is important, wherever clay-with-flint occurs, and some 162 parish churches in the south-east are faced with it.[33] Clay-lump walling, often set above the ground by flint 'pinning,' is a characteristic feature of the eastern counties, especially in Norfolk, which abounds in a suitable type of boulder clay. Many of the old brick cottages in this region are really clay-lump walls, faced with brick. Similarly, pantile roofs have tended to supersede the traditional reed or rye thatch in East Anglia.

The Cotswolds have the finest examples of buildings made from oolitic limestones. The medieval wool trade, bringing prosperity to the region, accounts for its fine architecture, although the Cotswold style is later, dating between 1580 and 1690.[34] Stone walling varies in each district according to whether the stone was quarried in thin layers or in blocks. In the former type, the stone was built in thin courses, and in the latter thick courses have been used. Again, local variations in the laminated slates at the base of the Great Oolite series, account for the varying pitch of the roof. The Stonesfield slates are in varying but medium size, and their roofs average a pitch of 55°. Where the slates are smaller, the roofs have been built at a steeper pitch to permit the rainfall to run off more effectively. The Northamptonshire slates have a larger and more regular size and so commonly the roof pitch tends to be lower to avoid stress.

In the south-east of England, the cob-walled farmsteads occur wherever the decomposed Devonian Carboniferous slates and shales give rise to surface deposits of stiff greyish clay, or in the tracts of New Red marls, from which cob-walls of bright red hue have been fashioned.[35] In west Somerset, the characteristic architecure of the ill-drained lowlands is 'spit and dab' work, comparable to the 'wattle and daub' house of East Anglia. Again, in the uplands of Devon and Cornwall, the cottages built of granite blocks or schist and roofed with heavy slates, reflect a different environment of severity and exposure.

Compared with the Midlands or the south, the buildings of the north of England are low-pitched and gable-ended, surmounted with plain squat chimneys and with an absence of eaves-projection. The predominant use of undressed stone, especially in the slate and schist country, adds to the feeling of austerity, enforced by the intractable nature of the building medium.[36] In Wales, the same simplicity of farm and store building materials is found everywhere, only diversified by the half-timbering which penetrates up the formerly wooded valleys.[37]

This example of English building materials indicates the close relationship that exists between the resources of the environment and the handiwork of man. The traditional house-type is clearly a complement of the landscape. But the medium of road and rail transport with the standardised importation of materials such as Peterborough brick and Welsh slate, have tended to efface the local and regional variations of architecture.

Factors Affecting the House-plan

So far the house has been considered solely as a shelter for man. It is also necessary, however, to study it as an instrument of his agricultural activities. The influences of climatic conditions, the local resources, the medium of building materials and the cultural traditions of the inhabitants explain the external appearance of house-types. But the plan of the house and the lay-out of the farm buildings can only be explained in terms of social and economic factors. Social factors are apparent in the tribal organisation and religious features of certain house-types. For example, in the Balkans, the co-operative existence of the family group or *zadruga* helps to explain the grouping of the numerous buildings around the residence of the head of the household.[38] Similar factors account for the distinctive arrangement of the Turkish settlement or *čiflik*, while in the Moslem houses of Albania, the basic division of the dwelling into the men's quarters (*selamlik*) and harem (*haremlik*) is understandable. Defence, too, explains the association of high-walled courtyards and houses erected near adjacent towers, as in the *kullë* of the Adriatic coast, the *alquería* of the Spanish Levante (Fig. 22), and many types in Western Europe. Apart from the social factors, however, the house-plan is closely related to the agricultural activities practised by its inhabitants.

Two fundamental types of house-plan have been distinguished by French and German scholars: the single, compact house (*maison-bloc* or *einheithaus*) and the multiple dwelling (*maison-cour* or *gehöft*). The former has human and animal accommodation under the same roof, the latter has them in separate buildings. At first sight, the distinction may appear to be a social one, dependent on the standard of living, with the former related to a peasant economy and the latter associated with the large farm unit. This comparison is often true. But the distinction is much deeper, associated with historical traditions and perhaps even ethnic factors, since the single unit farmstead may occur in areas where the holdings are large and the farms prosperous, such as in the North German Plain[39] (Fig. 20). Just as it was noted in the previous chapter that settlement types cannot be explained always by reference to any one factor of social, economic or ethnic significance, so the same is true with the variety of house-plans. The legacy of history in the regional landscape is too complex to explain the diversity by one set of factors alone.

Systems of House Classification and Their Distribution in Europe

The two fundamental types of house described in the previous paragraph have been subdivided by Demangeon.[40] The single, compact dwelling (*maison-bloc*) he divided into three types, the rudimentary house (*maison à terre rudimentaire*), the compact house (*maison-bloc*), and the vertical house (*maison-haute*). The second category of multiple dwellings (*maison à cour*), he divided into open farmhouse (*maison-cour ouverte*) and enclosed farmsteads (*maison-cour fermée*). Brunhes, in his *Human Geography*, criticised this classification. He saw that it often grouped house-types dissimilar in economic status, such as the Lorrainian farmhouse and the *bourrine* of the Vendée.[41] The agricultural functions to which the house-types corresponded did not coincide sometimes in examples within the same category of plans. Nevertheless, the classification is valuable and it has been further modified by Lefèvre in her system of house-plans.[42] The single dwelling she has divided according to the shape of its plan into three types: the long-house (*maison-bloc en longeur*) such as the Lorraine type, the broad-house (*maison-bloc en profondeur*) such as the Frisian and Saxon farmsteads, and the vertical house (*maison en hauteur*). The multiple house-types she divided into two categories: the grouped farmstead (*maison en ordre serré*) and the scattered farmstead (*maison en ordre lache*). The quadrangular and two- or three-building farms are subtypes of the farm, and the duplicate house is a special type of the latter, associated with the dual economy of Alpine villages.

Both these classifications are a useful basis of study but they are restricted in their application. Demangeon based his initial study on

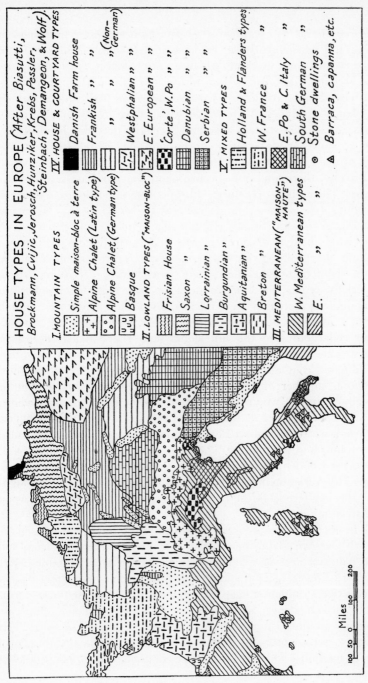

HOUSE TYPES IN EUROPE (After Biasutti, Brockmann, Cvijic, Jerosch, Hunziker, Krebs, Pessler, Steinbach, Demangeon, & Wolf).

I. MOUNTAIN TYPES
- Simple maison-bloc à terre
- Alpine Chalet (Latin type)
- Alpine Chalet (German type)
- Basque

II. LOWLAND TYPES ("MAISON-BLOC")
- Frisian House
- Saxon ,,
- Lorrainian ,,
- Burgundian ,,
- Aquitanian ,,
- Breton ,,

III. MEDITERRANEAN ("MAISON-HAUTE")
- W. Mediterranean types
- E. ,, ,,

IV. HOUSE & COURTYARD TYPES
- Danish Farm house
- Frankish ,, ,,
- ,, ,, ,, (Non-German)
- Westphalian ,, ,,
- E. European ,, ,,
- Corte', W.Po ,, ,,
- Danubian ,, ,,
- Serbian ,, ,,

V. MIXED TYPES
- Holland & Flanders types
- W. France ,,
- E. Po & C. Italy ,,
- South German ,,
- Stone dwellings
- Barraca, capanna, etc.

Miles
100 50 0   100   200

Fig. 20.

the *Enquête sur les conditions de l'habitation en France*, published in
1894, and subsequently on his own investigations. Since then an
enquiry into rural dwellings has been published in two volumes by
the French Ministries of Agriculture and Public Health, in 1939.
The classification of Lefèvre has been based on her own research on
Belgian house-types. More research will have to be done in many
parts of Europe to obtain adequate data for a detailed classification.
Fig. 20, however, is a tentative effort to indicate generally the distribution of main house-types in Europe.

Broadly, there appear to be five main zones of European house-
types. Throughout Northern Europe the multiple or farmstead
dwelling (*maison-cour*) is characteristic, occurring in Denmark,
Poland, the Baltic States, Scandinavia, Finland and Russia, and
associated chiefly with stock-rearing. The farm buildings, scattered
around the dwelling, are numerous even for the small holdings,
since the long winters necessitate much storage accommodation,
especially as hay, the chief fodder crop, is a bulky commodity. In
Scandinavia, there may be as many as six or more hay stores on each
farm, scattered about as precaution against fire[43] (Ill. IXa). An out-
door cellar cut into the hill slopes, and the Swedish *harbre* or
Norwegian *stabbhur* or granary raised above the ground, are other
buildings. From central Poland northwards, the steam bathroom or
laźnia is another characteristic building. The farmhouse itself is
usually a simple, wooden dwelling of two or three rooms. Sweden
still had one-third of its total rural dwellings in 1934 with only two
rooms, a bedroom and kitchen, and another quarter of the total had
two rooms and a kitchen.[44] The same accommodation characterises
the other wooden houses of the other countries, and there is surpris-
ingly little variation in the architectural features of the house throughout the coniferous forest belt, except in the local detail of wood
ornamentation.[45]

The second zone of house-types comprises the broad belt of the
North German Plain, the coastlands of Friesland and Holland, and
the plateaux and scarplands of Luxembourg and Lorraine. Here
stock-rearing is again predominant, but the milder winters do not
necessitate so much storage accommodation. The single unit farmstead (or *einheithaus*) is characteristic (Ill. IXb), although there are
several variations, such as the Saxon and the Frisian houses. Their
origin goes back probably to prehistoric times.[46] Essentially, the plan of
the Saxon house which appears a type common to all Aryan peoples at

an early stage of their development, is an enclosed corridor with the hearth at the end furthest from the main entrance, and flanked by cattle stalls and stables on either side (Fig. 19 E). The living quarters are built beyond the hearth. The Frisian house is built with a lower elevation, a long rectangular plan divided into two, with the dwellings on one side and the stables, byres and barn on the other side. Thus the Saxon house has been best adapted for stock-rearing, and the Frisian house for mixed farming, where the storage of crops is also important.[47]

The Lorraine farmhouse is intermediate between the two types. The ancient 'Saxon' layout can best be recognised to-day in the primitive sheep farmsteads on the moorlands of the North German Plain. It is also found on the plain of the lower Rhine as far south as Duisburg, but it is everywhere in retreat before the expansion of the Frankish or Middle German house-types[48] (Fig. 20). A comparable retreat of this house-type took place in Britain during the Middle Ages. Thus a law of 1419 expressly forbade the citizens of London to keep pigs and cows in their houses.[49] By 1577, Harrison noted that 'the mansion houses of our countrie towns and villages (which in champanie ground stand altogether by streets and joining one to another, but in woodland soils dispread here and there, each one upon the several grounds of their owners) are builded in such sort generallie, as that they have neither dairie, stable nor brewhouse annexed unto them under the same roofe (as in manie places beyond the sea and some of the north parts of our countrie) but all separate from the first and one of them from another.'[50] From the researches of Seebohm[51] and others, it appears that the single, unitary dwelling was once more widespread in North-west Europe than it is to-day.

The third zone comprises the mountain regions of Europe. Economic indigence accounts for the persistence in these areas of the single, unitary dwelling, although some types are more elaborate than others for a variety of social and economic reasons. Demangeon's distinction between the *maison-bloc élémentaire* and the *maison-haute* is applicable to this zone. In many parts of Hercynian Europe, the simple house-type is common, as in the *wohnstallhaus* of Spessart, Hunsruck, Taunus and Erzgebirge in Germany,[52] in the Ardennes, Brittany, the Central Massif, and in Wales, Scotland and Ireland. The Carpathian *stavoli*, the Alpine *chalet*, the Pyrenean *caserio*, the Apennine *seccatoi* and the *kucá* of the Dinaric Alps, belong to the second category, usually larger two-storey dwellings where hay storage and winter

I

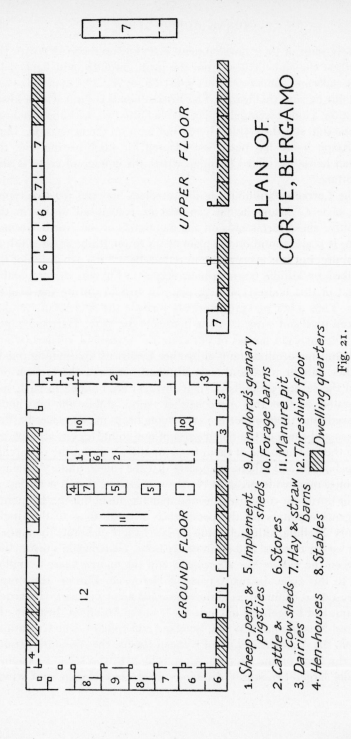

UPPER FLOOR

GROUND FLOOR

PLAN OF.
CORTE, BERGAMO

1. Sheep-pens &   5. Implement   9. Landlord's granary
   pigsties   sheds   10. Forage barns
2. Cattle &   6. Stores   11. Manure pit
   cow sheds   7. Hay & straw   12. Threshing floor
3. Dairies   barns   ▨ Dwelling quarters
4. Hen-houses   8. Stables

Fig. 21.

feeding of stock is a more vital part of the rural economy. In these mountain house-types, the animals occupy part of the ground floor, alongside the kitchen and hearth. The sleeping quarters of the family and the storage rooms are situated on the first floor, and often the hay loft is in the attic above (Ill. VII).

Over the loess belt of Central and Western Europe (Fig. 11), associated with the rich grain lands, there is the fourth zone of house-types. The characteristic feature of the houses is separate accommodation for man and beast. It is highly probable that this multiple type of dwelling has spread considerably beyond a formerly more restricted zone. It is prevalent in the Danube basin and extends into Bulgaria and Serbia (Fig. 20). It is predominant in the Frankish type of Germany and in Bohemia and extends across the loess lands of Hesbaye, Picardy and the Paris basin. In all these lands, cereal cultivation has tended to be of more importance than stock-rearing until modern times.

In this zone, broad distinctions can be recognised between the open farmstead and enclosed farmstead, or what Demangeon has called the *maison-cour ouverte* and *maison-cour fermée*. It is uncertain how far back one can trace this distinction. The *villa rustica* described by Vitruvius may have been either type according to the region concerned. The medieval granges farmed by the abbeys were often the origin of enclosed farmsteads which still persist in scattered enclaves such as in the plains of Burgundy, Caen and Yorkshire (Fig. 20). At different periods the multiple dwelling has changed from an open to an enclosed farmstead according to the exigencies of defence. Thus the Walloon *cense*, the Flemish *hofstede*[53] and the Alsatian farmhouse, were probably enclosed in the troublous times during and after the Thirty Years War. Along the Scottish-English marchlands the walled farmsteads express the same origin.

The fifth zone may be broadly accepted as Southern Europe. Here the vertical (*maison-haute*) rather than the low-lying house (*maison à terre*) is the rule, commonly associated with the nucleated villages and towns of the Mediterranean region. The traditional triad of wheat, oil and wine express a distinct agricultural economy where the processing and storage of tree-crops makes the dwelling a different instrument of agriculture from those previously considered. Typically, the wine cellars are located in the basement or in underground caves outside the village, the family live on the first floor or in part of the ground floor, and the crops are stored on the second storey. Distinctive accommodation such as the oil press (*almácera*), the carob bean store (*garrófera*) and the wine cellar (*bodega*) in a Spanish house reflects this emphasis on the tree-crops. A limited number of house-types are associated with the enclosed farmstead, such as the *alquería* of Valencia

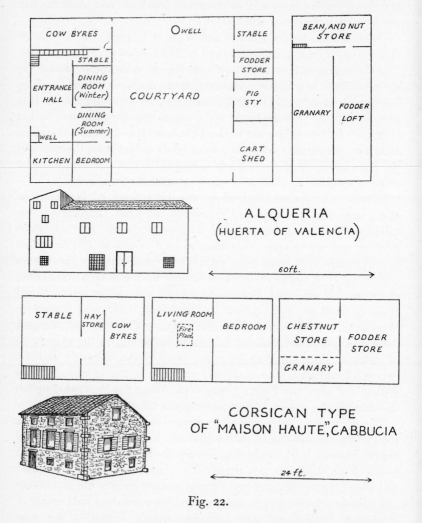

ALQUERIA
(HUERTA OF VALENCIA)

CORSICAN TYPE
OF "MAISON HAUTE", CABBUCIA

Fig. 22.

(Fig. 22), the *mas* or *masía* of Aragon, Catalonia, Provence and parts of north Italy, and the *boarie* of Friuili and Campania. Some of these farm sites are directly related with the Roman *villa rustica* but it is impossible to trace their subsequent evolution. A characteristic feature of the Mediterranean region is the *latifundia* system of large estates, using a large seasonal employment of labour to cultivate the Andalusian olive groves or ricefields of the Po valley. The seasonal labourers live in the villages and towns but the permanent workers are housed in large, enclosed farmsteads such as the *cortijo* of Andalusia and the *corte* of Piedmont, Lombardy and Venetia (Fig. 21).

This classification of European house-types only illustrates that within any one category there are endless variations of form, plan and building materials. Fig. 23 is included therefore to indicate the wide diversity of house-types which may be found in any one country. House-types suggest that the varied legacies of the past, preserved or modified by them to suit each economy and each environment, are as diverse as the personality of each region. The rural dwelling, like the agricultural systems themselves, belongs to a domain where a kind of collective conscience is more effective than individual initiative.[54] It is the understanding of this which makes the study of house-types of geographical significance. Vidal de la Blache in his classic study of Human Geography associated building materials with civilisations.[55] Their complex relations remind the geographer that the rural dwelling belongs as much to the world of the spirit as to its material environment.

SELECTED REFERENCES

Brunhes, J. *Human Geography*, abridged edition, 1947, Ch. 3.
Brunhes, J., and Deffontaines, P. *Géographie Humaine de la France*. Paris, 1926, tome 2, ch. XIV.
Demangeon, A. 'Essai d'une classification des maisons rurales,' reprinted in *Problèmes de Géographie Humaine*. Paris, 1942, pp. 230-35.
Demangeon, A. 'L'Habitat Rurale en France,' A. de G., vol. XXIX, 1920.
Demangeon, A., and Weiler, A. *Les Maisons des Hommes: de la Hutte au Gratte-Ciel*. Paris, 1937.
Dickinson, R. E. *Germany*. London, 1952, pp. 148-55.
Faucher, D. 'Evolution des types de maisons rurales,' A. de G., 1945, pp. 241-53.
Lefèvre, M. A. *Principes et Problèmes de Géographie Humaine*. Brussels, 1945, ch. VI.
Sorre, M. *Les Fondements de la Géographie Humaine*. Paris, 1952, tome III, ch. IV
Tricart, J. *Cours de Géographie Humaine—L'Habitat Rurale*. Strasbourg, 1950.
Vidal de la Blache, P. *Principles of Human Geography*. London, 1926, part II, ch. IV.

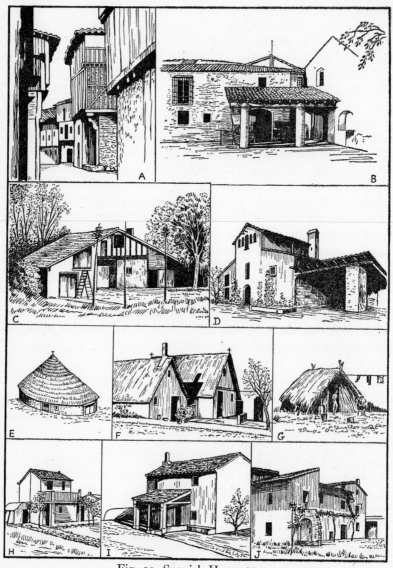

Fig. 23. Spanish House-types.

A. Street-houses in Salamanca. B. Aragonese Alquería. C. The Basque Caserío. D. The Catalan Masía. E. The Galician Pallaza. F. The Valencian Barraca. G. The Andalusian Choza. H. Murcian House. I. Farmhouse of Granada. J. Valencian Alquería.

Part III

URBAN GEOGRAPHY

CHAPTER SEVEN

THE GROWTH AND FUNCTION OF TOWNS

THE city is one of the most difficult subjects to study since it expresses most fully the complexities of civilisation. It would be false therefore to suppose that urban geography can analyse all the features of towns. The interaction of the focal values of the town site and the nodal values of its situation and its regional resources, are the chief concern of the geographer. Ratzel was the first geographer to recognise the distinction between the site and the situation of a town. In a study of Berlin he noted that the city had a site negative to its active expansion, but that its situation on the North German Plain was an important factor in its growth.[1] Where site and situation are both favourable, as in the examples of London, Paris and Istanbul, cities long famous in history may result. It is logical in this distinction to group together the features of situation, population growth and the function of towns; whereas site and urban morphology, although related to these first features, may be considered apart. Division in this manner has been made in the content of this and the following chapter.

The growth of a town is not a matter of chance. Its expansion from the nucleus of the original site will be influenced to some extent by the physical features of the relief and drainage. The development of its functions as a trading and commercial centre, with all the complexities of its administrative and cultural services, can be understood in relation to its regional resources and its national interests. A city may also develop in depth with increased specialisation of its services until the city itself becomes as much a geographical factor of growth as the conditions external to it. By the accumulative growth, according to the principle of compound interest, the city may then develop more servicing requirements within its boundaries than it provides for its tributary area.

Factors in the Theoretical Distribution of Towns

Unless urban centres have originated with a special function, such as federal capital, military garrison and naval base, health and seaside resort, or specialised type of manufacturing city, etc., they derive their sustenance from an area tributary to them. In the past, the limits of the tributary areas were sometimes defined specifically in town charters, but more often they were invisible zones fluctuating in their extent according to the pulse of trade and stage of growth in the

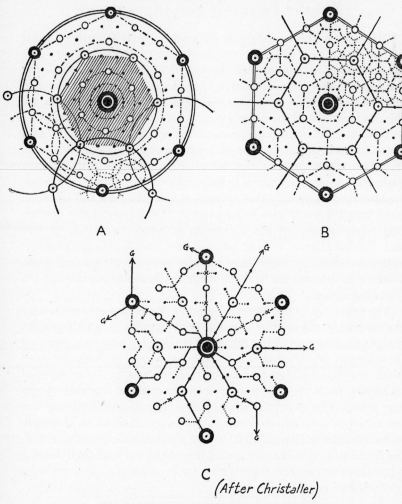

A

B

C

(After Christaller)

Fig. 24. Theoretical Distribution of Centres.

town. Some geographers, such as Christaller[2] and Kant,[3] have devoted much attention to this aspect of urban studies, and it is important to review their theories in the light of actual examples of town development. All stress the essential unity of a town with its region (*Ergänzungsgebiet*). Centres serve a pattern of areas, the size of which will depend among other things on the size of the urban centre and on the character of its services. A closely settled district will thus have a pattern of servicing centres (*Zentralen*) which ideally will be spaced at regular intervals. In a homogeneous land area where the relief does not interrupt the pattern, the tributary area will radiate from the centre, diminishing in the intensity of its influence the further away from the centre it is (Fig. 24, A). The tributary areas of surrounding centres, however, will intersect at the periphery and consequently the whole area will be more in the shape of a hexagon (Fig. 24, B).

In a rural district where the market is considered as the chief factor, such a regular mosaic of tributary areas and centres might perhaps be expected, provided the territory is homogeneous and fully settled. Transport, however, is a second factor to consider along with the market. At break-of-bulk points transport centres tend to form, and the pattern of centres will follow linear arrangements along the water, road and rail routes. The tributary areas of such centres will flatten along the route areas, wider at right angles and larger away from the route or coastline (Fig. 24, C). The most economic system of communication is one patterned on the hexagon, where the relationship between the length of communication and the adjoining area is most natural, and this system tends to characterise rural districts. The increased speed of transport and the growth of large regional capitals tends to give a different pattern of direct routes between the larger centres, missing out many of the smaller ones. The transport factor will thus bring about a disproportionate growth between the larger and smaller centres. The route network in such a pattern will tend to offer a different scale of choice, for which service centres will be preferred. Thus the normal hexagonal arrangement will tend to develop a hierarchy of regional capital centres and sub-centres with the sequence $1 - 7 - 49$ –, and the factor of transport may bring about a sequence of $1 - 4 - 16$ –.[4]

A third factor which complicates the distribution of centres still further is the specialised series of functions associated with mining and manufacturing industries. Towns located near mineral deposits or sources of power will tend to have an irregular distribution, which is non-geometrical since it is not related to the factors of distance but to such focal values as a coalfield. Thus mining and manufacturing industries emphasise the importance of point-production as distinct from production in area, which is associated with the factors of the market and transport. In modern specialised activities point-production is of increasing importance, accounting for the character of specialised types of towns such as those enumerated above, administrative capitals, health and holiday resorts, naval bases, and towns with special types of light industry. Many of these latter towns have been made possible by the development of electric power and more flexible modern means of transport. It is a criticism against Christaller's theoretical principles that he has laid too much emphasis on the function of servicing and not enough on the manufacturing functions of modern towns.

Most towns combine all three elements of markets, transport and manufacture, together with administration, though their complex functions may be weighted towards one more than another. Thus we can classify broadly such types as market towns, transport centres, manufacturing towns, holiday resorts, etc. The size of the town and the degree of its specialisation in certain functions tends to create a hierarchy. The form of the hierarchy or pyramid in any region will depend among other things on the degree of specialisation in certain types of services, the range of the population concentration and the form of local and national administration. The principle of servicing, for example, may be illustrated by the educational services required for a new town, as the Ministry of Education recently outlined in this country. On the average, a nursery school is needed for a unit of 2,500 inhabitants, a primary school for 5,000, a secondary modern school for 20,000 and a secondary grammar school and technical college for 60,000.[5] Similarly, there is the ranking of national administrative centres, such as the courts of law. In Germany, for example, a petty sessional court is needed for 20-30,000 inhabitants, a county court for about 80,000, a regional court or *landgericht* for 2-300,000, and a high court or *oberlandgericht* for 2-3,000,000.[6] Thus all public utilities, such as police and fire brigades, national administration, such as that of the church or government health services, and the facilities for amusement and other forms of private business all follow the hierarchical principle.

If these factors and principles determining the character, size and patterns of towns are complicated in theory, they are much more so in actual study. It is difficult if not impossible to develop a scheme of principles which will enable us to give a detailed explanation of all types of environments. The urban hierarchy of Britain, for example, is not explained by the same emphasis on servicing as Christaller gives for southern Germany.[7] Therefore the more systematic the theory of urban centres, the less likely will it be an adequate explanation of regional particularisms. Such theoretical concepts are as marginal to urban geography as abstract principles, formulated by economists, are to economic geography, though the research worker may be stimulated by them in his actual investigation.

A theoretical conception of urban relations is unsatisfactory since it views relationships along one plane only, that of space. Time too needs to be considered, and the attempt to focus both elements of space and time in town growth is one of the difficulties inherent in its study. In the history of town development, it is clear that many factors have been important, with varying stress according to the civilisation in which town life flourished. Thus it would be interesting for a comparative study to be made of the different forms of urban life which have risen and fallen in the civilisations of the world. In Europe there have been at least four chief phases of urban development: from the sixth century B.C. to the fourth century A.D., the period A.D. 1050 to 1350, the sixteenth and seventeenth centuries, and the modern phase initiated by the Industrial Revolution. Each historical period has expressed different values and emphasised certain functions of urban life more than others.

Factors in the Growth of Greek and Roman Towns

To the Greeks, town life was a manner of living in a political community. The size of the town was determined, at least in theory, by this viewpoint. As one Greek writer said, 'the city (or *polis*) must have a population which is self-sufficient for the purpose of living the good life after the manner of a political community. But it must not be so unwieldy that the members cannot maintain personal contact with one another.'[8] Hence Hippodamus, the Miletan town-planner, thought that 10,000 was the right number to have in a city population.* Hardly a score of cities, however, was as large as this ideal; even in the fifth century B.C. the majority of Athenians lived in the country, according to Thucydides.[9] As parasitical growths on an essentially agricultural population, Greek towns developed in at least three ways. Firstly, by the process of grouping political communities into a larger state, or synoecism, the town might become a

---

* It is not clear whether Hippodamus meant 10,000 citizens or inhabitants, probably the latter.

great capital, such as Athens became in the time of Pericles. Secondly, there were the federal capitals, such as Megalopolis. Thirdly, there were the cities developed as instruments of colonisation, both in the old colonies of Asia Minor, such as Ephesus and Miletus, and in the new colonies of Sicily and Italy, such as Selinus and Naples.[10]

To the Romans the city meant more than a means of living the good life or a means of trade with distant colonies. It was a microcosm of the State, complete with all the functions of its administrative, cultural and religious life. It was also the means whereby the defences of the Empire would be effectively integrated within a network of roads. Undoubtedly, this was aided at first by the existence of pre-existing centres, although the sites chosen by the Romans were often characteristically new and independent from native towns. From the cyclopean hill-towns of Tuscany and Latium the Roman state expanded beyond to the alluvial plains of the Po Basin, with a series of deliberately planted garrison towns. From the original twelve cities of Tuscany and the thirty cities of Latium, the Roman state created by the Augustan period a further three hundred and fifty towns in peninsular Italy and another eighty in northern Italy.[11] In Spain, the Iberian town-life was added to by the Romans and Pliny speaks of three hundred and fifty-four towns in the whole of the Peninsula, with monumental centres such as Tarragona, Sagunto, Merida and Coimbra. The establishment of Roman towns in Gaul, in addition to the numerous Post-Hallstadt native centres, meant that 30 to 40 per cent. of the population may be estimated to have lived in towns at the zenith of the Roman Empire.[12] More consciously perhaps than the Greeks, the Romans developed a hierarchy of urban centres, which ranged from the simple military camp, or *castrum*, through the small market centres around a local *forum* on a highway, to the great regional capitals or *civitates*. The close network of Roman roads made this possible and helps to account for the disproportionate size of its capital cities, such as Rome, Turin, Nîmes, Lyons, Trèves and Autun.

Factors in the Growth of Towns in the Middle Ages

In the resurrection of town life after the ninth and tenth centuries A.D., the ecclesiastical administration patterned on the old Roman provincial boundaries, and the defence needs of these unsettled centuries, together aided the revival of urban centres. During the Dark Ages, it was possibly only in Italy where town sites maintained any semblance of urban life, and this was the influence of the Church. There, some two hundred and eighty-six bishopric towns possibly survived. Defence was also important in the creation of towns. By the twelfth century there were thirty-two defence settlements or *castelnau* in the south of France.[13] In Scotland, during the thirteenth century, there were thirty-three 'royal burghs,' whose initial task was probably to provide military control over their region or sheriffdom. It appears more than a coincidence that certain groups of towns developed in Britain first as military garrisons in defence of territories which subsequently developed into trading centres: such are the Danish confederation of the Five Boroughs of Lincoln, Nottingham, Derby, Leicester and Stamford in Mercia; the four Scottish royal burghs of Berwick, Roxburgh, Edinburgh and Stirling first associated probably with northern Northumbria; and the five towns of the Ostmen along the Irish coast at Dublin, Wexford, Waterford, Cork and Limerick. Similar regional associations were developed in Germany. Military *burgs* appeared during the ninth and tenth centuries in many parts of Europe, such as those of the Flemish and Saxon coasts, those along the trade routes developed in Central and Eastern Europe, and some in Russia. These were the nuclei around which trade centres could develop.

Later, during the twelfth and fourteenth centuries more systematic erection of towns took place, as is evidenced, for example, by many of the Romance place-names.[14] These centres were established in zones of tension where the territorial rivalries of lords, city states or kingdoms, and the colonisation movements, with the creation of marchlands, made the erection of garrisons desirable. In the Iberian Peninsula during the Reconquest, several hundred settlements were erected along the successive series of frontiers, served especially by the valleys of the Ebro, Douro and Tagus. Indeed these 'castella' have given name to the important kingdoms of Castile and Catalonia. Rival struggles in Guipuzcoa, Navarre and Vizcaya account for the creation of some eighteen towns in the former province. Similarly in Italy rival city-states erected garrison towns along their frontiers, such as Castelfranco Veneto (1119) built by the Venetians against Padua, and Cittadella (1210-11) erected in turn by the Paduans against Venice.

On a large scale the same process went on in France. In the south, the Albigensian wars, the local rivalries of lords, and especially the Hundred Years' War between the French and English kings, account for the spread of many *bastides* and *villenueves*. Thus in the region between Guyenne and Languedoc, fifty towns were founded during this period, of which at least twenty were *bastides*.[15] Royal authority in France came to be associated with the erection of the fortified towns or *bastides*, but in other regions of France the erection of new towns by the nobility indicates the position of the French king as only *primus inter pares*. In Lorraine, Burgundy and Normandy there are examples of such establishments along their frontiers, such as Villenueve l'Archeveque and Villefranche in the Saône Basin.[16]

In Central Europe, the establishment of the successive German frontier provinces or *marklands* against the Slavs accounts for the creation of over three hundred towns in Brandenburg, Pomerania, Silesia and Bohemia. Thus to-day, most of the towns of Mecklemburg date from the mid-thirteenth century (e.g. Rostock) and in Pomerania of the sixty-three towns now existing, forty-one were founded between 1230 and 1300 (e.g. Stettin).[17] In European Russia there was also the development of new towns associated with the large commerical city republics, Novgorod, for example, having an outlying series of smaller towns created as defence centres such as Pskov, Tver and Torzhok.

The establishment of these settlements was an assurance of increased agricultural production in areas formerly devastated by war such as in southern France, or colonised on virgin territory as in Central Europe and Russia. It was also a guarantee of protection to an agricultural population so that many of these new settlements were erected in response to the petitions of the inhabitants themselves.[18] The study of the town charters reveals much about the methods of establishment of these medieval settlements. Many indicate they were based on the same legislative privileges as an earlier foundation, branching out like a family tree. In Germany, for example, many towns based their legislative liberties on those given to Lubeck and Magdeburg. The charters of London, Oxford, Northampton and Nottingham were frequently copied by other English towns. In France, Montauban was the example followed by many *bastides* in the south, as Breteuil in Normandy was used by towns of central and northern districts. Similarly in Spain, the charters of Pamplona and Huesca were copied in the grants made to many new towns during the Reconquest. However, in estimating the number of towns created within a specific period and region, it is necessary to distinguish carefully between actual foundation charters and charters of renewal or *novodamus*.

It would be false to suggest that defence alone was the creative principle of medieval town life. Indeed the original defence nuclei cannot be recognised to have had urban functions. It was the fertilising influence of trade which made urban birth possible during the later Middle Ages. Thus the development of the Scottish *burg* or the English borough from a military establishment in the tenth and eleventh centuries to a mercantile town in the twelfth and thirteenth centuries, was a process repeated throughout medieval Europe. At first, the merchants' suburb was attached to the military *burg*, or the ecclesiastical *cité*. Later it became the most active element in the development of the town, as is seen in the Spanish *burgo*, the Dutch *portus*, the German *neustadt*, and the Russian *torgoveia*.

Despite setbacks, such as the epidemics and wars of the fourteenth and fifteenth centuries, it may be said that the network of urban centres was already fixed in Europe. Military expediency had set up many incipient town centres, which later became redundant and were eliminated by the process of economic competition. In Europe, two developments took place, exemplified in Britain by interesting comparisons of municipal legislation, as seen in England and Scotland. According to English common law, comparable with that of many parts of the Continent, it was customary that no market should be established within a radius of six and two-thirds miles from an existing one.[19] This safeguarded against undue competition, and it is significant that in East Anglia to-day the radius separating market towns is still between seven and ten miles. Until the advent of modern rapid transport such a radius would be traditional with the length of time required to make a return journey between the hamlet and the market centre.* In Scotland the attempt was first made to carve up the whole country into territories, often very large, which were exclusively within the monopoly of the royal burghs for all matters

---

* In 1788 Condorcet suggested the same principle for the centres of French districts and provinces. He said, 'It is a real advantage that each community should be of such extent that in the space of a day, the citizens living farthest away from the centre can come there, transact their business for several hours, and then return to their homes; thus three leagues would seem to be the proper limit; a half-day's or part of a day's journey should be the maximum radius of a district; finally, a long day's journey should be that of a province, measuring from the centre to the farthest district. But at the same time it is to be observed that for these different divisions regard should be had to physical geography so as to combine only those parts between which communication is easy, and in which a similarity of climate and soil gives a community of culture, customs and habits; this is the prescription of nature.' —'Essai sur la Constitution et les Fonctions des Assemblées Provinciales,' in *Œuvres Completes*. Brunswick 1804, XIII, p. 231.

of trade and manufacture.* This became an intolerable control for the small settlements established on the lords' estates, so that between 1450 and 1707 the tributary areas of the royal burghs became punctuated with the rise of some three hundred new burghs, usurping many of their mercantile privileges (Fig. 25). This has resulted in many redundant centres and accounts for the anomaly of many small burghs, being to-day, no more than villages in size.

On the Continent, similar developments took place. In some territories, such as the arid plateaux of the Iberian Peninsula, it was difficult to obtain enough colonists for the poorer lands. In Andalusia, for example, it was stipulated that wherever possible the market towns should be from four to four and a half leagues in their radius from each other's influence.[20] In contrast, too many centres were established in Aquitaine and some of the *bastides* have declined in their importance. The framework of the provinces and lesser units have developed in some cases from the hierarchical arrangements of the settlements. In Spain, the hierarchy of *pueblos*, *partidos* and *provincias* dates back to the Reconquest. There, the trading area of a regional capital might form the original administrative framework. For example, the province of Salamanca had a royal town which gave it its name, controlling 105 villages and small towns, or *villas* and 408 hamlets, or *lugares*.[21] In Prussia there was also the defence district or *amtgerichtsort*, within which was centred a castle town.[22] Throughout the Middle Ages town-and-country relations were very close, even though the town set itself apart in its social and mercantile life from the country. The establishment of town houses by rural manors helped to effect this close relationship.

Whatever the original influence of town development, it was trade that sustained it. In Italy, the city-states had spectacular developments, owing to the expansion of their foreign trade. Venice and Milan, both had over 100,000 inhabitants in the thirteenth century, and Florence reached about 90,000 in 1239. The fortunes of cities, however, were very unstable. Thus Ypres, one of the largest cities of the Low Countries in the thirteenth century, with some 40,000 inhabitants in 1257, was reduced to 6,000 in 1486.[23] Epidemics of disease, war and the loss of trade, were such factors in the instability of towns. In many European towns, however, growth was much more

---

* There are examples of English towns having a trade monopoly, in a specified region such as Bury St. Edmunds with its control over the eight and a half hundreds, roughly equivalent to West Suffolk. But this was a monastic foundation with special privileges. St. Albans is a comparable example.

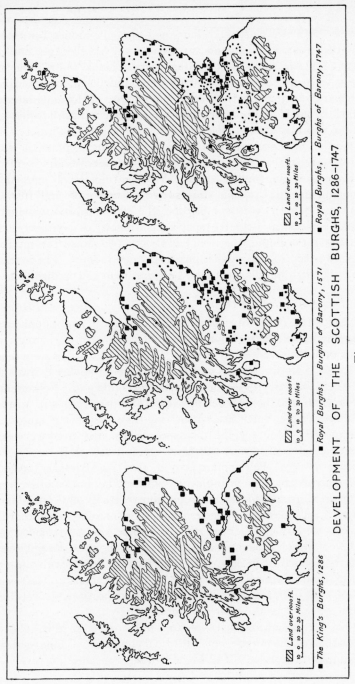

Fig. 25.

gradual and it was sustained. Paris was the only French town with
more than 100,000 inhabitants at the end of the Middle Ages, and the
average size was 8,000 to 15,000 for a large regional centre. The two
largest towns of the Low Countries were Ghent and Bruges, which
each had about 50,000 at this period, but no town of Holland exceeded
10,000. In the Holy Roman Empire some twelve to fifteen towns had
over 10,000 inhabitants; Cologne and Lubeck alone had more than
30,000.[24] The English towns, cut off from the Continental trade
routes, were small in comparison with the European trading centres.
At the end of the twelfth century, York had not much more than
8,000 inhabitants, Lincoln and Norwich 6,000 each and Ipswich
about 3,000.[25] In Northern Europe, the size of towns was much
smaller, consistent with the sparse distribution of population. In
Scotland, for example, Aberdeen had about 3,000 inhabitants in 1400,
Glasgow 4,500 in 1560 and Edinburgh 5,990 in 1565. The average
size of Scottish burghs must have been less than 1,000 inhabitants.

The Towns of Europe in 1600

Despite the factor of external trade, the local food supply was
undoubtedly one of the most important controls in the growth of
towns until the seventeenth century. Thus the great cities were those
which could grow in regions where agricultural productivity was high
and where the trade routes met, such as the Po Plain, the Netherlands
and Belgium, and the loess belt of Central Germany (Fig. 26). Around
the shores of the North Sea salt herring (first used about 1400) was
an important food for the townspeople. In the Mediterranean,
irrigation and polyculture sustained great cities, such as Naples
(238,000 in 1591), Palermo (104,000 in 1607) and Messina (100,000
in 1607). Foreign trade, manufacture and banking in that order were
the principal factors for the disproportionate size of some cities, such
as the great mercantile centres of Lisbon (110,000) and Seville
(100,000) with their American trade, but these were unstable factors,
the loss of which brought about the decay of the great Italian cities.
Bologna reached its peak in 1588 with 72,395, Venice with 139,459
in 1600 and Florence with 69,749 in 1642; thereafter their size
declined.[26] Constantinople, with about 300,000 inhabitants, was in a
unique category, as the capital of a great empire.

It has been calculated that some four million lived in towns of over
15,000 inhabitants in 1600, out of the total population of about eighty-
five million in Europe.[27] The highest urban concentrations were in

the Netherlands with 13 per cent. of the total population, and Italy with 12 per cent. Turkey also had 12 per cent. but Constantinople influenced this figure. Germany, France and England all had about 2 per cent. of their population in cities. The Scandinavian countries were only beginning to have any urban centres. Stockholm and

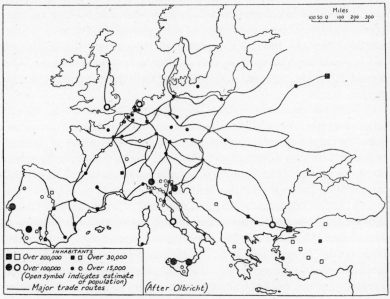

Fig. 26. Cities of Europe in *c.* 1600.

Copenhagen were the two cities of any size, while towns such as Helsingfors, established in 1550, and Götenburg erected in 1619, were not urban centres of importance. Similarly there was not much urban development in Slav territory (Fig. 26). Moscow had about 200,000 inhabitants, but it was chiefly the result of despotic rule and centralised government. Smolensk, the second city of Russia at this time, had only 15,000.

Factors in the Growth of Cities in the Sixteenth and Seventeenth Centuries

The period covered by the Renaissance and baroque town developments was one of constant readjustment to new forces of urban life. The sixteenth century saw the shift in trade from the Mediterranean to the Atlantic seaboard of Europe and, with it, the decline of the

Italian city-states. At the beginning of the sixteenth century, Europe had six or seven cities which had over 100,000 inhabitants, and at the end of the century there were about fourteen. During the seventeenth century, the great cities of Europe did not increase much in number, the baroque creations of Madrid and Vienna merely taking the places previously held by Antwerp and Messina in order of importance. It was a period of urban consolidation, when the capital cities and the great commercial centres multiplied their gains at the expense of the smaller towns. In France, the growth of Paris meant the decline of old regional capitals such as Nancy, Besançon and Toulouse. The formation of the national state thus implied the supremacy of the capital.

Among the important factors affecting the growth of the capital cities were the rise of nationalism, the closer integration of nation states by more efficient communications, the expansion of foreign trade and the development of trade and manufacture at the great courts of royalty. John Stow, writing in 1598 in answer to those who 'charge London with the loss and decay of many (or most) of the ancient cities, corporate towns and markets' in England, gives some illuminating reasons for the situation and expansion of London as a capital city. He describes the importance of navigation and foreign trade on the Thames and adds: 'As for retailers therefore and handi-craftmen it is no marvel if they abandon country towns and resort to London; for not only the court which is now-a-days much greater and more gallant than in former times . . . that the provision of things most fit for it may easily be fetched from thence; but also by occasion thereof, the gentleman of all shires do fly and flock to this city.'[28] By 1696 London was estimated to have 530,000 inhabitants representing one quarter of the total urban population of 870,000 in England.[29] Comparable developments were repeated in the great capital cities of Europe at this time. A general feature was the slacken-ing in the rate of growth after this period owing to immigration being offset by the very high death-rates in the cities.

Apart from the supremacy of capital cities like London and Paris as the head of the national state, the choice of other capitals differed widely. In some instances the capital was chosen to balance the interests of all the component parts or federation of states. For example, Warsaw was selected in the sixteenth century, as a com-promise between the old Polish capital of Cracow and the Lithuanian capital of Vilna, after the dynastic union of the two countries took place. Brussels was developed as the capital, near the boundary between the two regions of Walloon and Flemish Belgium. In other cases, the capital was selected as a rival to dominate other cities, such

THE GROWTH OF CAPITAL CITIES IN EUROPE, 1600-1900
(in thousands)

	1600	c. 1830	1900
London	60	1,500	6,580
Paris	90	800	2,660
Berlin	8	250	1,888
Vienna	30	340	1,675
Leningrad	—	330	1,267
Istanbul	300	420	1,125
Moscow	100	200	988
Budapest	10	90	732
Hamburg	12	130	706
Warsaw	8	120	638
Naples	200	380	564
Brussels	40	82	562
Amsterdam	50	221	521
Madrid	40	201	512
Barcelona	50	150	509
Munich	5	63	500
Milan	100	138	491
Rome	100	150	463
Copenhagen	10	104	378
Lisbon	110	260	357
Stockholm	10	79	300
Oslo	—	20	227
Prague	30	120	201
Athens	10	12	154
Helsinki	—	9	77
Belgrade	30	30	69
Sofia	30	40	68

(Statistics are based on Olbricht, Braudel, Arrowsmith and *The Statesman's Yearbook*.)

as Madrid, which met the rivalries of Barcelona, Valencia and Seville. Madrid was selected deliberately to check Catalonia. Similarly, Berlin, through the ambitions of its Prussian rulers, sought to dominate the

other great cities of Germany, of which it was supreme, long before
the unification of states in 1872. In true federation of states, however,
the capital has frequently remained of smaller importance than other
commercial cities, such as The Hague and Berne. Elsewhere, the
capital city remained small during this period because of the small
size of its territory as in the case of some of the German states. The
poorly developed resources of other countries explain the slow growth
of their capital cities. In 1600, Edinburgh had about 8,000 inhabitants,
Dublin 4-5,000, Copenhagen and Stockholm about 10,000 and
Warsaw 8,000, figures which compared unfavourably with the great
metropolitan cities of that period.

City Development during the Nineteenth and Twentieth Centuries

The population of Europe in 1800 was about 175 millions, of which
1·6 per cent. lived in twenty-two cities, each with over 100,000
inhabitants. This percentage appears small compared with modern
developments, but it was surprising there was even this urban population, in view of the long period of international warfare that Europe
experienced between 1610 and 1789. The phenomenal increase of
population during the nineteenth century, reaching 380 million at
the end of the century, is unique in world history. Between 1800 and
1890, the number of cities in Europe with over 100,000 inhabitants
increased from twenty-two to one hundred and twenty cities.[30]
Related to this great increase was a change from the spatial relations
between towns on the basis of trade, to an increasing emphasis on
the focal values of manufacturing industries, associated with the discovery of steam power and its use in the expansion of the factory
system. The spread of the railway plexus across Europe, the development of the coalfields and the continued increase of the capital cities
with the closer control and more intensive functions of central government, are three important factors in the general growth of towns and
the disproportionate expansion of the giant cities.

The distribution of European towns in 1830 is a useful landmark to
survey since this date was immediately prior to the development of
rail transport (Fig. 27). There were then 29 cities with over 100,000
inhabitants, 39 between 50,000 and 100,000 in size, and a further
298 between 10,000 and 50,000. The distribution of towns as first
shown in 1600 (Fig. 26) is re-emphasised, but Fig. 27 shows further
development in Western Europe, especially on the coalfields. By
1830, of the cities with over 100,000 only 8 (7 of these being in Great

Britain) were located on the coalfields and 16 were ports. The relatively high costs of inland transport and the slow speed of communications by such a medium as canals and natural waterways, imposed sharp limitations upon industrial concentrations. These handicaps were removed by the railway, leading to the growth of large manufacturing centres. The combination of this new form of transport, together with the added factor of point production, made possible by the steam-engine, caused the disproportionate growth of industrial centres. These features are well illustrated in Britain during the first half of the nineteenth century.

The accumulative effects of the Industrial Revolution in Britain were best demonstrated in the decade 1821-31 when the most spectacular increases of urban population took place in the areas of manufacture, especially at the seaports and iron centres. The next factor in urban expansion was the development of railway communications. Between 1830 and 1850, 6,600 rail miles were constructed in Britain and the industrial conurbations of the woollen and cotton towns of Northern England began to take shape. It is not always realised, however, that a third great source of urban expansion was taking place at the holiday and health resorts, which in the period 1801-51 had an increase of 254 per cent., the highest increase in England and Wales. This percentage increase was followed by the manufacturing towns with 224 per cent., mining and metallurgical towns 217, seaports 195, London 146 and the country towns 122 per cent.[31] This urban expansion was maintained by the mass of immigrants: in 1851, out of 3,336,000 people of twenty years and upwards, dwelling in London and 61 other towns in England and Wales, only 1,337,000 had been born in the town of their residence.[32] By the mid-nineteenth century the distribution of urban centres was fixed with a marked concentration on the coalfields. By 1900, of the 40 towns with over 100,000 inhabitants 27 were situated on the coalfields of the British Isles.[33] Since that period, the subsequent growth of towns has been associated with the urban sprawl across the earlier municipal boundaries and the creation of the conurbations, of which there are now six in England. These concentrate 16·9 millions, that is 41 per cent. of the total population of England, in an area of only 2,086 sq. miles.[34] Similar expansion has taken place in the Scottish conurbation. To-day, two-thirds of the population of Scotland are concentrated into the area occupied by Glasgow and within a twenty-mile radius of the city. These figures are certainly

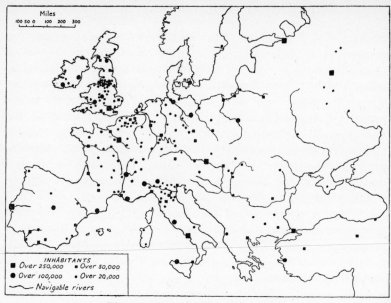

Fig. 27. Cities of Europe, *c.* 1830.

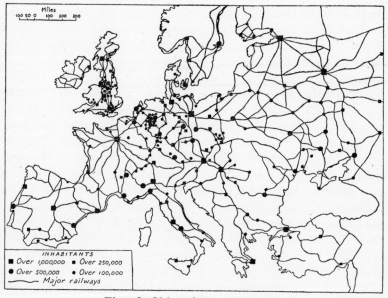

Fig. 28. Cities of Europe in 1950.

disproportionate to the size and distribution of population centres in the rest of the country and it is significant that the great increases of population in the conurbations have slackened substantially or even remained stationary during the last thirty years.

On the Continent, there have been marked regional differences both in the periods of greatest urban growth and in the intensity of city development. In Germany, the greatest increase of urban population occurred about 1861-4 when railway development was greatest but many great cities developed during the latter third of the century. There were eight cities with over 100,000 in 1871, representing almost two million. By 1891 the number had increased to twenty-four cities, with over five and a half million people.[35] Since then, another twenty-eight cities have been added to this list, representing in 1938, 30·7 per cent. of the total population. Unlike Britain, only two of the large German cities, with over 500,000 inhabitants, lie on a coalfield and many of the thirty-three towns with populations between 100,000 and 250,000 were important medieval towns. There are relatively few new towns exclusively related to the industrial developments of the last century. Similarly, in France, the seventeen cities with over 100,000 inhabitants did not increase appreciably until after the mid-nineteenth century. Only three of these are comparable to the British coalfield city and eight are ports.[36] The characteristic feature of French urban life is the dominance of Paris, the comparative absence of specialised manufacturing centres and the number of small provincial towns with spheres of influence over considerable areas.

To-day, there are in Europe some 300 cities with over 100,000 inhabitants with a total population of 112 millions. This represents the greatest urban concentration in the world since the total number of such cities is 700; Asia has 215 and the Americas 155 cities. Within Europe the cities of each country have been symptomatic of their different economic status, of their development during the last hundred years and of their general demographic structure. There is, however, one feature of city development common throughout Europe to-day, and that is the dominance of the primate city.[37] This is the supremacy of a national capital or commercial city in each country, crystallising in itself the national feeling. The importance of this feature is considerable when it is realised that some fourteen cities have been elected to the role of national capital since the

THE PRIMATE CITIES OF EUROPE, 1900-1950

1900

Primate city	Second city	Third city	
London, 6,580	Glasgow, 11	Liverpool, 10	
Leningrad, 1,267	Moscow, (988)	Moscow, 79	Odessa, 31
Berlin, 1,888	Hamburg, 37	Munich, 26	
Paris, 2,660	Marseilles, 18	Lyons, 17	
Naples, 563	Rome (463)	Milan, 89	Rome, 82
Madrid, 512	Barcelona, 99	Valencia, 40	
Vienna, 1,675	Graz, 8	Linz, 3	
Budapest, 732	Szeged, 13	Szabadka, 1	
Bucharest, 282	Iasi, 27	Galatz, 22	
Brussels, 561	Antwerp, 51	Liége, 31	
Copenhagen, 378	Aarhus, 13	Odense, 10	
Prague, 201	Limberg, 79	Brno, 54	
Istanbul, 1,125	Izmir, 17	Adana, 4	
Amsterdam, 520	Rotterdam, 64	The Hague, 42	
Stockholm, 300	Goteburg, 43	Malmo, 20	
Lisbon, 357	Oporto, 49	Braga, 6	
Warsaw, 638	Lodz, 49	Cracow, 14	
Athens, 153	Patras, 25	Trekkala, 14	
Sofia, 68	Plovdiv, 62	Stalin, 47	
Oslo, 227	Bergen, 31	Trondheim, 16	
Helsinki, 77	Turku, 45	Tampere, 34	
Belgrade, 69	Zagreb, 89	Nisch, 35	
Zurich, 153	Basel, 74	Geneva, 70	

1950

Primate city	Second city	Third city
London, 8,417	Glasgow, 12	Liverpool, 9·5
Moscow, 4,137	Leningrad, 77	Kiev, 20
Berlin, 3,187	Hamburg, 50	Munich, 26
Paris, 2,725	Marseilles, 23	Lyons, 16
Rome, 1,665	Milan, 70	Naples, 51
Madrid, 1,512	Barcelona, 85	Valencia, 35
Vienna, 1,760	Graz, 12	Linz, 10
Budapest, 1,058	Szeged, 12	Debrecen, 12
Bucharest, 984	Cluj, 11	Iasi, 10
Brussels, 964	Antwerp, 27	Ghent, 17
Copenhagen, 927	Aarhus, 15	Odense, 9
Prague, 922	Brno, 29	Ostrava, 19
Istanbul, 860	Ankara, 26	Izmir, 23
Amsterdam, 836	Rotterdam, 80	The Hague, 68
Stockholm, 733	Göteburg, 46	Malmo, 25
Lisbon, 709	Oporto, 37	Funchal, 7
Warsaw, 600	Lodz, 98	Cracow, 37
Athens, 481	Thessalonica, 41	Patras, 16
Sofia, 435	Plovdiv, 29	Stalin, 18
Oslo, 418	Bergen, 26	Trondheim, 13
Helsinki, 399	Turku, 26	Tampere, 26
Belgrade, 389	Zagreb, 74	Sarajevo, 30
Zurich, 386	Basel, 49	Berne, 37

(Statistics are based on *The Statesman's Yearbook*.)

The first figure in each column is the population of the primate city in thousands. The other two figures for the second and third cities are percentages of the primate city beginning of the nineteenth century. The table opposite summarises the growing status of the European capitals and may be compared with the table on p. 151, where the growth of these cities is recorded prior to the modern era.

Not all capital cities have enjoyed primacy and there are the important exceptions to what has been termed 'the law of the primate city.' The Hague and Berne are still smaller as the administrative capitals, than Amsterdam and Zurich as the commercial capitals. Rome and Madrid have only recently surpassed Milan and Barcelona respectively in their total population. Elsewhere in Europe, the primate city is always disproportionately large and clearly expressive of national development and feeling. As such, the capital city is usually the centrifugal force of internal migration. For example, in south-east England, population changes have been dominated by London, its pull fading out with smaller migration gains at wider radii from the metropolis. In other countries, such as Sweden, Denmark, Belgium, France and Hungary, the pull of the capital has dominated the movement of population. Elsewhere, as in Norway and Yugoslavia, the natural barriers of relief have checked the forces of centralisation and promoted the growth of regional centres. Vienna has suffered a reversal of the general trends of migration, first by the disruption of its former empire and, since the Second World War, by the military occupation. In contrast, Sofia and Athens have benefited from the international changes of refugees, and these have been the most important contributions to their growth in the inter-war period.[38]

It is thus apparent that the city-ward movement towards the primate centres of Europe has been a general tidal advance compared with which all other population movements have been mere ripples. In this unique tidal advance of city population it is clear however, that the historical movements of advance and retreat, through many and devious channels, need to be considered. No analysis of cities and their functions can be adequate without a historical interpretation, for there are few other subjects in Human Geography which are more dynamic in character.

SELECTED REFERENCES

Aurousseau, M. 'Recent contributions to urban geography,' G.R. XIV, 1924, pp. 444-55.
Blanchard, R. 'Une Méthode de Géographie Urbaine,' Rev. de Géog. Alpine, XVI, 1928, pp. 193-214.

Chabot, G. *Les Villes*. Paris, 1948.

Cornish, V. *The Great Capitals*. London, 1923.

Dickinson, R. E. *City, Region and Regionalism*. London, 1947.

Dickinson, R. E. *The West European City*. London, 1951.

Harris, Chauncey D., and Ullman, E. L. 'The Nature of Cities,' The Annals of the Amer. Acad. Pol. and Soc. Sci., 1945, pp. 7-17.

Lavedan, P. *Histoire de l'Urbanisme; Antiquité-Moyen Age*. Paris, 1926.

Lipman, V. D. 'Town and Country. The study of service centres and their areas of influence,' *Public Admin.*, XXX, 1952, pp. 203-214.

Mumford, L. *The Culture of Cities*. London, 1938.

Ullman, E. L. 'A Theory of Location for Cities,' Amer. Journ. of Sociol., Vol. 46, 1941, pp. 853-64.

Weber, A. F. *The Growth of Cities in the Nineteenth Century*. London, 1899.

Wycherley, R. E. *How the Greeks built Cities*. London, 1949.

CHAPTER EIGHT

THE SITE AND MORPHOLOGY OF TOWNS

THE town is both a historical and a geographical fact. It represents the complex activities of civilisations by its functions and growth of population. It is also the material expression of a created landscape. As a geographical fact in the environment of man, it is necessary therefore to study the site and the plan of towns. In the position of a town, the geographer would distinguish between the site and the situation of the settlement. Both are relative terms and they have to be considered together in explaining the value of the town's nodality. The focal values of the site are some of the most distinguishing features of towns. It is this which differentiates best the urban from the rural settlements. The latter are more influenced by the conditions of the environment within their regional context of such elements as population density and agricultural economy, and by the physical factors of relief, soil and water-supply. Regional patterns of rural settlement can often be discerned, appearing almost as the products of the soil, growing from the land in which they first took root. The qualities of site and nodality give to urban settlements a different emphasis in their study. Sometimes towns may be developed almost as alien importations, where a basic relationship between the environment and the urban centres may not exist. Where regional groups of towns suggest marked similarities of plan, growth and function, their unity is usually understood with reference to a common cultural background and a comparable historical context, rather than to any influences inherent in the natural environment.

On the map of Europe may be delimited a series of cultural types, representing the furthest advances of distinct cultural invasions, like strand-lines on the shore of history. Thus the Roman town with its geometrical plan, or the Moorish town with its irregular layout, provide contrasts in urban morphology in areas where these influences left effectively their imprint. The legacy of the Roman grid town along the Roman *limes* in the central nucleus of towns such as Strasbourg (Fig. 31) and Cologne (Fig. 30), contrasts with the medieval development of the Dutch and Flemish towns of which few had a Roman origin. In the Iberian Peninsula there is also a striking difference in plan between some of the northern cities where the Roman plan has been preserved, as in Saragossa (Fig. 30) and Lugo (Fig. 31), and the town plans of the south and east, such as Toledo, Seville, Granada and Valencia (Fig. 37) where the irregular plan of the Moorish centre is still characteristic. The cathedral cities of the Paris Basin, the commercial cities of the Low Countries and the military strongholds of Eastern Europe, each express distinct unity of intersts, so that the cathedral, town hall (*rathaus*) and castle (*kremlin*), may be taken as symbolic of their *raison d'être* and development.

Situation of Towns in Europe

In the previous chapter, reference was made to the relations between the trade routes and the location of European cities (see p. 149 and Fig. 26). In Southern Europe, the Mediterranean Sea has been the great trade route, and along its shores have risen, flourished and decayed the commercial emporia of three millennia, according to the rise and fall of its civilisations. The Greeks, Romans, Venetians and Turks have created coastal towns and ports, wherever acropolis sites and sheltered havens have been linked with trade routes. In times of piracy, towns have been pushed back from the coasts, leaving a legacy of abandoned coastlines or the development of twin settlements, a fortified port linked inland with the original town. Thus there developed Rome and Ostia, Athens and Piraeus, Cythera and Scandia in the island of Cythera, among many other examples. In the interior basins and fertile valleys they have developed usually in terms of local needs of provincial administration and commerce, often dating back to sites of Iberian, Etruscan and other early occupance. Such inland towns are frequently at considerable altitude. In Spain, for example, there are eighteen provincial towns situated above 2,000 ft. Where the inland basins are also strategic routeways, fortress towns have developed, such as Braganza (2,200 ft.) in Portugal, Burgos (2,850 ft.), Segovía (3,274 ft.) and Cuenca (3,028 ft.) in Spain, and Skoplje (816 ft.), Sarajevo (2,300 ft.) and Ljubljana (1,201 ft.) in Yugoslavia. In the North Italian Plain a series of towns are situated along the Emilian Way at the foot of the Apennines, such as Rimini, Faenza, Bologna, Modena and Parma. In the Danube Basin, towns have developed chiefly in three zones. Firstly, along the tributaries of the Danube a series of valley settlements have been located, especially in the Roumanian lowlands of Muntenia (Fig.

41). The wide belt of marshland along the river Danube has not favoured the growth of many towns there, except at a few strategically placed sites such as Belgrade and Budapest. These are not bridge-point settlements in their development but fortress towns, along the routes of invasion between mountain and plain, where the hills from the interior stretch out in fingers of higher land near to the flood plain of the Danube. Secondly, there is a marked concentration of small towns along the piedmont zone of the Carpathians and Balkan mountains, especially where minerals are also extracted, such as in the oilfields around Ploesti (Fig. 41). The third group of towns are located in the mountains, wherever enclosed basins linked by routeways provide the resources and markets for provincial capitals such as Cluj and Ostrava, and innumerable small centres.

The loess belt of Central Europe has influenced the location of a number of important cities, such as Cracow, Breslau, Dresden, Leipzig, Magdeburg and Brunswick. Another group occurs along the Rhineland and in the middle basins of the Main and the Neckar. A third group are scattered along the Alpine Foreland, including those along the Upper Danube, such as Vienna, Munich, Augsburg, Regensburg and Linz. Along the line of the Elbe and Saale valleys, a series of towns have developed from medieval fortress towns and bishoprics. In Eastern Germany, the numerous *Kolonialstadt*, associated with the expansion of the German marklands against the Slavs, have also developed. Finally, along the coastlines of the Baltic and North Sea, stretching from South Finland to the Dutch coast, ports, associated with the activities of the Hanseatic League have grown by their mercantile enterprises, notably Königsberg, Lübeck, Stettin, Hamburg and Bremen.

In France it is significant that the larger towns are nearly all located on the coasts or near frontiers. Furthermore, of these principal cities, the majority lie near the eastern or the continental frontiers, with only Bordeaux and Nantes situated on the Atlantic coast. The dominance of Paris in the north is a further feature, and of towns to-day exceeding 20,000 inhabitants only Chartres is situated within a sixty miles radius of the capital. In Belgium and in the Netherlands there is the greatest concentration of urban centres in Europe; where the medieval town reached its finest flowering under the beneficent influence of commercial and industrial prosperity. Three great concentrations of cities occur: in the provinces of North and South Holland; in the triangle linking Antwerp, Ghent and Brussels;

L

and in the belt which stretches from Maastricht through Liége to
Namur and Mons along the foot of the Ardennes.

Unlike many continental examples, where medieval concentrations
of towns and subsequent industrial expansion have gone together, the
situation of British towns shows revolutionary changes before and
after the exploitation of the coalfields. Primarily, distinction can be
made between the Lowland Zone of Britain, where town life began
early, and the Highland Zone, where it came much later, usually not
until the eighteenth century. Coastal sites were early of importance,
such as the Cinque Ports and Hull. Many more towns were developed
at the head of navigation and where river crossings were possible,
such as Bristol, London, Ipswich, Norwich, York and Newcastle.
An interesting series of towns developed at the head of navigation on
rivers which breached the Jurassic escarpment with its numerous
trackways, such as Lincoln, Grantham, Stamford and Northampton.[1]
Others were situated along frontier zones, such as the Thames valley
settlements of Oxford, Abingdon, Wallingford (Ill. XI) and Reading,
between the Danish and Saxon Kingdoms of Mercia and the West
Saxons, respectively, and also the Welsh border towns. In Scotland
(Fig. 25) and in Ireland, there was a concentration of towns along
their east coasts because of the orientation of medieval trade. The
Industrial Revolution changed the value of many of these aspects of
nodality with the concentration of many new towns at the ports
and on the coalfields (see pp. 152–3).

Town development in Northern Europe has been located particularly along the coasts. All the chief towns of Denmark are ports, and
most of these are concentrated in east Jylland where they have grown
naturally at the head of fiörd sites.[2] In Scandinavia, the mountain
barriers and the poverty of the interior lands have resulted in the towns
turning their interests seaward in search of mercantile enterprise. The
ancient towns of Norway, such as Tønsberg, Stavanger, Bergen and
Trondheim, are all coastal ports. Similarly, in Finland, the five
medieval towns of any importance such as Åbo and Viborg, were
located on the littoral. In contrast, the fertile plains of south-west and
central Sweden attracted some urban settlements, in the lands away
from the coast, such as the ancient capital of Lund and the towns of
Uppsala, Enköping and Strangnäs in the Mälar plain, often situated
at the intersection of an esker and a stream.[3] North of latitude 60°, most
of the towns have developed since the seventeenth century as metallurgical centres, lumber towns or fishing ports.

The Sites of Towns

It is more difficult to generalise about town sites than it is to describe their situation. Each town site is, in a sense, unique. It is also clear that the site possesses only relative values, which depend upon the reasons for the town's initial developments, its role and functions, its needs of defence and its communication with other centres. Sometimes the site may become inconvenient for the further growth of the town, indicating the powerful influence of geographical inertia. At least three aspects of the site have significance for the student of urban geography: the topographical features, as elements of fixation for town development; the influence of topography on the plan of the town; and the created landscape of the town as it modifies the original site by urban expansion.

The first of these considerations, the elements of fixation on the site, is closely related to the original causes of town creation. Chief among these elements have been the sites of strongholds, fords and bridge-points, the confluence of rivers, and road junctions. Many Mediterranean towns have been located near a fortified hill which was neither too high nor inaccessible. Athens, for example, began on the Acropolis site, and by classical times had spread all round, forming a circle centred on the stronghold.[4] The fortified hill nucleus has been the origin of countless sites later imbedded within the town plan. Madrid commenced as a Moorish fort or *almudaina*, overlooking the gorge of the Manzanares 130 feet below. From this site the small Moorish settlement or *almedina* expanded and alongside the new town of the sixteenth century was created.[5] Similarly, Barcelona expanded from the hill fort of Montjuich, and Narbonne grew alongside the stronghold of Montlauris. Edinburgh, in the thirteenth century, clustered on the castle slope well protected by its steep site (Fig. 34).[6] In some cases the distance between the acropolis site and the town made them separate settlements, as in Fiesole and Florence. A deliberate transfer from the restricted site of Old Sarum to the new town of Salisbury in the Avon valley is an example of another variant.[7] Again other town sites have been fixed by a fortified hill and a sheltered haven on the coast, such as Nice, located between the Château and the harbour of St. Lambert.

The large number of towns located at bridge-points or ford crossings suggests the importance of this element of fixation. The Celtic name of Amiens—Samarobriva—explains the origin of this town, as it was located at a crossing of the river Somme. On the right bank of

X*a*. Polder Town, Elburg, Holland.

X*b*. Hill Top Town, Montecompatri, Italy.

the river was placed the citadel, on the island of St. Lieu was the original nucleus of the town, and on the left bank later developed the medieval town, all linked by the bridge across the Somme and its two tributaries, the Avre and Selle. The Roman names of Maastricht and Utrecht—*Trajectus ad Mosam* and *Trajectus ad Rhenum*—indicate the origin of these river towns at fords of the Meuse and Rhine respectively. Similarly *Pons Aelius* suggests the origin of Newcastle on the fortified left bank of the Tyne near the Roman Wall, while Carlisle occupies a comparable site where the Roman Wall pivoted on the defended crossing of the Eden. Famous examples of bridge towns are Saragossa (Fig. 30), Seville, Florence, Pavia, Turin, Geneva, Grenoble, Limoges, Rennes, London, Dresden, Stettin, Frankfurt-am-Main and Breslau. Many other towns have developed at the confluence of two rivers, such as Granada, Segovia, Teruel, Milan, Parma, Lyons, Le Mans, Metz, Liége, Ghent, Coblenz, Mainz and Belgrade. Sometimes, where the river is broad, twin settlements have developed on either bank, such as Beaucaire and Tarascon on the lower Rhone, Mannheim and Ludwigshafen on the Rhine (Fig. 29), Buda and Pest on the Danube.

Water defences have served the strategic sites of many towns by the use of meander spurs, islands and marshes. Meander spurs have been the sites of Toledo on the Tagus (Fig. 29), Besançon on the Doubs, Charleville-sur-Meuse, Luxemburg on the Alzette and Prague on the Vltava. Island sites on rivers are exemplified by the Cité of Paris, the Ile Saint-Géry of Brussels, the Alt Kölln of Berlin, the Dominsel of Breslau and the Stadsholmen of Stockholm (Fig. 29). There are numerous examples of towns situated on low-lying sites, defended by river marshes. There are the north Italian towns of Cremona, Mantua and Ferrara, Dutch examples such as Amsterdam (Ill. XIII), Rotterdam, Delft and Arnheim, as well as many others such as Oxford, Lille, Melun, Strasbourg, Hamburg and Warsaw.

Road sites and junctions have also been important elements in the fixation of towns. The Roman road plexus has fixed many of the communication centres of Europe. In Italy, the Emilian, Flaminian and Egnatian roads are lined with market towns and regional centres.[8] Milan, the *Mediolanum* or 'centre point' of Roman times, is an excellent example of a route centre, at the crossing place of communications between Central Europe, through the Alpine passes and the Mediterranean, as well as between the Adriatic and Western Europe. In the plain of Languedoc the Roman road (Via Aurelia) has fixed the position of several towns: Nîmes was placed where access to the Cevennes was possible; Montpellier where the sea was approached close to the highway; Beziers at a river crossing;

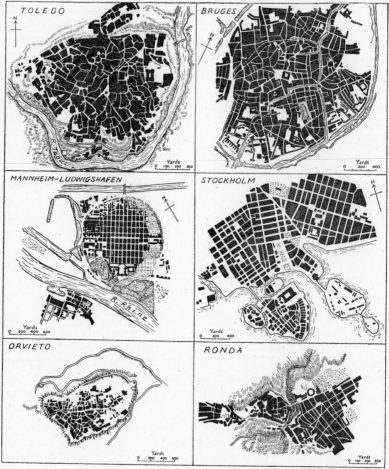

Fig. 29. Types of Urban Sites.

Narbonne at the road junction to Aquitaine; and Perpignan where the pass of Perthus could be gained across the eastern Pyrenees. Autun and Dijon are other examples of Roman and medieval road crossings.

The influence of the topographic site on the plan of the town is illustrated in many of the above quoted examples. Fig. 29 shows examples of such influences. Some of the most striking examples are the hill-top towns. Many of these settlements have been contained by the steep gradients, allowing of no further expansion on the site. Tuscan towns such as Arezzo, Perugia and Orvieto, and the Latium town of Montecompatri (Ill. X*b*) well illustrate such features. Enna in Sicily is one of the best examples, lying on a steep hill at 3,068 ft. with the railway station in the valley, 1,086 ft. below. Other famous hill-top towns are: Cacares and Segovia (Spain), Evora (Portugal), Beziers, Laon and Cassel (France).

Restricted island sites also give marked individuality to town plans such as Peñiscola off the coast of Castellón in Spain, Syracuse and Augusta on the Sicilian coast, Gallipoli in the Gulf of Taranto, Chioggia in the Po delta and Mitilini on Lesbos in the Aegean Sea. Venice, the famous example, has now extended over some 120 islands, served by the Grand Canal together with 45 other canals, and spanned by about 400 bridges. Copenhagen, though not originally on an island site, expanded in the sixteenth century on the fortified island of Slotsholm and in 1618 Christian IV laid out the town of Christians-haven on the adjacent island of Amager, the whole plan of the city to-day being much influenced by the waterways.[9]

The Morphology of Towns—Roman Town Plans

The physical factors alone are inadequate to explain the features of urban morphology, since the town is as much the expression of history as of geography. The Greek town plans have little imprint on the lay-out of modern cities in the Mediterranean, but the Roman legacy has been great. The influence of the Roman grid plan is still apparent in a large number of European towns. The relative import-ance of some of these Roman colonial cities and garrison or *castrum* towns can be assessed from the area occupied by their original sites.

In the North Italian Plain and the south of France, the Roman legacy of towns is very marked. Further north it is much less so, although the Roman *limes* along the Rhine valley and the Danube had towns of considerable size between Cologne and Regensburg. The absence of much town development in the Low Countries during Roman times meant that the original town sites of this region were generally of a later date, associated with the development of trade in the twelfth and thirteenth centuries. The considerable size of the Roman towns in Britain has been a significant influence in the sub-sequent morphology of many of them.

The Roman town plan was deliberately executed and measured with exactitude. Hygenus, the Roman architect, considered the ideal cam town should be 2,400 × 1,600 ft., since any greater length might endanger defence by indistinct signals along its walls.[11] Turin thus

AREA OF SELECTED ROMAN TOWNS[10]

Town	Area of site in acres	Town	Area of site in acres
Southern Gaul		*Low Countries*	
Nîmes	660	Tournai	28
Lyons	328	Louvain	11
Toulouse	239	Brussels	7
Poitiers	103	Antwerp	7
Vienne	88		
Northern Gaul		*Britain*	
Autun	494	London	330
Metz	168	St. Albans	200
Orleans	60	Colchester	150
Rheims	148	Canterbury	c. 50
Troyes	38	Silchester	104
Dijon	26	Chichester	103
Amiens	19	Winchester	138
Paris	19	Dorchester	68
		Exeter	91
Rhine Limes		Cirencester	240
Trèves	494	Gloucester	46
Cologne	230	Caerwent	44
Mainz	228	Leicester	105
Worms	165	Wroxeter	170
Bonn	60	Chester	56
Strasbourg	48	York	50
Basle	12	Carlisle	c. 50

fulfilled these requirements almost exactly: it was 2,400 × 2,220 ft., and Aosta also was comparable with 2,440 × 1,920 ft., giving them areas of 94 and 81 acres respectively. The street axis of the *cardo* and *decumanus* usually orientated east to west and north to south respectively, established the gridiron into which the street blocks

were divided parallel with each other. Turin is the best example of a
city which has maintained the Roman gridiron, preserved almost as
clearly as a fly in the amber. The Roman plan divided into blocks or
insulae, measuring 242 × 262 ft. and 262 × 393 ft., is still preserved
in the modern layout of the streets (Fig. 30).

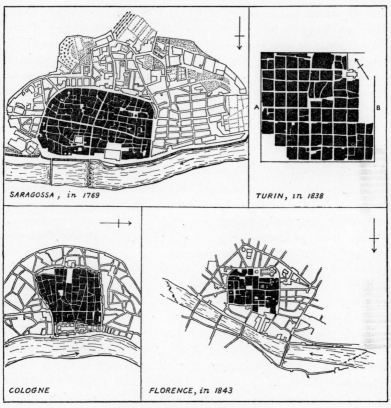

Fig. 30. Roman Town Plans.
(Areas in black indicate Roman site.)

The relation between the Roman plan and the existing lay-out of
the town is not always clearly traceable, even though a central grid
system is apparent. In several of the English examples of Roman
garrison towns, with areas between 150 and 50 acres, the outline of
the plan has been altered, as in Colchester, Chester and York. In
some cases it may be the influence of a bridge site which has shifted

with destruction of the site by inundations. Thus the curve of the High Street in Perth towards the bridge across the Tay may be a possible example. Again in other towns, the whole Roman plan has been so shifted that the existing central grid is no longer superimposed on the original plan. In Florence, the gridiron Roman plan of the Imperial era is clearly seen, the *cardo* running due north and the *decumanus* east-west (Fig. 30). But the centuriation of the Florence basin is aligned south-south-west/north-north-east and west-north-west/east-south-east; and this has led scholars to speculate why Florence itself does not correspond to this alignment, as do the other towns of the basin, e.g. Prato.[12] In the south of Spain many of the original Roman plans have been erased by the subsequent haphazard and tortuous street plan of the Muslim towns, such as Seville, Cordoba, Toledo and Valencia, whereas at Saragossa the Roman site of 116 acres has been preserved intact (Fig. 30).[13]

Medieval Town Plans of Spontaneous Growth

The Roman influence on many town plans to-day does not mean, however, that there has been a continuity of urban functions on the same sites. Apart from examples in Italy, it was general throughout Europe that the Roman sites did not continue with an urban life during the Dark Ages. The ecclesiastics often continued to occupy the *cité*, a portion of the site which usually remained aloof from the subsequent re-development of the town. In France, where the relation of the Roman site to the medieval settlement has been carefully studied, we know that the latter occupied only a fraction of the original plan: Bordeaux occupied one-third, Nîmes one-seventh, Perigueux one-thirteenth, and Autun only one-twentieth of the Roman site.[14] Even to-day, towns such as Merida in the south of Spain and Trèves in Germany still occupy only a small proportion of the Roman town area.

A characteristic feature of many of the evolved town plans, as distinct from those created in a single plan, is the cellular growth of such settlements. This is a characteristic particularly of the Germanic towns. Brunswick, for example, consisted of five nuclei (Fig. 31). Around the original *burg* of Dankerwarderobe were grouped the suburbs: Alte Wik, a feudal village; Hagen, a settlement founded in the mid-twelfth century; Neustadt, first mentioned in 1257; and Sack, built in 1300. The five quarters of Brunswick remained as separately walled entities until 1697.[15] At Rostock there were three

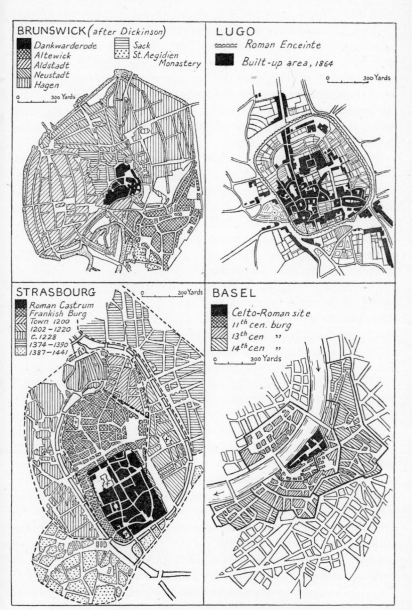

BRUNSWICK *(after Dickinson)*

- Dankwarderode
- Altewick
- Aldstadt
- Neustadt
- Hagen
- Sack
- St. Aegidien Monastery

0   300 Yards

LUGO

~~~~ *Roman Enceinte*

Built-up area, 1864

0   300 Yards

STRASBOURG

- Roman Castrum
- Frankish Burg
- Town 1200
- 1202 – 1220
- C. 1228
- 1374 – 1390
- 1387 – 1441

0   300 Yards

BASEL

- Celto-Roman site
- 11th cen. burg
- 13th cen "
- 14th cen "

0   300 Yards

Fig. 31. Types of Town Growth.

nuclei: the Alstadt, founded in 1218 around two churches; the Mittel-
stadt in 1232; the Neustadt added in 1252; all united within one wall
in 1265.[16] Similarly, at Königsberg the castle was erected in 1255
and three small settlements were added, in the Altstadt, Löbenicht
and Kneiphof, which gained their municipal rights in 1286, 1300 and
1327 respectively.[17] In these and many other examples the origin was
the castle, followed by the market place, the latter being the focal
point of each nucleus, around which each settlement developed
independently from the others.

Sometimes the different nuclei were settled by different ethnic
groups. Pamplona, capital of the Christian kingdom of Navarre,
developed in this way. There was the Navarrese settlement of the
indigenous population called the *Navarrería*, granted a market in
1087. Then rival settlements with immigrant 'foreigners' were established at San Cernín in 1129 and at San Nicholas in the second half
of the twelfth century. The central market and wall enclosing the
three settlements were not established until the fifteenth century and,
prior to this unification, there was much rivalry among the three
nuclei. It is characteristic of the Spanish town plans to have the
Morería and the *Judería* (Moorish and Jewish quarters) apart from the
rest of the town.[18] In some cases, such as at Ronda, they were also
physically separate, since in Ronda a gorge 400 ft. deep separated the
old Moorish city from the Mercadillo or Christian quarter (Fig. 29).

The same cellular development of a group of settlements within a
town is apparent in many towns of Eastern Europe. There, however,
the urban plan was related closely to the fortress and even to fortified
churches. The *gorod* or churches were usually the only stone buildings
in the Russian town apart from the fort or *kremlin*. Thus in Peskov, a
town near Novgorod, each quarter clustered around its church, which
was used for the storage and protection of goods held by the guilds.
The plan of Novgorod is also characteristic of other Russian towns.
The bridge point across the river Volkhov was guarded by the
kremlin, erected in the ninth century. On the left bank was the
ecclesiastical quarter or *sophia* on the right bank the merchants'
quarter. The town was divided into five units or *kanats*, each with its
own administration. Even the very extensive lands of the republic of
Novgorod, stretching towards the Urals, were administered separately
by these five *kanats* of the city.

Apart from the activities of these merchant burghers, the ecclesiastical foundations were an important contribution towards urban

XI. Wallingford, Berks.

XII. Winchelsea, Sussex.

creation. In some towns they are the direct cause of town beginnings. In St. Andrews, Scotland, the abbey church was built in 1112 on an earlier Culdean site and the bishops' burgh was established about 1144. The motif of the plan consists of two streets radiating from the Cathedral. The trade of the town was largely seaborne and associated with important pilgrimage traffic from the Continent. There are many examples of bishopric towns whose creation was associated in the first place with the establishment of the church. Among some famous examples are Canterbury, Lichfield and Coventry in England, Rheims, Chartres and Laon in France, Liége, Malines and Tournai in the Low Countries, Bremen, Cologne, Munster, Würzburg and Augsburg in Germany, and Trondheim and Lund in Scandinavia. In a few instances the town has grown up within the walls of a monastery as in Moissac in the Garonne valley. Apart from such specifically ecclesiastical settlements, the grant of ecclesiastical holdings within many towns was a contributory factor for their successful growth.

Medieval Town Planning

Town planning was not possible on a large scale in the Middle Ages because the resources of the states were small and the life of the people predominantly agricultural; but a great number of towns were deliberately created by the exigencies of war and for the effective occupation of newly conquered territories. This has been discussed in the previous chapter. Methods of town planning varied according to local circumstances, but the description which Leland has given us of Winchelsea, in Sussex, is typical of a new town planned near an old site. This settlement had been destroyed by the sea, 'whereupon, A.D. 1277, the King sent thither John Kirkely, Bishop of Ely and Treasurer of England and vewid a plot to make the new towne of Winchelsey on, the whiche was at that time a ground wher conies partily did resorte. Sir John Tregose a Knight was chief owner of it, and one Maurice and Bataille Abbey. The King compounded with them and so was there VII score and ten acres limitted to the New Towne. . . . Then in the tyme of the yere aforesayde the King set to his Helpe in beginning and waulling New Winchelsey and the inhabitants of Old Winchelsey took by a little and a little and builded at the New Towne. So that within the VI or VII yere afore expressid the New Towne was metely well furnished and dayly after for a few yeres increased' (see Ill. XII).[19] The development of Salisbury was comparable. But more often the new town was built in a new district where the success of the settlement depended on the attraction of settlers.

The plans of these created towns vary widely, but certain types were most commonly developed. Variants of the simple street plan, allowing for the subsequent expansion of the town, are the commonest type. In Scotland 'the King's highway' provided the axis of settlement along which the burghers built their houses. The stunted size of many of the small burghs has meant that the plan has not been much modified from the original. In the *villenueves* of the south of France and in Spain, a parallel development of streets or an elliptical arrangement of streets centred on the main street axis, is a common motif. Vitoria, the capital of the Spanish province of Alava, established in the twelfth century, is a good example of the elliptical street plan, also illustrated in Bilbao and other towns of northern Spain (Fig. 32). In eastern Germany and in Eastern Europe a rectangular fortress and a church alongside it provided the nucleus for many town plans. These may be double street plans, rectangular grids as in Prussia and in Czechoslovakia (e.g. Pilsen, Fig. 32) or two parallel streets in spindle form as in Silesia.

It is impossible to trace the origin of the grid plan to any specific cause other than convenience of exact measurement. The first grid plan of medieval France is Montauban in the Tarn valley. It was created by the Count of Toulouse in 1144. Its trapezoid shape is made to fit into the topographical site of a peninsula composed of high terrace gravels overlooking the river. The most remarkable and therefore the least typical of the *bastides* of southern France is Montpazier, erected in 1284 (Fig. 32). It was designed as a rectangle 400 by 200 metres with two large squares near the centre for the cathedral and market causing breaks in the otherwise regular alignment of the parallel streets.[20] Aigues-Mortes is another well-known rectangular *bastide*, built in 1240-6. Its plan is influenced by the factor of local climate; its main streets are so orientated as to break the force of the prevailing wind from the sea (Fig. 32).[21] In England, apart from Winchelsea already mentioned, regular grid plans are apparent in Ludlow, and more clearly in Salisbury.[22]

Though these planned medieval towns are interesting examples of urban creation, they are not the most important group. By far the commonest type of town is that which has grown gradually without any pre-determined design. In general, the plans of such may be divided into three categories, nuclear, linear and radial. The nuclear town plan has already been discussed. The street plan and its variants account for most of the linear types. The single street axis, as in many

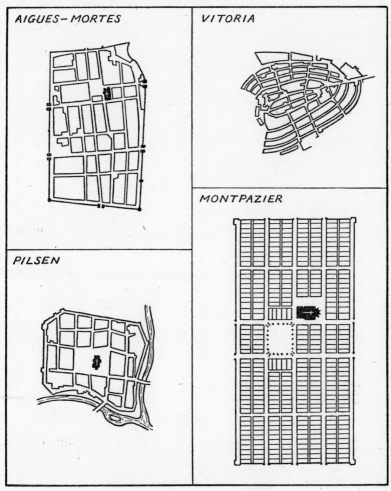

Fig. 32. Medieval Planned Towns.

Scottish burghs, is related both to the stunted size of these towns and to the importance of 'the king's highway.' Where encroachment took place in the broad central street, a parallel street would be formed, as in Stirling. Forked street plans, as in many English market towns,

M

XIII. Amsterdam.

such as Carlisle, and cross-road plans as in some of Alfred's towns of Wessex, e.g. Oxford, are other types of comparable axial development. In Italian towns, Stia and Pietrasanta represent a comparable evolution. The street plan is also characteristic of Bavaria, the Tirol and eastern Franconia. Thus most areas where it was developed were thinly populated areas which only required small local market centres.

The radial arrangement is a curious and composite series of town plans. Some are the result of deliberate planning, as in the case of Milan, where the original Roman plan was erased completely in the new town, created after the fire of 1162. Others represent a natural growth, such as the hill-top towns of Central Italy, where the topographical contour explains their lay-out. The streets follow the contours in such examples as Urbino, Siena, Foligno, Montecompatri and Cerveteri.[23] Again some suggest the radial arrangement around an important focus, such as a palace, church or market place. Aachen is planned around the former imperial palace, later the market place. Many of the towns with a nuclear growth are centred on the market place, such as Rostock previously mentioned. Many of the towns of Flanders, Holland and Westphalia are planned radially from the guildhall and market, e.g. Middleburg, Malines, Bruges (Fig. 29), Brussels and Douai. In England, medieval Bristol clustered radially around the guildhall. The ease with which canals could be constructed as moats of defence as well as navigable waterways, possibly explains some of the examples noted in the Low Countries such as Amsterdam (Ill. XIII).

The Renaissance and Baroque Town

Medieval town planning was followed in the sixteenth century by the Renaissance development of towns, first in Italy and later in France. This led to the great activity of baroque town planning in the seventeenth and eighteenth centuries throughout the courts of Europe. The movement was first developed when the Italian and French theorists made popular their abstract conceptions of new towns for military fortresses. Such were Scamozzi's ideal town, and Palissy's plan inspired by the shell of the mollusc. Leghorn, laid out in a grid plan, was one of the earliest creations, built by the De Medici family in the fifteenth century. A later grid plan was Vitry-le-François, founded in 1545. Palma Nova in Venezia, built in 1593, was a radial plan for a fortress which was one of the most idealistic plans (see

(*Aerofilms Ltd.*)

XIV*a*. Palma Nova, Italy.

(*Aerofilms Ltd. K.L.M.*)

XIV*b*. Naarden, Holland.

Ill. XIV*a*). Along the eastern frontier of France other fortresses were built, such as Philippeville and Charleroi. A number of French ports (such as Le Havre, Brest and Rochefort) were also erected in the sixteenth and early seventeenth centuries; while in Norway the port of Fredrikstad built in 1567 is comparable. At Nancy, a new town was founded in the grand manner in 1587 and dovetailed into the existing medieval plan (Fig. 33); Willemstad, founded by Prince William I in the Netherlands, is another example. In Germany a few refugee centres were built at this time, such as Freudenstadt, founded in 1599 in the Black Forest.

The change from the Renaissance to the baroque was from military planning to the more aesthetic creation of capital cities, to the embellishment of existing towns and to the extravagant practice of landscape design. This gave rise to the great activity of baroque town planning during the seventeenth and eighteenth centuries. Madrid, Munich, Vienna, Budapest, Warsaw, St. Petersburg (Fig. 33) and Copenhagen were all associated with such creative activity, while other great towns such as Dublin, Edinburgh (see Ill. XV), London, Paris, Lyons, Bordeaux, Florence, Rome and Naples felt its modifications on their old plans. Such cities witnessed the spirit of this age in their formal lay-out, the emphasis on public squares and ornamental gardens, the rigid planning and the uniformity of design. As Mumford has said, 'town plans changed from medieval diversity to baroque uniformity; from medieval localism to baroque centralism and from the absolutism of God and the Catholic Church to the absolutism of the temporal sovereign and the National State.'[24] The multiplication of small towns tended to cease in most parts of Europe and in their place great capital cities grew parasitically on the provincial towns, their size out of all proportion to the total population of their country. The whimsical fancy of a ruler chose a site such as the hunting lodge of the Retiro or the gardens of the Trianon for the development of a Madrid or a Versailles. The site was usually an arbitrary choice, although its nodality was recognised in the interests of government control.

This movement of baroque planning was associated with three objects: the foundation of new towns alongside the royal residences; the embellishment of towns with the ideas of the new planning and the improvement of defences in the fortress towns. The first of these was the most extravagant. In the creation of Versailles is exemplified the characteristic features of the baroque: the dominance of the royal

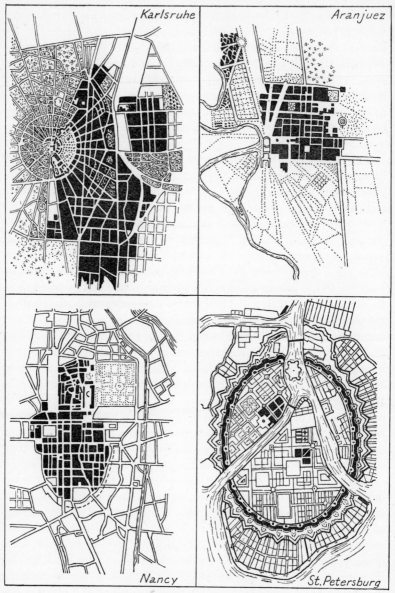

Fig. 33. Baroque Town Plans.

residence, the suggestion that the town created is only part of the greater whole and the counterbalance of streets of the town by the more extensive avenues that radiate from the palace. The same features were copied in Aranjuez, the summer residence of the kings of Spain (Fig. 33). Rastatt built in 1689 was a German example of the same plan. At Karlsruhe, founded in 1715, was developed the most ambitious design of this type (Fig. 33). The subjection of the town plan to the grand design was clearly enforced, and of the thirty-two radial axes only nine were streets.[25]

Each country developed baroque planning according to its resources. In France, apart from the town creations of Versailles, Nancy, Charleville, Nice and the new ports, Vauban erected or refortified about 150 towns on the eastern frontiers. The Dutch engineer Van Coehoorn is responsible for other fortified towns such as Naarden, Elburg (Ill. Xa) and Doesburg. Naarden, fortified in 1675–85, is a particularly good example (see Ill. XIVb).[26] In addition many of the larger towns were embellished with new squares, broader streets and encircling boulevards. In Spain, Aranjuez and El Escorial were the chief creations, with developments in Madrid and Barcelona. In Germany, refugees were settled in Mannheim (1607) and a number of smaller towns. The small kingdoms and principalities of Germany achieved such efforts as Potsdam, Dresden, Munich, Nuremberg, Hanover, Weimar and Erlangen. In Norway, there are also the examples of Christiania (1624) or Oslo, and Kristiansand (1641). All were the embodiment of the despotic power of their rulers. In Russia, St. Petersburg was perhaps the most daring creation (Fig. 33). Founded in 1703 by Peter the Great, it already had 80,000 inhabitants by 1750. Such towns fully expressed the view *l'état c'est moi*.

The Morphology of Town Growth

Apart from the legacy of town plans formulated by natural growth or creative development, it is necessary to consider a further historical element, that of subsequent growth. The establishment of a palisade or ditch around the town indicated in the most primitive form the identity of the original centre. The first wall built around the town, often grouping a series of urban nuclei, was the next stage, still discernible in many town plans. The enclosure made by the walls or *enceinte* might be built closely around the original settlement as in the case of many English towns, or it might be extended over a large area in order to enclose two or more suburbs.

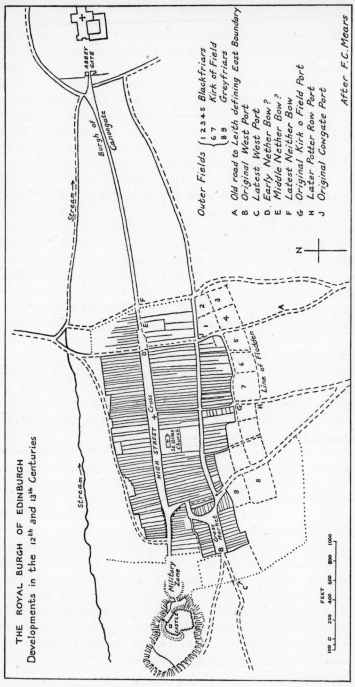

THE ROYAL BURGH OF EDINBURGH
Developments in the 12th and 13th Centuries

Outer Fields { 1 2 3 + 5   Blackfriars
               6 7   Kirk of Field
               8 9   Greyfriars

A Old road to Leith defining East Boundary
B Original West Port
C Latest West Port
D Early Nether Bow?
E Middle Nether Bow?
F Latest Neither Bow
G Original Kirk o'Field Port
H Later Potter Row Port
J Original Cowgate Port

After F.C. Mears

Fig. 34. Medieval Plan of Edinburgh.

Where the *enceinte* included a large area, the rural appearance of the town has been marked in many examples. Thus in the French towns of Dijon, Rheims and Provins, the original enclosure of the twelfth century has been sufficiently large to absorb all subsequent expansion until the modern railway era. The Spanish town of Lugo

(*Kemsley Picture Service*)

XV. Edinburgh.

still has 34 acres of farmland enclosed within the ancient Roman site (Fig. 31). The rural appearance of such towns is attested for example by the name 'couture' (*cultura*) in Rheims and Douai, and by 'kouter' in Ghent.[27] Even after the Middle Ages the burgesses have lived close to the soil and their houses have sometimes remained also as farm-yards. The influence of the town lands on the subsequent plan of the settlement is often very striking. Usually distinction was made in the charters of *terra burgalis* or the holdings owned individually by the burghers, the *terra campestris* or common arable held by the town, and the *terra communalis* or common grazing lands. Even small towns might have lands of considerable extent, such as Norwich with 8,000 acres in the sixteenth century, Bedford with 2,164 acres, Northampton 1,520 acres and Glasgow 1,810 acres. In many towns, the distribution of these lands has influenced the plan and its development, as in the cases of Newcastle-upon-Tyne, Lincoln, Stamford and Brighton. In Edinburgh the medieval pattern of rigs and burgess strips behind the frontage of the houses is still visible in its wynds and closes, a feature common to other Scottish towns (Fig. 34). Thus the town fields were encroached upon as trade superseded agriculture as the primary occupation. In a plan of Edinburgh in 1742 there were 186 wynds and closes which represented the built-up area enclosing the rigs and paths, many still the original rood size of the rigs, 450 × 25 ft.[28]

Few British towns expanded sufficiently to have a second *enceinte* of walls, but on the Continent the stimulus of trade and the dangers of invasion made this frequently necessary. Thus the successive series of *enceintes* is a second element in the morphology of growth. This has been summarised for selected examples in the following table:

Growth of Medieval Towns in Western Europe*

Town	Area of Roman site in acres	First medieval enceinte *and date*	Later enceinte
Saragossa	117	*c.* 120 (1118)	
Avignon	49	98 (1234)	2,624 (1370)
Marseilles	69	53 (1121)	160 (1298)
Bordeaux	79	25 (1227)	679 (1326)
Paris	19	300 (*c.* 1250)	1,053 (14th cen.)
Troyes	38	103 1254)	238
Strasbourg	48	170 (*c.* 1150)	484 (1541)
Basle	12	*c.* 160 (1080)	325 (*c.* 1400)
Geneva	12	37 (1364)	143 (1475)
Bonn	137	103 (12th cen.)	—
Cologne	230	137 (*c.* 948)	962 (1180)
Aix-la-Chapelle	–	120 (*c.* 1150)	420 (14th cen.)
Brussels	7	189 (*c.* 1134)	1,177
Ghent	–	192 (end of 11th cen.)	1,555 (16th cen.)
Bruges	3	168 (*c.* 1089)	1,033 (16th cen.)
Louvain	11	144 (*c.* 1149)	984 (16th cen.)
Antwerp	7	77 (12th cen.)	*c.* 1,500 (1540-3)
Amsterdam	–	625 (1342)	1,812 (1593)
Berlin	–	175 (13th cen.)	900 (17th cen.)

* Data derived from a number of town studies, especially Ganshof and Lot.

Apart from towns which have remained stunted in their growth, or those created rapidly by industrialism in the nineteenth century, cities have grown by three clearly recognised stages. The first, or nuclear stage, is represented by the central area of the modern city, often demarcated by broad avenues following the alignment of the old walls, such as the *Ringbahn* of Berlin and the inner boulevards of Paris. The second, or formative stage, is represented by the expansion of the city during the nineteenth century. Two factors of special importance during this period have been the establishment of the factory system and the development of communications, especially the advent of the railways. The former has established the industrial areas on the periphery of the central area, to be later engulfed by the expanding city, while the latter has determined the framework of all subsequent expansion along the main lines of communication. The third stage of the city, that of modern rapid growth, is related closely to the introduction of motor transport.[29]

Prior to the advent of the automobile, the radius to which a city might be normally expected to expand was about five miles. The automobile increased this radius by at least three times, enabling a city to absorb the satellite centres within its expanding boundaries, a feature clearly demonstrated in all the great European cities. For example, the ramparts of Vienna were dismantled in 1857 and the city further extended to 108 sq. miles in 1905. By 1938, a vast area of 460 sq. miles was within the jurisdiction of Vienna.[30] Greater Berlin (the *Stadtkreis*), created by law in 1920, covered an area of 341 sq. miles, compared with 24 sq. miles in 1871 or 11 sq. miles in 1841. Similarly, Greater London, which now covers 695 sq. miles, had 115 sq. miles when it was unified under the administration of the County in 1888, and 58 sq. miles in 1860.

Urban Zones

The three stages of city growth, mentioned above, have left their imprint in the urban land use. Usually three distinct zones can be recognised: the central area, bounded by the inner ring of communications, the suburban, or outer ring, and the satellite development of dormitory centres which commute their workers to the city each day. Recognition of such urban zones is now established by town-planning legislation in many countries.[31] Since the city is a dynamic organism in constant change, the zones reflect changing patterns of land use and population migration. In general, high land values and taxation in the central area of a city cause centrifugal tendencies of population and industry, and increasing specialisation in the use to which the central area is developed. The latter is related to centripetal force, since the central area will tend to gain more in terms of volume of trade and income from land and buildings, from the extended radius of city influence, than it has from the centrifugal movements of population and business. In contrast, the peripheral area of a city tends to show attractive qualities for increased immigration because of the large areas of cheap land and adequate transport facilities.[32] The former is the more important influence at first, but as traffic congestion in the central area becomes worse the latter factor is an important influence in the centrifugal tendency. These general features will now be illustrated by specific examples.

The central area of great cities has been very congested until recent decades. Thus the *Ringbahn*, enclosing inner Berlin, had 2·5 million inhabitants in an area of 33·5 sq. miles, or 60 per cent. of the city's population within 10 per cent. of its area.[33] But decline of the population within the central area is now common to all great cities. The City of London had 128,129 inhabitants in 1801, whereas in 1939 there were less than 10,000.[34] Similarly, the old town of Rotterdam, which reached a maximum of 69,500 in 1869, had only 21,000 in 1930.[35] This decline has been clearly developed in great capitals such as Paris, Berlin, Vienna, Budapest and Rome, as well as in most large cities. The decline, starting at the centre, has now worked outwards, affecting the inner ring quarters. The inner districts of Rotterdam reached a maximum of 200,600 in 1920, but they had dropped to 167,600 in the following decade. The commercial centre of London had 125,000 inhabitants in 1850 but by 1900 this had dropped to 60,000. The larger unit of the County of London reached its peak figure of 4,521,000 in 1911, but by 1936 it had declined to 4,141,000. Similarly, in Budapest there was the same movement. Between 1880 and 1935, the inner ring districts, or *beltekek*, declined by some 1 to 5 per cent., whereas the outer ring districts, or *kultetek*, increased by as much as 50 per cent.[36]

The tendency to increase the specialisation of land use in the central area and push the residential quarters further out is also general. This has been well shown in a comparative study of Stockholm between 1880 and 1930.[37] In 1880, the southern Norrmalm district was the best residential quarter in the centre of Stockholm, and business enterprises were located south of it. Since then, commercial quarters have displaced the better-class residences, which in turn have pushed the poorer-class residential and industrial quarters further out of the city. Stockholm has now four concentric zones of land use; the financial centre, the shopping and residential quarters of the city, the densely built residential zone and the sparsely built suburban zone.[38] Similarly, Prague has developed three well-defined economic zones. There is the commercial city on the right bank of the river Vltava in the central area; the administrative castle town on the left bank, stretching from the centre into the peripheral belt; and the outer manufacturing ring, including most of the peripheral belt and part of the satellite ring beyond.[39]

Urban zones are geographical features which can be readily discerned in any city plan of urban land use. Generally, the central area consists of certain specialised groups of districts such as banking, commercial offices and government institutions.[40] On the periphery of the central area are often quarters of luxury shops such as tailors, jewellers, etc., and distinct from them the large general stores. Light industry and certain trades which demand storage space, such as furniture dealers, tend to be localised in the periphery of the inner ring. Heavier industries are localised near the railways and canals on the outskirts of the city, associated with poorer residential districts. The better-class residential districts usually divide into two categories: those related to high land values near the centre of the city, or those on the suburban fringes with high-class amenities.

Cities can be studied systematically as important and complicated geographical regions, albeit small in areal extent. And, as in all forms of organisms, the analysis of the complex features of a city's anatomy and physiology are mutually interrelated. No one aspect of urban study is thus an adequate explanation in itself of all the complexities of man's greatest achievement, the city.

SELECTED REFERENCES

Clark, C. 'Urban Population Densities,' Journ. of the Royal Statistical Society, Series A, Vol. CXIV, Part IV, 1951, pp. 490–496.
Clouzot, E. 'Le Problème de la formation des villes,' La Géog., vol. 20, 1909, pp. 165-76.
Dickinson, R. E. The West European City. London, 1951.
Fleure, H. J. 'City Morphology of Europe,' Journ. Roy. Inst. of Gr. Brit., 1932.
Fleure, H. J. 'Some types of Cities in Temperate Europe,' G.R., 1920, pp. 357-74.
Ganshof, F. L. Étude sur le développement des villes entre Loire et Rhin au Moyen Age. Brussels, 1943.
George, P. La Ville. Paris, 1952.

Haverfield, F. *Ancient Town-Planning*. Oxford, 1913.

Lavedan, P. *Histoire de l'Urbanisme; Antiquité—Moyen Age*. Paris, 1926.

Sorre, M. *Les Fondements de Géographie Humaine*. tome III, *L'Habitat*, Paris, 1952.

Tout, T. F. *Medieval Town Planning*. Manchester, 1934.

Wycherley, R. E. *How the Greeks Built Cities*. London, 1949.

(Note: For individual town studies see the references in the volumes of the Géographie Universelle. There is also a good bibliography in R. E. Dickinson, *The West European City*. On English towns see the list of references in M. R. G. Conzen, *Geographie und Landesplanung in England*. Bonn, 1952. A useful list of town plans is contained in *Catalogus Mapparum Geographicarum ad Historiam Pertinentium*. Warsaw, 1933, pp. 212-291.)

CHAPTER NINE

TYPES OF EUROPEAN CITIES

THE two previous chapters have sought to emphasise that town studies can only be adequately analysed in a space-time context. Generalisations about towns tend to become unreal whenever one or other of these is ignored. The space context suggests that a town must be studied in relation to its own regional features. Often the site of a town is circumstantial and one of several other alternatives could have been selected. But the situation of the town usually has more insistent influence on the development or decay of the urban settlement. The time context expresses the dynamic qualities of a town, whose changing values and techniques employed may vary greatly in the growth of a town. Thus the particularisms of place and the legacies of time together express the individuality of towns so that classifications at best remain loose frameworks for general study.

The town is a living being and as such it adapts itself to changing needs. Primarily towns have been developed to answer the social needs of man and to benefit him with communal amenities. Defence has been one of the most primitive of these needs; even modern words such as the English 'town' or Russian 'gorod' mean originally fortified enclosures. Many examples have been quoted in chapter seven of towns which have developed as military centres. The spiritual needs of man have clearly expressed themselves in the large number of ecclesiastical centres, bishopric and monastic towns. Educational values have led to the growth of university towns such as Oxford[1] and Cambridge. These social needs alone, however, would not have created towns the size of modern cities.

Superimposed on these social factors of town growth have been the results of the second great need of man, commercial intercourse. The city states of Italy and the towns of the Hanseatic League have reflected the great stimulus which trade has played in city development. The function of exchange itself has been a variable, dependent on the form of transport and the system of commerce. Thus commercial cities, before and after the Industrial Revolution, express two different systems of growth, although many European cities have adjusted themselves from the one to the other in their historical development.

Since the era introduced by the factory, modern transport and mobility of labour, new forces have been active in the creation of city life. Point production has developed the great conurbations and industrial cities with economic structures never known before. The political functions of the state have created an institutional life in the capital cities such as even the baroque capitals never had. New social needs have expressed themselves in the creation of the seaside resort, the inland spa and other recreational towns.[2] In consequence, European towns are polygenic, sometimes expressing the legacy and momentum of previous functions adapted to changing conditions of life, at other times modern phenomena created to meet new requirements.

In this chapter, four cities have been selected to illustrate distinct types of urban development. Paris is the brilliant example of a national capital whose two thousand years of history have not exhausted its virility. The political factor has given Paris a momentum which it has never lost, although it may now appear to have reached the limit of the national resources available for it. Valencia, on the east coast of Spain, represents the growth of a Mediterranean city, dependent on the productivity of its irrigated land. By its urban sprawl across the surrounding agricultural land it now threatens to destroy what has been the *raison d'être* of the town. Birmingham, in the English Midlands, is a third type, a phenomenon expressive of the Industrial Revolution, which has created an urban landscape hitherto undreamt. The fourth city, Brighton on the south coast of England, ranks as one of the most outstanding examples of the modern holiday resort. Brighton illustrates in its growth that irrational forces may sometimes be as powerful a force in urban creation as the logical forces of nodality and regional resources. In these four types, varying and changing values illustrate some of the complex relationships between man and nature.

Paris

Paris is an example of a great capital city, whose urban landscape and concentration of population express gigantic creative forces. Such a city may be studied from almost an infinite variety of aspects. Paris may be reviewed representatively as the national pageantry of France, each building, monument and square commemorative of events in the history of the capital. It may be considered as the emblem of power and the head of the state, its changing fortunes reflecting the checks and expansions of a great nation. It may be represented as the full flowering of European culture, enriched with all the cultural endowments of such leadership. It may be described therefore as the dwelling-place and inspiration of its great men, the background of the national biography. It may also be viewed as the demographic heart of France, pulsating with the resources of man-power and intellectual life which are drawn from the furthest limits of the nation. With such a variety of aspects in mind, Mirabeau could thus reflect and say, 'Paris is a Sphinx, I will drag her secret from her'; but no man has yet succeeded fully.[3] All the geographer can attempt to find out about Paris is the analysis of its urban landscape, which in itself expresses forces beyond the compass of his subject.

Paris is what Paris has made. It represents in its conurbation about 14 per cent. of the total population of France, or 5·5 million in-habitants. On less than 123,000 acres of land it has concentrated more than one-quarter of the total urban population of the nation. Within its bounds it employs about one-fifth of all the industrial workers of France. The small department of Seine, which is absorbed by Paris, has 1,250,000 workers, who utilise in their labours 20 per cent. of the steam power of France, consume 12 per cent. of the total electrical energy, and enjoy 39 per cent. of the industrial and com-mercial benefits of the nation.[4] Within the city proper there are 2,725,000 inhabitants on an area of 19,274 acres, the highest densities of population to be found in any European capital. The quarter of Saint-Gervais with 995,000 inhabitants is one of the most densely populated districts to be found in any city.[5]

The services necessary for such a concentration of population are impressive. Some two million cubic metres of drinking water are consumed daily by the city, carried in 1,864 miles of pipes. The city is drained by a system of sewers 1,180 miles in length.[6] About four million cubic metres of gas are consumed daily. A network of electric cables 7,456 miles long transmit the power of 2,500 million kilowatt-hours which are used daily. There is a plexus of 1,240 miles of bus routes, with one-sixth of all the public vehicles of France. There are also 118 miles of the underground *Métropolitain*, which pierce under the Seine in five tunnels.[7] In all this material development Paris is to-day the result of creative forces rooted in the nineteenth century. Paris has celebrated two thousand years of history, but it is in the last century, 1850 to 1950, that it has gained four million citizens and created the landscape of a great capital and industrial city.

The Site of Paris. It is just below the confluence of the Marne with the Seine, at a point where a river crossing was fixed by a north-south route running north through a hill gap, that Paris has grown. Before the Capet kings selected Paris as their capital they had tried successively Angers, Tours and Orléans as their residence. It was the routeways which favoured the site of Paris, integrating the territories of

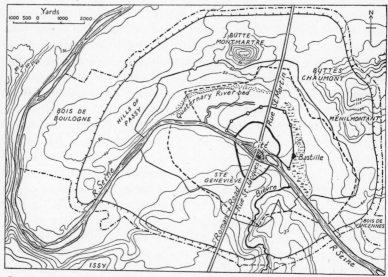

Fig. 35   SITE AND GROWTH OF PARIS *(after Crone, Demangeon, and Ganshof).*

━━━━━ *Wall of Philip Augustus 1180–1210*   ‑ ‑ ‑ ‑ *Limit of building decreed in 1674*
o—o—o *„ „ Charles c.1370*   ━━━━━ *Wall of Farmers-General*
══════ *„ „ Charles IX to Louis XIII*   ⊥⊥⊥⊥ *Fortifications 1841–45*
                 ‑ ‑ —‑ ‑ .*Actual limits of City*

their kingdom. Concomitant geographical conditions made the site of strategic importance. Forests surrounded the site of Paris on the high terraces and plateaux, but the basin of the middle Seine is a converging point for all the small streams of the Yonne, Aube and Upper Seine, as well as the Marne and Oise. These valley communications helped to link the county of Paris, France and Vexin together, while the lowland sill stretching southwards to the Loire connected the Frankish capital with the county of Orléans. The grain lands of Beauce and Vexin, as well as the vine terraces of the Seine, provided the sustenance for its inhabitants.

Downstream from Paris begins the first of a dozen wide meanders which cover the distance of 140 miles from the city to the sea. In this meander belt the valley trough is well defined, bounded by steep terraces, into which the Seine has incised its course 200 ft. below the chalk plateaux. At the site of Paris, however, the Seine valley changes in aspect. Here the left bank valley terraces decline in elevation and the right bank slope is dissected into a series of buttes. These right bank hills form a semi-circle of heights 75–100 ft. above the river, beginning at Passy and running through Montmartre, Chaumont and Belleville, and returning closer to the river at Menilmontant (Fig. 35). On the left bank a spur from the hills of Issy projects close to the Seine, partly dissected by a small tributary, the Bièvre.

Three significant features of the site have influenced the morphology and growth of the town. In order of development these are, the islands within the Seine, the plateau to the south of the Seine, and the open amphitheatre to the north. Associated with these features have been the three elements of the medieval town, the *Cité*, the *Université* and the *Ville*. Lutetia, the Romano-Gaulish town, was a bridge-head settlement which connected these three elements of the site. It was built along the artery of the Roman road which is still followed by the alignment of the Rue de St. Martin on the north bank, and the Rue de St. Jacques on the south side of the river, linked by the Petit Pont across the Ile de la Cité.[8] Most of the Roman public buildings were erected on the slopes of Ste. Geneviève on the south bank, including the palace, amphitheatre and aqueduct, but the forum and temples were built on the Ile de la Cité, one of several islands in the Seine.

During the early Middle Ages, ecclesiastical foundations were concentrated on the plateau to the south, and later in the thirteenth century it also became the site of the University colleges. On the Ile de la Cité the imposing Gothic pile of Nôtre Dame was built between 1161 and 1235, together with the royal palace. The right bank dips northwards to a quaternary course of the river which was marshy ground and checked any expansion in this direction.[9] Le Marais, as the eastern side of the meander bed was called, was only drained during the twelfth and thirteenth centuries, and another two centuries elapsed before the upper course was built over by the expanding town (Fig. 35).[10] The most destructive floods of the Seine have frequently retraced their old course, such as those of 1296, 1658 and 1910. The northern site, between the abandoned meander and the bank of the Seine, became the merchants' quarter in the development of commerce from the twelfth century onwards. The association called 'les marchands de l'eau' (established in 1108-37) developed the river trade between Burgundy and Rouen and also the commercial links with the fairs of Champagne and Flanders. Close to the road junction or 'croisée de Paris' on the north bank, a river port was built on a site now occupied by the Place du Chatelet, and nearby was erected the Hôtel de Ville.

The Growth of Paris. The wall of Philip Augustus (1180-1210) first gave individuality to the medieval town, enclosing an area of 300 acres on both banks of the river (Fig. 35). The town became surrounded subsequently with suburbs which enclosed ecclesiastical foundations, situated on the principal roads leading out of the walled town. Such were St. Germain l'Auxerrois, St. Merry, St. Paul, St. Marcel, Ste. Geneviève and St. Germain des Près, situated in order from the north-east to south-west of the town. The filling-in of these villages and their junction with the town formed the circular plan of the late medieval capital.[11]

The second *enceinte*, the wall erected by Charles V in 1368 and enclosing a site of 1,053 acres, was built wholly on the north bank.[12] It was expanded, not with general consideration for the town, but with the idea of enclosing the Louvre and the principal municipal buildings of the thriving *Ville*. It followed closely the segment of the meander plain to the north, and the Bastille was planted in the marsh on the east. The wall of Louis XIII (1631) completed the expansion around the meander arc to the north-west. Because these extensions to the town all took place on the north bank, the subsequent growth of Paris was also irregular and the chief developments continued on that site.

The next expansion of the walls had a fiscal rather than a strategic reason. The 'Mur des Fermiers-Généraux' was built between 1784 and 1791 to facilitate taxation of *octroi*. The new *enceinte* covered an area of 6,603 acres and extended northwards to the foot of the Butte Montmartre and Belleville. Portions of the old ramparts became the inner circle of boulevards and in turn the *octroi* fortifications were transformed in the 1840's into the boulevards and 'places,' such as Étoile, Clichy, Trône and Maine. The city had now 557 miles of streets. The population in 1841 was 935,000. Before the Siege of Paris, for military reasons, a new extended area was included within the city, making a total of 12,668 acres. This was fortified from the northern heights beyond Belleville and Montmartre and southwards to the hills of Issy and Gentilly. The wall of the Farmers-General then became the outer boulevards of the city. In the period 1860-1875 the sewerage system was modernised and completed with a network of 860 miles of drains, and the market garden area of Gennevilliers was established in association with the waste disposal.[13] As in the medieval town, there was still a small amount of agricultural land within the fortifications and this stood the city in good stead during the Seige in 1870. During this period the population had risen to nearly one and three-quarter millions, partly the result of including a number of suburban towns within the new *enceinte*, such as Belleville (57,000), Montmartre (35,000), La Chapelle St. Denis (40,000) and Vaugirard (37,600).

In the modern period, the city has not developed uniformly but is determined by the tentacular expansion of its suburbs along the lines of communications. The greatest development of built-up area has been to the north-east of the city in the meander spur of the Seine with a population concentration of 450,000. To the north, in the low col between Montmartre and Belleville and beyond, the location of the canals of St. Denis and de l'Ourg, and the main railway terminals of St. Lazare, du Nord and de l'Est have attracted great industrial quarters. Urban sprawl now follows the two railways towards Pontoise and Creil. Eastwards the urban area spreads out towards the confluence of the Marne with the Seine. Industrial quarters tend to be concentrated on the plain, and residential quarters on the high land. The hills to the south have been preserved largely for residential purposes, extending towards Versailles and St. Cloud. A marked feature of the land use of Paris is the extent of woodland. The woods of Vincennes, Meudon and Boulogne push their way into the city. The forests of St. Germain and Montmorency, further west and north, remind us how forested the landscape of the Parisian environs has been until modern times.

The Zones of Paris. Modern Paris is a great economic complex like Greater London, or 'Gross Berlin.' The geographical factors of site and nodality have remained durable controls of the city's growth, but since the mid-nineteenth century, economic forces have been the more apparent. These have been, in particular, the development of the factory system, the highly developed functions of specialised servicing and the outward growth of the city with changing use of the central areas. Within a radius of 20 miles from Nôtre Dame there are to-day 81 communes in the department of Seine, 386 in Seine-et-Oise, 107 in Seine-et-Marne and 83 in Oise, a total of 656 communes with nearly 7 million people.[14]

In this great urban agglomeration there are three well-defined zones: the *Ville*, the Suburban Zone and the *Banlieue*. Within a radius of 3 miles from Nôtre Dame is the city with its 2·8 million people. The city may be divided into two concentric rings, corresponding to the outward growth, which are marked by the boulevards. The first, the central area, comprises 28 quarters. It consists chiefly of commercial and shopping districts and the home of highly special-ised craftsmen such as tailors, jewellers and leather-workers, all interlocked with densely populated districts. The second ring of development comprises 30 quarters which extend to the former fortifications of the outer boulevards. In the north this consists chiefly of industrial quarters and elsewhere of residential and commercial areas. A third ring forming part of the Suburban Zone has 24 quarters, mostly industrial and working-class districts except for the high class residential area of Passy in the south-west. The following table shows that there has been a marked displacement of population from the central area outwards:

PERCENTAGE OF POPULATION IN THE CITY, 1861-1921[15]

	Central Area	*Middle Zone*	*Outer Zone*
1861	37·5	41	21·5
1921	13	44	43

The quarters of Temple, la Bourse and L'Hôtel de Ville in the central area, had densities of 245 to 320 persons per acre in 1860. To-day, they have 100 to 200 per acre. La Bourse has shown the most noticeable decline in density, decreasing by over 35 per cent. between 1896 and 1931. Opéra and Luxembourg had 175 to 200 per acre and now have 60 to 100 per acre. This decline is associated with two factors: the spread of financial and business houses and luxury shops, and the development of city transport services facilitating daily travel from places further removed from the centre. Towards the Suburban Zone densities are still relatively low, but they have had the highest increases of population. For example, between 1896 and 1931 Passy and Vaugirard have increased by over 150 per cent. and several other quarters increased by 65-120 per cent.

The limit of the Suburban Zone corresponds to the radius of 3 to 9 miles with a population of two and a half million. Its boundary corresponds to the limits of the city transport facilities. The *Banlieue* or outer zone has a radius of 9 to 18 miles and it is associated with the expansion of the railways, the *Métro* and bus routes. The limit of daily work is about 12 to 15 miles by autobus and 22 to 25 miles by train. Some 95 per cent. of season-ticket holders live within 12 miles radius of the city centre.[16] Thus in comparison with other great capital cities there is a greater concentration of population in the central area of Paris, and the city itself has an area a quarter the size of the administrative County of London.[17]

Valencia[18]

A characteristic feature of the Mediterranean is the agricultural town which appears almost to have grown out of the soil, dependent on irrigation for its continued productivity. Its *Huerta* is the largest (173,000 acres under irrigation) and most densely populated (over 800,000 inhabitants) of all the irrigated plains of the Levante coast of Spain. The city lies in the centre of its *Huerta* or *Vega* and, as one writer noted at the beginning of the nineteenth century, 'all the habitations which surround it seem as if they were part of it, and we imagine that we see the largest town in the world.' Valencia has developed with its changing landscape, so that the proud achievement of its irrigation systems, the reclamation of the lagoonal marshes and the changing pattern of land use, have had marked influence on the growth of the city. There has been an increase of 131 per cent. in the irrigated area since the end of the eighteenth century. Some 31,200 acres have been reclaimed from the marshes of the Albufera lagoon to the south of the city for rice cultivation. Another 47,000 acres are now watered by pumped supply from wells, half of which is utilised for the orange groves to the west and south-west of the city. In the Huerta surrounding the city the intensity of cultivation is such that two to three crops are grown annually on the same land, while the diversity is such that forty-one crops are listed as commercially important. The municipal boundaries of Valencia still include 28 sq. miles or 54 per cent. of the total urban area under irrigation, principally for horticulture. The land is cultivated to the very limit of the built-up area and because of the high land values there is little adjoining suburban growth, except for some ribbon development along the main roads; the suburbs form a ceinture of small towns and villages on the edge of the irrigated plain, between the hill lands of dry-farming practice (*secano*) and the *Huerta* (Fig. 36).

The Site and Nuclear Area. The site of Valencia is on the south bank of the river Turia where the important Roman road between Andalusia and Italy, the Via Augusta, crossed the shallow ford of the

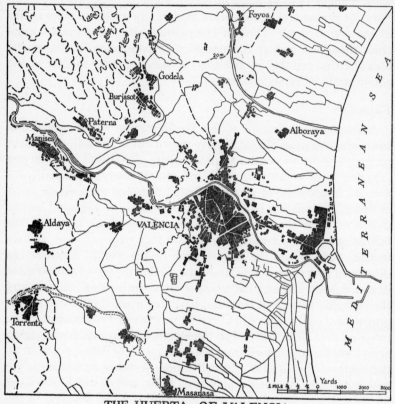

THE HUERTA OF VALENCIA

Fig. 36.

river (Fig. 37). Another road met here from the interior, but it was not an important road junction. The road to the west was of only local significance because of the difficulty of transverse communications across the north-south ranges which constitute the edge of the Castilian Meseta. Indeed it was only in 1946 that Valencia was put into more direct railway communication with Madrid. Nor was the primitive site of Valencia a strong defence point, being without the natural advantages of the neighbouring hill-towns, such as Liria and Sagunto. Hence the early site had not the military significance which Liria had for the Iberians or Sagunto for the Romans.

The primitive site was probably an island consisting of alluvial sands and gravels with a few patches of diluvial deposits, 30 to 55 ft.

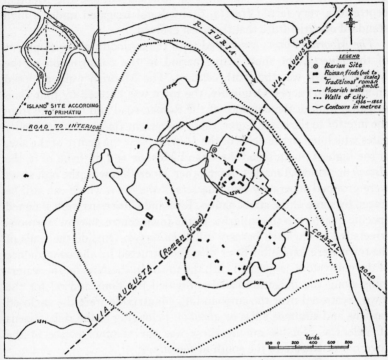

THE SITE AND ENCEINTES OF VALENCIA

Fig. 37.

above sea-level (Fig. 37). Around it the river Turia bifurcated, with the main stream to the north of the site, and this influenced the subsequent plan of the Moorish town.[19] As a Roman settlement Valencia is first mentioned in 138 B.C. and rebuilt in 75 B.C.[20] It had no *castrum*, however, and the traditional ambit of the Roman walls given as 2,656 ft. and enclosing an area of 109 acres, is uncertain, for there is no evidence of continuous walls and not all the remains are found *in situ*.[21] It was overshadowed by the large Roman town of Sagunto, 12 miles to the north. Alluviation was rapid and the coastline

has been extended seaward over two and a half miles since the first
century A.D. This has not favoured the site with a natural harbour, and
the modern port has only been constructed since the end of the
eighteenth century. Thus the early site of Valencia was not favoured
by any marked advantage of nodality or defence which could have
given it importance. It was only as Valencia became the Moorish
centre of a very fertile *Huerta*, drained and irrigated under a high
standard of agriculture that the town evolved.

The Moorish Town. Associated with the agricultural development
of the *Huerta*, the most active period in the construction of the
Moorish town was the tenth century. The Moorish walls enclosed
an area of 293 acres. Originally, the town was entered by four *Babs*
or gates, built at the entrance of the Roman road and the route from
the interior to the coast. Later, there were eight *Babs* and nine smaller
gates which led to the fields of the *Huerta*. Near the centre of the site,
at the highest point, stood the Grand Mosque and, in front of it, the
Aswak or principal market. As in other Moorish towns, the industries
were grouped separately into quarters of the town which can still be
traced by some of the street names. Jews and Christians were assigned
specific quarters in the suburbs. In the town centre, narrow, tortuous
streets led to enclosed bazaars called *kaisariya*. Outside the walls of
the town were four suburbs or *rabad* constructed for the convenience
of the cultivators, associated with the town. In the *Huerta*, the water-
mills along the irrigation canals provided the flour and oil for the
town. Scattered over the surrounding countryside were the enclosed
gardens and summer villas or *almunias* belonging to the rich citizens
of Valencia. Notable among these was the summer palace of the
governor at Ruzafa to the south of the city.[22]

The Post-Conquest Town. The subsequent town maintained several
features of Moorish origin. The narrow, tortuous streets remained;
even in 1762 there were 428 streets, 131 squares and 12 quarters for
the 9030 houses of the town. The grouping of the crafts and
industries into distinct quarters also persisted until the eighteenth
century. At least sixteen mosques were converted into churches and,
on the site of the Grand Mosque in the centre of the town, was built
the cathedral. By the end of the Middle Ages, about one-sixth of the
area of the town was occupied by the lands and buildings of the twelve
parish churches and the seventy-six religious houses, hospitals and
colleges. The religious character of the town was an indication of the
wealth it had acquired as an agricultural and commercial centre quite

apart from its functions as a cathedral and university city. The guilds, religious in origin, were developed in association with the parish churches.

After the Reconquest, with the change in political orientation from south to north, and with the economic links with Catalonia instead of with Andalusia, the main gateway of the town was built in the north wall and bridges were constructed across the River Turia. The town grew rapidly in the fourteenth century, so that a new wall was built to include the silk factories to the south of the town and the woollen mills and merchants' quarters to the east and west; to avoid congestion in the centre, the market was moved beyond the old Moorish walls, and several of the central streets were re-aligned. The new *enceinte* of 1386 enclosed an area of about 737 acres which sufficed to contain the town's expansion until the walls were destroyed in 1865. An interesting feature of the post-conquest town was its social structure. The Christian settlers, who settled in the town, divided themselves into quarters or *barrios*, according to whence they had come. Several quarters with settlers from places in Catalonia and Aragon were established, and the north quarter of the town is still called *Los Serranos* after its Aragonese settlers who had come from the mountains of Teruel.[23]

The sphere of influence of the medieval town is clearly known. The limits of the *Vega* or *Huerta* corresponded with those administered by the Tribunal of Water, whose seven canals supplied the irrigation water derived from the river Turia. An eighth canal was used to flush out the sewers of the town and to water its gardens. The Tribunal has met regularly since the Middle Ages at the front door of the cathedral to settle water disputes. The limit of the Tribunal's jurisdiction is followed approximately by the municipal boundaries and in the town's records constant reference is made to Valencia and its *Vega*. The one-league radius of Valencia was marked with boundary stones; within this area Valencia was the acknowledged authority for all purposes of trade and even jurisdiction. For example, one recurrent problem was the periodic outbreak of malaria associated with rice cultivation. In 1562, and at intervals during the following centuries, it was prohibited to grow rice within the one league's radius of the town. Because of the economic integration of town and county individual villages of the *Huerta* were taxed with the town and the *gobernación* of Valencia extended four or five leagues inland. According to a municipal law, it was forbidden within a four-league radius of Valencia to buy wheat, which was not for the use of the city or for the needs of the surrounding villages of the *Huerta*. Valencia was always deficient in cereals, other than rice, so that the four-league radius was of great economic significance to its municipal granaries at Burjasot (Fig. 36).

The Modern City. It has been demonstrated that the growth of Valencia was related to the use made of the productive *Huerta*. The economic developments of the nineteenth century emphasised this relationship: the introduction of the steam pump to supply well water to the orange groves and to regulate the drainage of the rice-fields, the use of artificial fertilisers, and the development of road, rail and port facilities, served to integrate the agricultural wealth of the coastal plain and the prosperity of the city on a commercial basis. The retail area of the city's markets for daily supplies of fruit and vegetables corresponds roughly with the traditional *Vega* or *Huerta*. From the dormitory suburbs, at the edge of the *Huerta*, comes a considerable proportion of the city's labour. These limits correspond thus with the *zone du voisinage* of Valencia.

Since the middle of the nineteenth century the city has expanded greatly. In 1852, a broad avenue was built around the medieval *enceinte* and in 1865 the walls were removed. By 1911, a new planned town had developed on the south side of the city, to include the *Huerta* villages of Patraix and Ruzafa. The port developed for the export of the agricultural products of the plain was linked with the town by a highway along which much building has been located. To-day, the built-up area of the city comprises 3,700 acres and the population has increased from 82,000 at the beginning of the nine-teenth century to over 500,000. The centre of the old town is being transformed as wide streets push their way across the areas once tightly packed with dwellings and narrow streets. The industrial zone of Valencia and its port of El Grao occupies 1,633 acres with timber yards, metal foundries, chemical works, ship-building yards and factories for the making of boxes for fruit exports, furniture, food and liqueur industries.[24] To-day, the city occupies about 20 per cent. of the area of the traditional *Huerta*. Therefore Valencia and its satellite centres threaten to destroy their *raison d'être* by the rapid sprawl of the built-up area across the irrigated plain. According to the present trend of growth, the built-up area is likely to double in the next fifty years. It is therefore essential for the well-being of the region that further growth should be restricted to dormitary centres further west on the poorer, unirrigated hill lands, such as at Torrente, Manises, Paterna and Burjasot (Fig. 36).

Birmingham

As the example of an industrial city, Birmingham is outstanding. A creation of the Industrial Revolution, it has become the industrial hub of the Midlands and the second city of Britain. In cities of long history, such as Paris, it is easy to point out the geographical advantages of the site and the elements of nodality, whether at a bridgehead, a crossing of routes or at a transfer point. Cultural features in many medieval towns, such as the church, the castle or the palace, have focused the growth of their plan. But in Birmingham none of these influences is obvious. Its position on the valley slopes of the River Rea only provided the meadow land, arable and heath of a Domesday manor. Its bridge-point across the marshy tract of the flood plain only warranted its role as a small medieval market, its horizon of the world being bounded by a day's journey. The situation of Birmingham near the South Staffordshire coalfield, and its regional trade, only permitted its growth in the seventeenth century as an industrial village, but it was not much larger than other Warwickshire market towns. The factors involved in the modern development of Birmingham are more indirect, and they have worked slowly below the surface of its history. In its vicinity charcoal was available from forest lands, water was abundant, and iron ore was mined. These facilities for metal industries, together with large numbers of workers willing to be trained in these industries, laid the foundations for Birmingham's subsequent greatness. The vast superstructure of modern Birmingham, however, has been constructed by its captains of industry such as Boulton, Thomason, Cadbury and Chamberlain, and its inventors such as Baskerville and Watts.

Birmingham is essentially a modern creation. It was made a borough with its own corporation only in 1838. The town had an irregular, quadrilateral plan without any *enceintes* of growth, except for the embryonic nucleus clustered around St. Martin's Church and the streets between Deritend and Digbeth. Its population was then only 186,000, surrounded by a number of manorial villages and a wide expanse of heathland. It was made a city in 1889, a University town in 1900 and the centre of a bishopric in 1904-5. A century after its borough charter, there was a new city, covering an area sixty times that of the early nineteenth century, with a population of over a million (Fig. 38). A vast transformation had taken place in the urban landscape.

THE GROWTH OF BIRMINGHAM
1731 — 1946

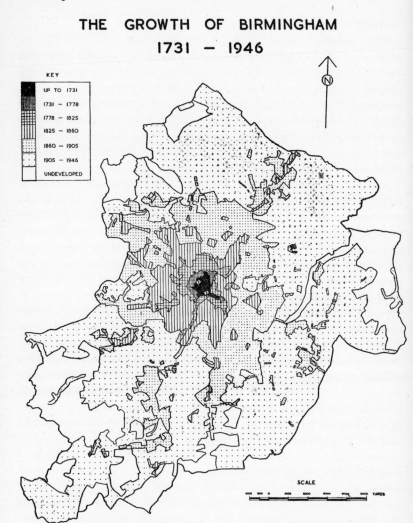

Fig. 38. The Growth of Birmingham, 1731–1946 (*from Wise*).

The city now sprawls over 51,147 acres, of which 42·8 per cent. are built upon by housing and another 6·7 by industry. The corporation of the city employs 35,500 (the total population of a medium-sized town) to maintain its services, and it has been responsible for 113,000 new houses between 1919 and 1939, housing a population the size of Swansea. Birmingham has the greatest gas and omnibus services controlled by any one municipality in the world. A network of streets 900 miles long is serviced by 153 miles of bus routes. There are 1,352 miles of sewerage, 1,500 miles of water mains and 1,886 miles of electric cables. Gas is served over 195 sq. miles and water over 182 sq. miles. There is a frontage for industrial sites along the 160 miles of canals in the vicinity of the city. The water supply for the city is brought by aqueduct 73 miles from the Welsh Hills, which has to tunnel through 12 miles of obstructions.[25] All this is the epic story of man's creation of a new landscape on a marshy valley floor and an exposed heath plateau.

The Situation of Birmingham. Birmingham illustrates the changing values which geographical location may have within the historical context. The position of the medieval settlement was of regional significance only for a radius of some twenty to thirty miles. The plateau, about 300 ft. above sea-level, is the Midlands watershed of the Tame-to-Trent and Stour-to-Severn drainage systems. At first, this had no geographical significance. The poverty of the Midland centres, isolated from the coastal trade of the rest of Britain, merely resulted in the development of a local trade such as the salt from Worcestershire, the manufactures of Coventry and the iron from Staffordshire. This Midlands traffic, keeping to the higher ground wherever possible, could only cross the flood plain of the Rea at two points, at Duddeston and Deritend. The former served Tamworth, Lichfield and some villages to the south. The latter crossing, less marshy, served the other market towns and villages, and so Birmingham drew to itself most of this traffic. As the focus of routes across the Midlands plateau, Birmingham had become a busy market by the end of the Tudor period, a strategic centre during the Civil War and an important industrial village in the eighteenth century.[26] The exploitation of the Thick Seam in the South Staffordshire Coalfield a few miles to the north-east, and the expansion of the iron-smelting industry on the Birmingham plateau, continued to increase the nodality of the town.

Birmingham overcame its isolation from the rest of the country, first by the development of canals and then by the railways. Canal construction was not easy because of the steep gradients, and the early waterways that were built did not venture to cross the plateau. The canals were designed for two purposes: to provide cheap transport of local coal, iron, limestone, clay and heavy manufactures within the growing industrial district, and to link it with the chief water routes of the nation. The Birmingham Canal (1769) connected the South Staffordshire coalfield with Birmingham, while the Staffordshire-Worcestershire Canal (1772) linked the district with the Severn waterways. The Trent-Mersey Canal (1777) later connected the Thames (1790) with the Midlands.[27] By the beginning of the nineteenth century the district was integrated by waterways into one great manufacturing complex, with Birmingham as its hub. Then the railways hastened the process of centralisation on Birmingham. The network of railways begun by the Grand Junction Railway (1837) and the London-Birmingham Railway (1838) was completed in the early 1850's. Subsequently, the improvement of road transport has completed the process. The centrality of Birmingham to-day commands much of the industrial pulse of the nation; it lies 90 miles away from Liverpool and the Mersey, 100 miles from the South Wales seaboard, and about 130 miles from Hull and Southampton. Within a radius of 20 miles it has a purchasing population of about three millions.

The Factory System and Development of Birmingham. The growth of Birmingham has been reflected in its utilisation of local and regional resources and by the increasing importance of point production.[28] The settlement grew without a charter and its crafts were therefore unshackled by the restrictions of guilds. In 1650 it had 1,500 inhabitants and at the end of the century 15,000. The tanning and textile medieval trades were surpassed by the later industries of metal manufacture. There were 178 smiths' hearths in the town in 1683 and a century later there were a great number of workshops. In 1781 there were 104 button workers, 40 platers, 40 toymakers, 26 jewellers and 14 locksmiths. Brass manufacture began in the same year and by 1800 the trade of gunsmiths had been fully developed. The economies of large-scale production were less important in these small workshop industries than in textiles or heavy industries, and it was not until the third quarter of the nineteenth century that large factories were developed with standardised production.

Certain trades tended to concentrate in quarters of the town, such as the gun quarter around St. Mary's Church immediately to the north of the town and the jewellery quarter in Hackley around St. Paul's Church.[29] These and other small domestic industries made the industrial character of Birmingham with all its slums and inadequate housing a feature of the mid-nineteenth-century town. The urban blight was such that there were some 2,000 fetid and filthy courts in the 1830's, 20,000 middens in the 1850's and the 48,000 back-to-back houses were supplied, if at all, with water, nine-tenths of which was polluted.[30] In these conditions the congested population 'lived the lives of the savages of Ceylon.' The activities of the commissioners and subsequently of the corporation did much to change the landscape of the central area with the rise of public buildings, the widening of streets and the clearance of slum property, while the railways altered appreciably the sites of the station terminals.

Although the small workshops have continued to thrive, the great expansion of Birmingham since the third quarter of the nineteenth century has been associated with the foundation of large factory units employing several thousand workers on the outskirts of the built-up area. The Birmingham Small Arms factory at Small Heath (1861), Cadbury's new site at Bournville (1879), the General Electric Company's plant at Witton (1901) and the Austin motor works at Longbridge (1904), among others, have become the nuclei for the spread of the city and the employment of its expanding population (Fig. 39).[31] The location along the canals with cheap transport and the available sites of cheap land on the surrounding heathlands have been the major factors in the spread of industrial districts. Thus along the canals at Selly Oak in the south-west, in the north-west and north-east, new suburbs have grown with long ribbons connecting them with the town area. The valley of the Tame has become industrialised and in the inter-war period there has been a spectacular growth of the built-up area to the south, east and north.

The heathland environs of Birmingham have enabled it to spread in a way that no other British city could afford. In 1911 it had an area three times the size of Glasgow and twice the size of Manchester, Liverpool or Belfast.[32] To-day, Birmingham has an average density of 20·6 per acre and one-third of its area is as low as 7·7 per acre. The central wards of the city have only 45 to 50 per acre. However, the features of decentralisation common to all large cities are apparent in Birmingham. In the centre, Market Hall Ward had a density of 136 per acre in 1871, which declined to 33 in 1948, while the suburbs increased from 1-5 to 20-30 per acre. In loosening up its central densities the city area has expanded to an area of 51,150 acres, of which 40 per cent. is not built-up.[33] In 1938 one-seventh of the housing was in the central area, while two-sevenths were in the middle ring and four-sevenths in the outer ring. Such low housing densities are in striking contrast to the high congestion in Paris or to the strict control of agricultural productivity in the Valencian *Huerta*.

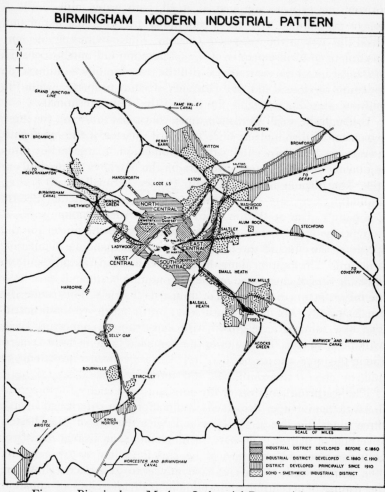

Fig. 39. Birmingham Modern Industrial Pattern (*from Wise*).

The despotic influence of rulers in the creation of baroque capitals and the insensate impulse of the Industrial Revolution in urban sprawl are both well known. It is not always realised, however, that other towns were being created during the same periods by the development of tourism. The medical profession started the movement to the inland spas and seaside resorts, followed by the leadership of royalty and fashion in their subsequent growth. The publication of Gruner's *Eisgebirge des Schweizerlandes* (Berne, 1760) started the popularity of the mountain health resorts in Switzerland, just as Russell's *Dissertation on the Use of Sea-water in the Diseases of the Glands* (London, 1752) influenced public opinion towards the popularity of the English seaside centres. Often the observations of the medical profession on the local climate and the health values of certain sites for towns were a fantasy, but their advice influenced the selection of locations for new towns.

Towns affected by these movements may be classified into three categories. Firstly, there are the inland spas built around medicinal springs, such as Bath, Cheltenham, Harrogate and Tunbridge Wells in England,[34] Carlsbad, Kesselbrunnen and Marienbad in Germany, and Royat (near Clermont-Ferrand) and Lourdes in France. Secondly, there are the holiday resorts which may be subdivided into two groups. There are the ancient ports or fishing harbours which have become the nuclei for holiday towns such as the Riviera towns of Cannes, Antibes, Nice, Monaco, and San Remo, and the Channel coast resorts of Ostend, Margate, Hastings, Brighton and Weymouth. There are also new towns developed on convenient sites for the metropolitan or industrial cities such as Le Touquet for Paris, Southend for London and Blackpool for the Lancashire towns. Thirdly, there are the winter sports centres, such as St. Moritz, Davos and Zermatt; Switzerland alone has 70 of these centres.[35] Many of these towns combine health and recreational functions.

Brighton

An outstanding example of a holiday resort is Brighton on the Sussex coast. As Brighthelmstone in 1760, it was a small fishing town covering an area of about 80 acres and housing some 2,000 inhabitants.[36] To-day, it has about 150,000 and it has sprawled over an area of 12,565 acres. The city is a great pleasure resort where theatres and cinemas can accommodate about 28,000 persons. There are over 3,500 shops with a total frontage of 11·1 miles.[37] Together with Hove adjoining it, some 200,000 visitors can be received at any one time. Compared with Blackpool's 4,000 boarding houses and 240 hotels and inns, Brighton has 1,167 boarding houses and 607 hotels.[38] This difference measures the social contrast in the character of these two towns.

Position and Site. Brighton has developed as London-by-the-sea, since it is only 50 miles from the capital and its nearest point to the south coast. The development of its communications has been an important factor therefore in exploiting its position. In 1792, the coach journey took 9 to 11 hours between London and Brighton, a time reduced to 3 hours, 40 minutes by 1834.[39] The coming of the railway in 1841 made day excursions popular. Finally, the electrification of the railway in 1933 has given added advantage to Brighton as a dormitory of London.

The original site of Brighthelmstone was the foreshore, but the remains of this fishing settlement finally disappeared in two storms at the beginning of the eighteenth century. The nucleus of the present town was built on the cliffs, at a point where the confluence of two combes provided a level site, called the Steine. This site was first occupied in the fourteenth century, forming a small rectangular plan around the market place. Modern Brighton, created after the mid-eighteenth century, has grown along the valley sides of the two combes, as well as to the east and west of the original nucleus where the 50- and 100-foot raised beaches have provided suitable building sites.

Growth of Brighton. The medical profession provided the first stimulus to the growth of Brighton. The practice of drinking salt water and bathing in the sea was advocated by them and this was begun on an official basis at Brighton in 1750. Dr. Richard Russell settled there in 1753 and advocated the treatment of sea-bathing. Dr. Anthony Relham emphasised the healthy climate of the resort, and advertised the virtues of the chalybeate spring nearby. The second stimulus was provided by the patronage of royalty. The names of Charles II and Tunbridge Wells, George III and Weymouth, and Princess Caroline and Southend, are linked in the same way as those of the Prince of Wales and Brighton. Royal residence brought society to Brighton and it became fashionable to spend the summer months there.[40]

The peak period of Brighton's growth was in 1822-28; in 1826 alone, 500 new houses were in course of erection. Between 1821 and 1831 the population census noted an increase from 24,429 to 40,634 and the number of dwelling houses increased by 95 per cent. Some two and a half miles of shore were now overlooked by boarding houses and, between 1822 and 1825, amenities along the sea-front were enhanced by the Royal Pavilion, the chain pier and promenade. During this period, most of the development took place to the east

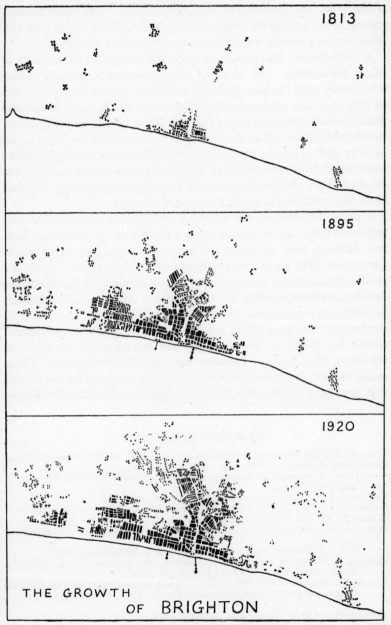

1813

1895

1920

THE GROWTH
OF BRIGHTON

Fig. 40 (*from Gilbert*).

of the town and northwards along the combes, with more limited growth to the west of the Steine. Kemp Town, Brunswick Town and other regency estates were planned and partially developed.[41]

A lull followed this expansion until the coming of the railway in 1841. Henceforth, the increase of population continued uninterruptedly until the later part of the century: 46,000 in 1841, 65,000 in 1851 and over 90,000 in 1871. Expansion of the town proceeded mostly to the north and west (Fig. 40). Hove, which had only about 100 inhabitants in 1801, developed in the Victorian era, with 2,500 in 1841 and 11,000 in 1871. Since then the increase of population has slowed down and much of Brighton's subsequent increase has resulted from the extension of its municipal boundaries, whereas Hove has continued to expand to 65,000 in 1946.

To-day, Brighton is not wholly a recreational town. It has also industrial functions as well as being a dormitory for London. These two features have helped to increase its population from about 100,000 in 1881 to its present figure of nearly 150,000. There are small light industries and railway works in the town, while some 2,750 London workers also live there.[42] Brighton still maintains however, its distinctive character, both by its architectural legacy and its recreational functions. What politics have done for Paris, agricultural wealth has produced for Valencia, and industrialism has done to transform Birmingham, pleasure has created for Brighton. These examples only indicate how varied and complex may be the factors that have been employed in the development of the urban landscape.

SELECTED REFERENCES

Crone, G. R. 'The Site and Development of Paris,' G.J., XCVIII, 1941, pp. 33-47.
Demangeon, A. *Paris, La ville et sa banlieue.* Paris, 1933.
—— *France Economique et Humaine, Géographie Universelle*, tome VII, part 2, 1948, pp. 785-840.
Dickinson, R. E. *The West European City.* London, 1952.
George, P. *La Ville. Le Fait Urbain à travers le Monde.* Paris, 1952, pp. 117-46.
Gilbert, E. W. 'The Growth of Brighton,' G.J., CXIV, 1949, pp. 30-52.
History of Birmingham: Gill, C. *Manor and Borough to 1865*, Vol. I. Birmingham, 1952.
—— Briggs, A. *Borough and City, 1865-1938*, Vol. 2. Birmingham, 1952.
Houston, J. M. 'Urban Geography of Valencia—the Regional Development of a Huerta City,' Trans. I.B.G., 15, 1950, pp. 19-35.
Jurgens, O. *Spanische Städte, Ihre bauliche Entwicklung und Ausgestaltung*, Abhandlungen aus dem Gebiet der Auslandskunde, Univ. of Hamburg, Band 23, 1926.
West Midland Group, *Conurbation.* London, 1948.
Wise, M. J. (edit.) *Birmingham and its Regional Setting: A Scientific Survey.* British Assoc. 1950.

Part IV

POPULATION STUDIES

CHAPTER TEN

THE GEOGRAPHICAL INTERPRETATION OF POPULATION DATA

THE unique rate of growth of population in Europe and its expansion overseas is one of the most challenging events of modern times. Since the systematic recording of vital statistics began towards the end of the eighteenth century, many principles have been formulated in population studies by demographers to account for and to predict this movement. The geographers' contribution however, has been more in the understanding of population distribution of the earth's surface than in the formation of biological laws. Three aspects of study belong most properly to the field of geographical research: the distribution, density, and arrangement of population. Each of these studies is essentially descriptive and their basis is the population map. It is necessary therefore to consider first the value of the population map as an exact tool of the geographer.

Cartographic Representation of Population Data

The population map has two important values for geographical study. Firstly, it expresses in cartographic form the interactions of physical, social and economic conditions in terms of space and time relations. The comparative study of other distributions already mapped, such as relief, rainfall and resources, both potential and actual, provide the descriptive material which the geographer can compare and study deductively. Such work forms the basis of most geographical knowledge. Secondly, although the influences upon human activities in any given region cannot be measured precisely, the population map has a statistical basis which serves as the most accurate index available of such influences. The scale of the map, the accuracy of the census figures and the skill and detailed knowledge of the compiler will determine its reliability, but usually it is the most accurate form of representation.

Population maps are of two kinds, according to whether absolute or relative data are compiled. The first method of using absolute data shows the actual distribution of population, or the arrangement of rural and urban population, by some symbol, usually the dot. The second method is the relation of population or buildings with area or resources and is a density map. Both types of map have two variables: the scale of the base map and the scale of the dots or shading. The value of the method chosen usually depends therefore on the choice of scales.[1] The dot map has been used successfully on both large and small scale maps. Medium scale maps are often better suited to shaded methods. The reasons for this will now be considered.

There are three types of dot map used to show the distribution of population. Firstly, there is the uniform dot map first used by Sten de Geer in 1906 and later elaborated in his well-known map of Sweden (1 : 500,000 with one dot equal to 100 persons).[2] In this method a number of dots of uniform size, in proportion to the number of population, is plotted to indicate exact location. The method is unsatisfactory, however, when the region has a wide range of densities and the concentration of dots in an area leads to black-out effects. The method also tends to give undue prominence to scattered rural population. The second method is the use of the dot, with other symbols for the large urban centres. Sten de Geer, in his map of Sweden, combined the simple dot distribution with the use of spheres for urban centres and the 'dot net' for intermediate densities. Granö, in his map of Finland (1 : 1,000,000 with one dot equal to 100 persons) combined the simple dot distribution with the use of squares and triangles.[3] Similar representation is used in Söderlung's map of Europe[4] (1 : 4,000,000 with the dot equal to 5,000 inhabitants) and at the other end of the scale in Tammekann's map of Estonia[5] (1 : 200,000 with the dot equal to 50 persons). The third type of map has used the proportional dot, in which the area of the dot is proportional to the numbers plotted. Four variants of this system have been used: the square and circle, and the three-dimensional representation of the sphere and the cube. Its disadvantage however is that the map is elaborate to construct and the proportional spheres do not always give a good visual appreciation of the numbers involved.

All these variants of dot maps are best used on large scale research maps. Such methods have been successfully used by Sten de Geer and Granö when land use distributions have been plotted on the same map. But the dot map often suffers from pseudo-accuracy because of the question of where the dots are to be placed, whether over the dwellings or over the cultivated lands. This is a big problem in many rural districts, such as in Mediterranean countries where the holdings may be scattered at a considerable distance from the settlements.

The method is also not very successful for showing detailed distribution of population in built-up areas.

The second, or relative study of population statistics, was first made possible by Buffon in the eighteenth century, when he conceived the idea of population density,[6] now one of the most important concepts in geography. Density of population is best depicted by the shaded method on medium scale maps and is most successful in regions of high densities, such as the industrial areas. For such maps, two problems arise: the correct visual impressions of colour or shading and the choice of scales used in the densities. Certain colours graded according to the spectrum may not appear rightly graded to the eye. The scale of densities adopted on a map will depend on the absolute densities recorded and accordingly arbitrary, arithmetic, geometric and logarithmic scales may be used. On small scale maps the latter two scales are usually better, but on large or medium scale maps it is advisable to adopt the density scales according to the geographical conditions of the regions. Thus different types of land use, fishing or other extractive industries may show a normality of densities best adopted on the map.

The shaded method, to show population density, is used effectively in both cartograms and maps proper. The cartogram uses the large units of the census, such as county or province, which have no direct relation to the spread of population. Since de Martonne first attempted to show population density by natural regions in his classic study of Wallachia,[7] three methods have been used. In the plates of the *Atlas de France*, Demangeon and his collaborators have shown the population distribution by grouping communes according to their densities. A second method has been used in the Ordnance Survey Map of Population in Britain (1 : 1,000,000). The parishes and wards have been used as units of density but the boundary lines have been 'particularised' according to the relief features, the uninhabited tracts and built-up areas, etc. A third method has been adopted with varying accuracy in the use of isarithmic boundaries between densities. Known densities are plotted at frequent intervals and isarithmic lines are joined by interpolation, a method used successfully by Wallis in his map of Hungary[8] and by Romer for Poland.[9] Robert in a map of population in Brittany related zones of density to distance from the sea. Maps constructed by formulæ, such as those of Barnes and Robinson,[10] Kant,[11] and those already discussed in chapter five, are examples of the same method. All these methods of cartographical representation have their values and it is the task of the geographer to use his tools selectively. Generally however, the more complicated the map the less likely it is to tell a true story or to make geographical analysis possible. Each map must be regarded as a separate piece of work suited to the region and the subject concerned.

Factors Affecting the Limits of Settlement

When a suitable map of population has been constructed the next problem is to interpret it. This is a three-fold task and demands the study of the limits of settlement, the analysis of population density and the synthesis of regional demographic types. The remainder of this chapter will be devoted to these three aspects of study.

There are in Europe* some 1,355,200 sq. miles which are unproductive and most of the total population of 403 millions is concentrated in a small proportion of the total area. As we have seen in chapter four the long process of settlement has altered the landscape in varying degrees, and spread throughout its area. It is safe to assume therefore that throughout most of Europe, the inhabited areas are the same as the habitable areas or *Oecumene*. The chief factors, which have affected the uninhabitable areas or *Anoecumene* of man, have been latitude, altitude, aridity and marsh.

In Northern Europe, the settlements tend to follow the coasts and the distribution of population forms a molecular pattern of nucleated settlements, isolated by wide expanses of uninhabited waste. Lapland, for example, stretches over 150,000 sq. miles but the total population is only about 32,000 inhabitants or one person for every 4·6 sq. miles. Latitude and climatic conditions are commonly attributable for such low densities. This explanation is only indirectly true, since modern settlements established by Russian colonists demonstrate that man can live well within the Arctic Circle, provided food supplies are available. Biological conditions are therefore the controlling factors.

In the great mountain systems of Europe, meagre food supplies are also the limiting control in the *Oecumene*. Compared with the upper limits of settlement in the Andes and in Asia at over 15,000 ft., the maximum limit in the European mountains is about 6,500 ft. and consequently the physiological limit is never reached in Europe. The tree-line has also no significance because the climatic limit is not properly attained. The tree-line is therefore not to be equated

* Excluding the U.S.S.R.

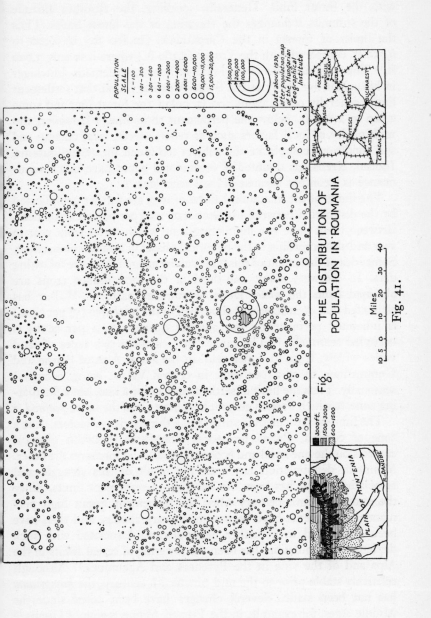

POPULATION
SCALE

· 1 – 100
· 101 – 300
○ 301 – 600
○ 601 – 1000
○ 1001 – 2000
○ 2001 – 4000
○ 4001 – 6000
○ 6001 – 10,000
○ 10,001 – 15,000
○ 15,001 – 20,000

500,000
200,000
100,000

Data about 1930,
after population map
of the Hungarian
Geographical
Institute

THE DISTRIBUTION OF
POPULATION IN ROUMANIA

Miles

10 5 0   10 20 30   40

Fig. 41.

3000 ft.
1500–3000
600–1500

TRANSYLVANIAN ALPS

PLAIN OF MUNTENIA

R. DANUBE

SIBIU
BRAȘOV
FOCȘANI
RÂMNICUL
SARAT
BUZAU
BUCHAREST
PITESCI
SLATINA
CARACAL

with the forest limit. Generally speaking, the absolute altitude of the summits influences the elevation of the forest limits. Thus the limits of forests in the Carpathians (12,800 ft.) is 6,500 to 6,750 ft. compared with the Vosges (4,160 ft.) where it is only 3,000 ft.[12] This variation affects the limits of human settlement. Flückiger in his exhaustive study of the Swiss Alps has found that settlement limits generally occur about 300 ft. below the forest line and some 2,500 to 2,800 ft. below the permanent snow line.[13] However, the multiplicity of local factors such as relief, aspect, local climate and soil conditions complicate the subject too much for generalisations. Indeed, Krebs has doubted if vegetational zones have much significance as a concept because of local variations.[14]

The limits of the mountain habitat of man are further complicated by the distinction between his temporary and permanent settlement. Between them there is a fluctuating zone which varies from year to year and also according to the historical phases of human colonisation. Some idea of the extent of this zone can be gauged from the following data. In Norway, about one-third of the total fodder crops are obtained from the *saeter* lands or summer pastures. Walser has estimated that in Switzerland about half of the total area (54 per cent.) is inhabited permanently but another quarter (24·2 per cent.) is occupied seasonally.[15] The range between these two types of land varies widely, from 61·6 per cent. in the Swiss Alps of Sarine and Gummennen to 32·2 per cent. in central Valais, being occupied seasonally. Thus the limit of settlement is never a line, but a fluctuating zone, to which French geographers have given the name *plafond*.[16]

The limit of settlement is subject to a third series of factors. It is a zone of combat, Ratzel termed it *kampfsaum*, between physical controls on the one hand and economic and social forces on the other. Mountain depopulation has been the result of this struggle and associated with it has been the lowering of settlement limits. Since the mid-nineteenth century when the movement began high permanent settlements have become temporary abodes, and then have been abandoned with further depopulation. Associated with such depletion of population, has been the lowering of cereal limits in the Alps and of the vine in the Pyrenees and Apennines.[17] Although relatively stable prior to the mid-nineteenth century, the *kampfsaum* has not been static. Several changes have been noted since the Middle Ages, for example, in the French Alpine region of Oisans.[18]

Within this dynamic framework, the limits of settlement are

influenced by the factors of latitude, relief, aspect, soil and climatic conditions such as exposure to wind, snow, avalanches and floods. The influence of latitude is noticeably apparent in the Scandinavian mountains. Because of the combined factors of altitude and latitude, permanent settlement in Norway is found rarely above 1,900 ft. The influence of latitude is such that the alpine zone is at 1,600 ft. in Lapland, 3,000 ft. in Dalecarlia and 3,800 to 5,500 ft. in the Storefjelds of southern Norway. It also appears to be a factor in the Iberian Peninsula: the upper limit of permanent settlement is 3,200 ft. in the Iberian Mountains, over 4,500 ft. in the Central Sierras and between 4,800 and 5,500 ft. in the Sierra Nevada.

Relief conditions have more apparent relations with population distribution. As the distribution of population usually follows the valleys, the limit of permanent settlement will depend upon the height of the valleys above sea-level. Thus in the French Alpine Foreland the limit of settlement is only about 2,500 ft., whereas in the Central Alps of Savoy and Dauphine where the valleys are higher, the limit is about 5,200 ft. and rises to over 5,900 ft. in the Austrian Alps. Longitudinal valleys have usually higher densities of population than transverse valleys and consequently the upper limit of settlement is often higher in the former. A comparison of the Alps and Carpathians is instructive in this respect. The Carpathian valleys, with their marked absence of longitudinal trends, have lower densities and the limit of permanent settlement is nowhere above 4,000 ft.

Insolation and aspect are important factors, influencing the range of the *Oecumene*. It has been estimated that Swiss settlements on the sunny slope of the valley or *adret* are, on an average, some 230 ft. higher than those on the shady side or *ubac*.[19] In the Hohe Tauern, where the absolute limit of settlement is 7,600 ft. and the average is 6,700 ft., 90 per cent. of the population are concentrated on the *adret* slopes. Similarly, in the Upper Rhône Valley, some 86 per cent. are on the sunny slopes.[20] Miss Garnett has given examples of other Alpine valleys in her monograph.[21]

None of these factors enumerated can be considered independently. All play their role in an intricate relationship of control. Sometimes other unexpected influences may enter into this complex. For example, the limits of settlement in the Austrian Alps are usually as much as 600 ft. higher than those in the neighbouring Italian valleys. The explanation appears to be that the Austrian habitations are dispersed while the Italians favour nucleated settlements. Consequently, isolated dwellings on the Austrian frontier can avail themselves of sites too limited for Italian villages.

Two other factors which affect the *Oecumene* of Europe are aridity and marsh. In the Mediterranean lands, drought is an important factor, but it is a relative control on the density of population rather than a well-defined limit to the habitable areas. In the great steppe lands of the Danube basin, such as the plains of Barangan in Eastern Roumania and also in the 17,000 sq. miles of steppe in Spain, the densities of population are everywhere less than 25 per sq. mile. Ill-drained lands with their associated dangers of malaria have also been checks on population densities in the Mediterranean. In the great stretch of fluvial marshes along the Danube Delta and in the 18,000 sq. miles of waste in the Pripet Marshes, densities are very low. However, their fishing resources do not make them, strictly speaking, part of the *Anoecumene* of Europe.

Definition of Population Density

The concept of population density is a study in averages, where the numerical relations between the numbers of population and the area which they inhabit have precise meaning. However, as the function of two sets of variables, density of population is not a simple concept. The ratio of total population to the total area may be quite meaningless since the relationship between man and area is usually highly complex. More detailed definition of these terms is therefore necessary.

In the first place it is essential to know what is meant by 'population.' It may mean the total rural, the agricultural or the urban population, each a variable in itself, dependent upon the demographic structures of each country and on the detail available in the national censuses. Thus the term 'rural population' is difficult to define according to a fixed standard, especially as the economies of European countries vary so widely. The Committee, entrusted by the International Statistical Institute to define the term, have decided to call 'rural' those administrative areas of a census which have at least 60 per cent. of their total population dependent on agriculture.[22] Such an arbitrary definition is only useful, however, for the comparison of international statistics. The term 'agricultural population' is even more difficult to define, although in its widest sense it usually embraces all those engaged in agriculture, certain agricultural industries, forestry and freshwater fishing, together with their dependents.

Again definition of the term 'urban population' is relative and not absolute.

In the second place, the concept of 'area' may mean a number of things to the geographer. Usually it refers to the total area of an administrative unit for which census material is available. It may also mean the computed area of a natural region such as de Martonne used for his study of population in Wallachia. It may mean the altimetric zone between two contour lines such as Anfossi[23] and Marinelli[24] have calculated for the population densities of Corsica and Sicily respectively. 'Area' is also defined in terms of the natural resources of a region. It may thus be applied to the habitable area, as Roberts calculated in the French Alps.[25] It can be defined in terms of the exploitable or usable area, and also as the cultivated area. In Scotland, the exploitable area can be measured by the limit of the head-dyke standing like an upper tide-mark along the bounds of past cultivation. There may be as much as 50 per cent. difference in the Scottish Highlands between the exploitable and the cultivated areas.[26] All these variable concepts of area need to be studied to understand fully the distribution and density of population and of its changes.

Factors Affecting Population Density

If population were a free agent it would respond directly to a number of geographical agencies. The flow of population from mountain districts into the plains, the thin spread of population in areas of drought or cold, and the mosaics of varying densities patterned by soil conditions, would be expressions of such forces. Apart from these intrinsic factors of the environment there are other extrinsic forces which have had more importance in determining the population map of Europe. Political frontiers have controlled the flow of migration. National tariffs and policies related to the different standards of living, have influenced the agricultural conditions and farming systems, and these in turn are important factors on the densities of rural population. Above all, as we saw in chapter seven urban growth has been the most disturbing factor against the even spread of population densities. We must admit therefore that physical explanations cannot account completely for all the complexities of population density, although they may indicate and elucidate a great many of them.

Despite the mobile and complex character of European population, certain well-marked zones of uniform densities stand out on the

population map (Fig. 42). The low densities associated with the
mountain systems across Europe, and with the adverse climatic
conditions of Northern Europe, comprise two well-marked belts. In
sharp contrast, there is the dense rural belt of population associated

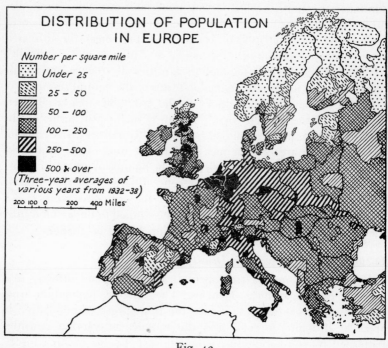

Fig. 42.

with the loess soils, a feature already considered in chapter five. In
Northern France and in Germany, this belt is partially merged
with the industrial constellations of urban population, but across
Polish Galicia, the Danubian Plain and the black soils of Ukraine it
is the outstanding feature of the rural landscape, fading out to the east
in the steppes of Russia (Fig. 42). The coalfields, the historical zones
of dense populations such as Holland, the Rhine Valley and the North
Italian Plain, and the modern capital cities, have together provided
the heavy rash of high densities in Western Europe. All these broad
features, which cut across all political frontiers and which have
contributed to the civilisation of Europe, are quite understandable.
It is in the detailed analysis of any one region that the study becomes
more difficult to understand.

Figs. 43 and 44 demonstrate that there are at least two Europes, divided between the Vistula and the Adriatic into an Industrial West and an Agricultural East. Urban growth in varying degrees has been largely responsible for this distinction. As a result, the rural densities of population have been much influenced by the relative intensity of urban penetration into the countryside. Apart from this factor, the chief controls in the densities of rural population in the West have been the type of farming practised, the pattern of land use and the size of farms. Soil fertility is a factor of variable importance depending on other controls. In Eastern Europe, rural densities are subject to rather different standards, where the high birth-rates, the low standards of living and the legacy of historical causes are often of permanent importance. Some of the densest population of Eastern Europe is in mountain districts and in areas of poor soils, a situation quite contrary to the principles of economic opportunity in the West where dense rural population at least suggests that it pays to utilise good soils intensively. Somewhat intermediate between the two are the scales of population densities in Southern Europe. Drought and the low standards of living, together with the relative impact of industrialisation in the more favoured regions, are the primary factors which influence densities there.

The Demographic Types of Europe

It is now possible to consider in more detail the character of population densities in different European environments. Fig. 45, showing the distribution of demographic types in Europe, is a synthesis, compiled with reference to the normal population densities of each region, the dependence of the rural population upon agriculture, the degree of agricultural productivity, and the balance between migration and natural increase.* Broadly, there are at least nine demographic categories according to which Europe can be divided, whose features are summarised in the table on p. 230.

Features of Urban and Industrial Densities

Categories one and two can be considered together since they represent relative conditions of urban growth, according to the pull of metropolitan centres, industrial areas such as the coalfields, or smaller urban centres. Something has already been said about these

---

* Figures obtained in appendices of Kirk, D., *Europe's Population in the Inter-war Years*. Princeton, 1946.

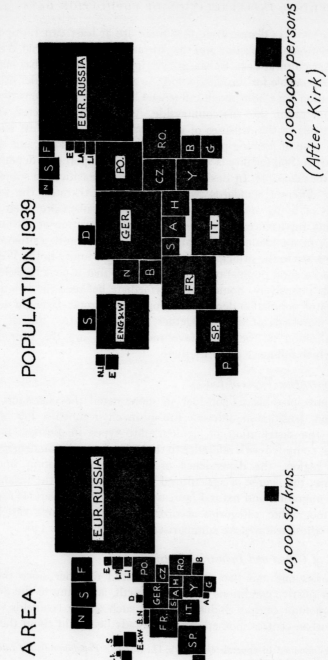

Fig. 43. Area and Population in Europe, 1939.

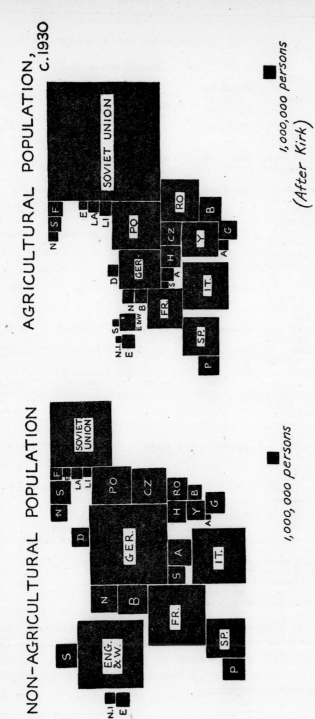

Fig. 44. Non-agricultural and Agricultural Population in Europe, c. 1930.

DEMOGRAPHIC TYPES IN EUROPE BEFORE 1939

Category	Population densities per sq. mile	Percentage of population dependent on agriculture	Coefficient[27] of agric. productivity	Migration* Type
I Areas dominated by city growth	over 2,000	1–15	over 250	C_2 C_3
II Areas of high urban population	over 1,000	15–35	100–300	A_2 A_3 B_1 B_2
III Areas of medium densities and high agric. productivity	500–1,000	25–40	150–400	variable chiefly A_2 A_3 B_1 B_2
IV Areas of medium densities and medium agric. productivity	100–500	40–80	75–150	ditto
V Areas of medium densities and low productivity	100–500	40–80	20–75	ditto
VI Areas of low but balanced population with adverse resources	1–100	25–75	75–150	B_1 B_2
VII Areas of unbalanced population with adverse resources in W. Europe	1–100	25–75	50–100	A_1 A_2
VIII Areas with signs of agrarian over population	100–500	50–90	20–50	A_2 A_3
IX Areas of Rural Colonisation	—	50–75	40–60	C_1 C_3

* Migration types have been arranged by Kirk as follows:

A_1 Depopulation through migration exceeding natural increase.
A_2 Out-migration more than half but less than total natural increase.
A_3 Out-migration less than half the natural increase.
B_1 Small out-migration.
B_2 Small in-migration.
C_1 In-migration less than natural increase.
C_2 In-migration more than natural increase.
C_3 Repopulation through migration.

influences in chapter seven. They can be summarised therefore by reference to four characteristic features relating to their distribution: their concentration at power resources, the steep population gradients, their cyclic character of change and the features of their agricultural population.

The first characteristic of these two categories is their markedly irregular distribution of population, patterned by conurbations, cities and a zonal arrangement of suburbs and satellite towns. Unlike rural densities, where the spatial distribution reflects the normality of density, site and nodality emphasise the depth of concentration in

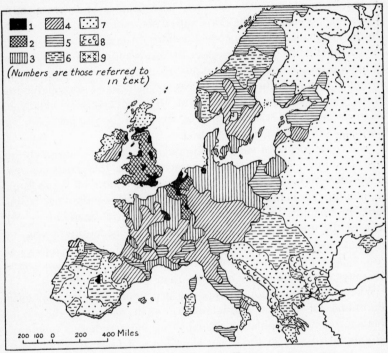

Fig. 45. Demographic Types in Europe, *c.* 1930–39.

urban population. Consequently the latter does not mean so much in terms of area as in terms of its occupational structure and its economic opportunity. The classification of their population according to occupations shows that a minimum importance is attached to agricultural industries. In the suburbs of Paris, for example, only 1·5 per cent. is engaged in agriculture. In industrialised countries, the percentage ranges from 5 in the United Kingdom to 25 in Germany. Inversely, the tertiary population comprises 37·5 per cent. in the suburbs of Paris. It ranges from 47 per cent. in the United Kingdom to 33 per cent. in Germany. The industrial groups comprise the bulk of the wage-earners, ranging from about 47 per cent. in the United Kingdom to 41·5 per cent. in Germany.

The role played by manufacturing industries in these two categories suggests the emphasis which power resources have had on the grouping of population. In Western and Central Europe, some 87 per cent. of the population is located at the sources of power, 70 per cent. on the coalfields and 17 per cent. near sources of hydro-electric power (14 per cent. in the Alps and 3 per cent. in Scandinavia).[28] On the coalfields there is a concentration of some 600 towns of over 10,000 inhabitants. In this respect Britain is unique, for it has over 25 million people distributed in densities above 1,000 per sq. mile on its eight major coalfields. The largest coalfield of Germany, the Ruhr, had 6,800,000 inhabitants in 1939, concentrated chiefly in fourteen cities. It was responsible in 1937 for 70 per cent. of Germany's iron and steel production.[29]

As a consequence of such high population densities dependent on this economic activity, a third characteristic is the sharp contrast in the densities between neighbouring areas. Some of the steepest population 'gradients' are found in Britain where the coal basins flank the uplands. In the industrial belt of Central Scotland, 74 per cent. of the total population of Scotland are concentrated within 15 per cent. of its area.[30] In North-East England, there are densities of over 25,000 per sq. mile along the banks of the Tyne, whereas a few miles inland the moors have less than 50 per sq. mile.

Where the population is thus so dependent on the geological conditions for mineral extraction, a fourth feature is the cyclic character of their population changes. Mining may have a long continuous history, as in the Harz Mountains of Germany, but more often there is a cycle of youth, maturity and old age, which may be rejuvenated at any stage by new mining techniques and new sources of supply or demand. These three stages are associated respectively with rapid expansion of production and high immigration, maximum production with variable increase of population, and decline of both production and population. Fig. 46 illustrates these cyclic features for the coal and iron fields of West Cumberland.[31] In this region, the most notable difference between the populations of the coalfield and the ironfield have been the greater fluctuations in the latter. Sporadic distribution of the ore bodies has led to an initial rush of miners to an area where rich deposits have been discovered and rapid decline of population has set in as soon as the workings have been

exploited. In industrial areas, apart from the coalfields, the movements of population are more complex and it is impossible to
generalise their features.

The agricultural population of industrial areas has distinct characteristics. The percentage of population dependent on agriculture

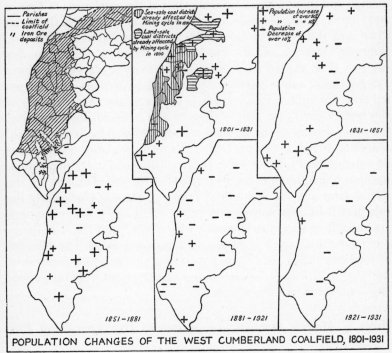

POPULATION CHANGES OF THE WEST CUMBERLAND COALFIELD, 1801-1931

Fig. 46.

tends to be highest in the least favoured lands, chiefly as a result of
the decline of agricultural labour in industrialised areas. Such areas
are, for example, the Welsh counties, the German provinces of
Mecklenburg, Pomerania and Bavaria and the central and south-
western departments of France. Agricultural productivity *per capita*
is very high, ranging from a coefficient of 250 to 400 (Utrecht with
407 is the highest in Europe). These high outputs are associated with
rationalised agriculture, high average yields and efficient marketing,
in relation to the competitive influences of urban productivity. Under
such conditions rural densities may be very high, reaching 2,000 to

2,500 per sq. mile in some of the horticultural lands of North and South Holland.

Areas of Medium Densities and High Productivity

This category is transitional between areas predominantly industrial and those which are rural. Most of the rural areas of France and Germany, the piedmont zone of Alpine Europe such as the Swiss Plain and the Austrian Lowlands, as well as parts of Catalonia, Bohemia, Moravia, south Sweden and Denmark belong to this category (Fig. 45). In these areas, productivity is everywhere above 150 *per capita* and population densities range between 150 and 400 sq. mile. Conditions in Denmark best express the characteristics of this type, where 85 per cent. of the total area is potentially productive, the mean density of the agricultural population alone is 100 per sq. mile of farmland, and 31 per cent. of the total population is dependent on agriculture. Professor Vahl, in his analysis of Danish population, has shown that the chief factors responsible for such densities are the size of farm and the intensity of farming, stressing particularly the role played by pigs and poultry in the economy.[32] Soil conditions are variable in importance, usually only a significant factor in determining densities when physical conditions are difficult. The densities of total population vary closely according to the urban penetration into the countryside.[33] Migration movements, apart from the general city-ward trend, are inarticulate.

Areas of Medium Densities and Medium to Low Agricultural Productivity

These categories are the most widespread in Europe, ranging through several types of environment. The Mediterranean lands, the Central European plains of Hungary, Poland and Eastern Germany, and the East Baltic States are represented. All these areas have percentages of rural population above the average for Europe (48 per cent.) but it is difficult to consider their range comparatively, since statistical definition of the term 'rural' varies from country to country. Rural densities tend to reflect averages, which are dependent on the types of economy practised and on the birth-rates.

In Southern Europe the density of population has at least three characteristic features. There is a striking normality of density wherever the monocultural features are marked. Secondly, the

emphasis placed on tree-crops and the relief features of Mediterranean lands emphasise the zonation of densities. Thirdly, irrigation and
other factors account for steep population gradients. The first feature
is well marked in Spain where monocultures of wheat, vines and olives
occur in different regions.[34] This, together with the degree of aridity
and relative urban influences, affect the range in rural densities. The
steppe lands have densities between 1 and 25 per sq. mile, the wheat-
lands of Castile range between 25 and 60, the mixed vine and wheat
lands of Aragon average densities in some areas as high as 60 to 100,
and the lands of Andalusia which specialise in oleiculture may have
up to 150 per sq. mile or more.

To avoid the threats of floods, malaria, and formerly of piracy,
much of the population along the Mediterranean coasts is concentrated on the hill slopes between 600 and 1,200 ft. Here the chief
tree crops are grown as an added incentive for this altitudinal concentration. In Tuscany, about two-thirds of the population are concentrated between 100 and 1,600 ft., while in Sicily, the slopes of
Mount Etna with their fertile lava soils have densities between 900
and 1,500 per sq. mile, at 2,500-3,000 ft., compared with only 10 per
sq. mile at 300-600 ft.[35] In Corsica, which has a mean elevation of
1,800 ft., there has been traditionally a concentration of population
between 900 and 2,500 ft., reaching 250 per sq. mile in some favoured
parts (Fig. 47).[36] In the Chataignerie district of the north-east, which,
as its name suggests, has been the chief area of sweet chestnut forests,
there is still a marked concentration of villages between 1,800 and
2,500 ft.

The third feature of the Mediterranean lands is the steep population gradient between adjacent areas, a reflection of contrasts in
the terrain, especially between irrigated and non-irrigated lands.
The interior lands of Valencia, for example, have densities as low
as 20 per sq. mile, while the irrigated plain of the *Huerta* has
densities rising to over 1,000 per sq. mile.[37] Drainage too accounts
for marked differences in comparable environments. The Roman
Campagna and the Pontine Marshes have 65 to 130 per sq. mile
while the plain of Campania, to the south, has between 1,300 and
1,600. Although these high densities are exceptional to this category
they act as 'pull' factors on areas of low density, coupled with the
'push' factors of adverse physical conditions in the poorer areas.
Migration, seasonal and permanent, is thus a marked feature of the
Mediterranean countries.

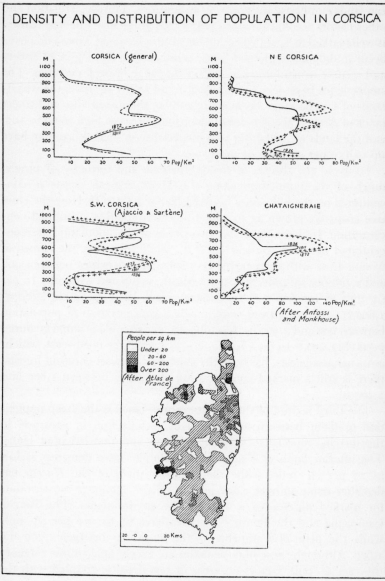

Fig. 47.

The central plains of Poland and Hungary are transitional in demographic character between the high productivity of the west and the signs of agrarian overpopulation in the east of Europe. Some 40 to 50 per cent. of the population is dependent on agriculture. Productivity oscillates between 75 and 150, less so towards the east where more people tend to be supported in the farming population group than is necessary. These features are found both in the fertile loess belt where grain occupies more than half the cultivated area, and in the less fertile rye and potato belt.

In the East Baltic States, where the percentage dependent on agriculture oscillates between 50 and 70 of the total population and productivity is 75 to 100, the rural densities usually reflect closely the soil conditions and the relative extent of forest and cleared land. Thus in Estonia, for example, the contrasts in terrain between the southern or 'emergent' region, and the northern or 'submergent' region (which was subjected to the last Baltic marine transgression) expresses itself in all the human geography of the state.[38] In the southern half, more than 50 per cent. of the area is under cultivation and rural densities are over 75 per sq. mile. In the northern half, less than 30 per cent. is under cultivation and densities are all less than 50 per sq. mile. These features are similar in the other states of Lithuania and Latvia. Southern Lithuania, however, shows some symptoms of over-population.

Areas of Low but Balanced Population with Poor Resources

It is difficult to demarcate this category distinctly from some of the areas included in the previous type. However, the Fenno-Scandinavian lands best exemplify the features of this category. Finland, central and northern Sweden, Norway and Iceland, with unfavourable climate, soil and problems of transport, have all shown that it is possible to bring about a satisfactory ratio between man and adverse conditions of land. All have average densities well below the total European average of 110 per sq. mile (Sweden 33, Finland 30, Norway 25 and Iceland 2). More than half of Norway lies over 2,000 ft. with the snowline between 3,300 and 6,000 ft. Only 2·7 per cent. of the land is under cultivation and the available farmland is about 3·3 per cent. of the total area. The distribution of population is emphatically a coastal location and in the interior the pattern of settlement reflects the hydrography. In Sweden, the densely populated districts of between 100 and 200 per sq. mile constitute about 7 per cent. of the total area while the cultivated area is 9 per cent., the difference of 2 per cent. being related to the scattered tracts and cultivated peat lands.[39] Swedish densities are more closely related to soil conditions than to altitude or climate. There is no evidence of pressure on the land since the percentage of population dependent on agriculture is relatively low (see Fig. 44) and many find their livelihood in fishing and forestry. Also there is a wide difference between the cultivated area and the agro-forestal area, as the following percentages indicate respectively: Finland 7 and 82, Sweden 9 and 66, Norway 3 and 28. Emigration reached its peak at the beginning of this century and, although there is the usual city-ward migration, the rural areas have remained relatively well balanced and are maintaining their densities.

Areas of Depopulation with Adverse Resources in Western Europe

In contrast, maladjustment between man and land has been a feature of certain mountainous districts on the Atlantic borders of Europe, such as the Scottish Highlands, Western Ireland, Brittany, parts of Spanish Galicia and Northern Portugal. In these areas of poor acid soils, broken relief and wet climate, overpopulation and subsequent emigration have been closely related to physical controls, although specific historical events have been the operative factors. The narrowness of the inhabited tracts amid a vast expanse of sea, mountain, and peat bog would have led to overpopulation at some period, especially as the natural increase of population has been high. The introduction of the potato about the mid-eighteenth century postponed the pressure on the land until later, but the demographic events of the nineteenth century were all the more catastrophic. In the Scottish Highlands the clearances, associated with land use changes, effected the emigration overseas of many thousands, and there has been an absolute decline of over half a million since 1861. The hunger drive of the mid-nineteenth century in Ireland had displaced overseas some three million emigrants by the end of the century. On a smaller scale there has been the displacement of Bretons and Gallegans. Climate and leached podzol soils are in tacit agreement for the continuance of poverty in these regions.

Regional variations, however, are quite marked. Possibly conditions are worst in the congested districts of Western Ireland,[40] where 80 per cent. or more may be dependent on agriculture, with low productivity coefficients ranging between 50 and 70. Conditions are comparable in parts of Galicia where the percentage of population dependent on agriculture is usually lower though the total densities are higher.[41] In Tras-Os-Montes in north Portugal, productivity is at a minimum but densities are relatively low.[42] From all these areas marked emigration, with unbalanced structures in their age composition, are still characteristic features. Galicia and Western Ireland show signs of agrarian overpopulation.

Depopulation is also a feature of the Alps and the Apennines where the movement became significant by the 1870's.[43] The prevalence of limestone, crystalline and schistose rock surfaces accounts for vast uncultivated tracts, concentrating the population in the more favoured valleys and intermontane basins. Causes of depopulation have been both economic and psychological, the disparity between the standards of the plains and mountains being an important inducement to migrate.

Areas of Agrarian Overpopulation in Eastern and Southern Europe

Frequently related to the above category is the condition of agrarian overpopulation. This term is relative, depending on such variables as the standard of living, the level of productivity, the density of rural population and the resources available. Much has been written on this subject and it would be out of place to consider it further here.[44] The areas which have the most marked symptoms of agrarian overpopulation are the Dinaric Mountains of Yugoslavia, parts of Slovakia and Carpatho-Ukraine, south Poland, Western Hungary, Bulgaria, the Roumanian province of Bukovina, Albania and most of Greece, especially the islands, Epirus and Peloponnesus (Fig. 45). According to Moore, all these areas have over 50 per cent. of their agricultural population as surplus or redundant. These and other less over-populated areas had some 17·5 million people in excess of production requirements in 1938, according to Bicanic.[45] Among the factors responsible are an undue dependence upon agriculture, with 80 per cent. or more of the population dependent on it in some areas, together with low productivity, high natural increase, restricted overseas migration, and social and economic conditions particular to each area. Average provincial densities range from 350 per sq. mile in south Poland to 90 in Albania and Western Greece. Across the Great Plain of Hungary[46] and the lowlands of Roumania densities are remarkably uniform with averages of 200-300 and 100-200 per sq. mile respectively. Productivity is low, reaching a minimum in Albania, which has a coefficient fifteen times less than that of Denmark.

The range of geographical conditions and the causes of over-population in these areas have wide variations. In south Poland, although the climate and the fertile loess soils are more favourable for agriculture than the northern half of the country, the symptoms of overpopulation are most expressive.[47] The high rural densities, with farming densities as high as 250 to 350 per sq. mile, are chiefly responsible. In the karst regions of Yugoslavia,[48] the Carpatho-Ukraine and the uplands of Bulgaria and Greece, adverse conditions of relief and the low percentages of cultivated to total area are important factors. In Greece, nearly half the population lives in a mountain environment.[49] Before the war about half the area of Hungary and Greece and a third of Roumania was in farm units over 50 hectares (123 acres) in size. Similar conditions of latifundia in Andalusia, Sicily and south Italy account largely for their excess rural populations. These and other factors have presented some of the greatest social and economic problems which Europe now faces.

Areas of Colonisation

Finally, the map of Europe is represented by some small areas of marked recolonisation. As a forced measure, this movement has been the consequence of war refugees. The first of these planned movements took place in 1923 in the exchange of nationalities between Turkey and Greece. Some 1,300,000 refugees from Turkey, Bulgaria and the U.S.S.R. were settled in Greece, mainly in Macedonia and Thrace, of whom 47 per cent. were agricultural.[50] The occupation of south Karelia by the Russians in 1940 effected the migration of several thousand colonists into central and northern Finland. A third transfer of population took place in 1942 when some 238,000 left the Italian Tyrol for Austria. Poland has received an influx of several transfer movements. Since 1939 it received 134,000 from Eastern Poland (in exchange for 40,000 White Russians), 214,000 entered South Poland from Roumania and another 130,000 entered from the Baltic States.[51] Apart from these international transfers of population there have been many more unofficial migration movements from east to west, especially in Germany. Pressure on the land has been severe in several regions, especially in south Poland and parts of north Germany, whereas active colonisation in pioneer lands has been stimulated in Finland and eastern Poland.

Conclusion

In conclusion, it is apparent that the term 'density of population' has various interpretations. At one end of what may be termed the 'population spectrum,' urban densities do not convey real significance in themselves. They merely reflect a highly complex development of economic activity, whose occupational structure in depth is more significant than the actual areal sprawl. At the other end of the 'spectrum,' there are the rural densities, which reflect symptoms of agrarian overpopulation. Such densities do not indicate balanced man-land ratios and the term 'density' is best considered in relation to agricultural productivity. Between these two extremes are densities which reflect in varying degree a relative balance between the optimum population[52] and the available resources. It is in these categories that the concept of 'density' has most significance. Even in these categories, however, a geographical explanation of the distribution and density of population in terms of physical conditions is inadequate. The symbiosis of man and his habitat is a complex of social, economic and political control, which no one social science can fully explain by itself. The geographer can only emphasise his point of view of space-time relations, as a contribution towards the total understanding of this complex.

SELECTED REFERENCES

Aurousseau, M. 'The Distribution of Population: A constructive Problem,' G.R., II, 1921, pp. 563-92.

Back, C. D. J. 'The Construction and Interpretation of Statistical Maps,' Austral. Geog., 2, No. 2, pp. 29-37.

Demangeon, A. 'La question du surpeuplement,' in his *Problèmes de Géographie Humaine*. Paris, 1942, pp. 35-52.

Fawcett, C. B. 'Some Factors in Population Density,' Rept. of Proc. of I.U.S.I.P.P., 1932, pp. 191-7.

Fawcett, C. B. 'Population Maps,' G.J., LXXXV, 1935, pp. 142-59.

George, P. *Introduction à l'Etude Géographique de la Population du Monde*, Paris, 1951.

Kirk, D. *Europe's Population in the Interwar Years*. Princeton, 1946.

Monkhouse, F. J., and Wilkinson, H. R. *Maps and Diagrams*. London, 1952, chapter six.

Peattie, R. *Mountain Geography*, Cambridge, Mass., 1936.

Stevens, A. 'The Distribution of Rural Population in Great Britain,' Trans. I.B.G., 1946, pp. 23-53.

Tulippe, O. *Cours de Géographie Humaine—Géographie de l'Habitat*, tome IV, Liége, 1944.

Tulippe, O. *Cours de Géographie Humaine—Monographies Synthetiques*, tome II, Liége, 1946.

United Nations. *Demographic Yearbook*, 1952.

Vidal de la Blache, P. 'La Repartition des hommes sur le globe,' A. de G., XXVI, 1917, pp. 81-93, 241-54.

Q

GLOSSARY OF WORDS USED IN THE TEXT

Acropolis. A hill stronghold which was the nucleus of many Greek towns at their formation.

Adret (Fr.). Like the German term *Sonnenseite* and the Italian *Adretto*, the word refers to the sunny slope of a mountain valley, facing more or less southwards. It receives more light and warmth than the shaded slopes because of its exposure for a longer period to the sun's rays.

Agglomerated settlement. A settlement or pattern of settlements which are loosely or irregularly grouped. Examples are the French *villages en ordre lache* and the German *haufendorfer*.

Agro-forestal area. Total area under crops, grass and forest cover.

Almedina. The residential quarters of a Moorish town.

Almudaina. The stronghold of a Moorish town and usually the nucleus of its early growth.

Altimetric zone. An area, following the contours, at the same height above sea-level.

Angerdorf (Ger.). A village with a central village street widened by a green and oval in shape, common to Eastern Germany and parts of Poland.

Anoecumene (Gr.). The uninhabitable areas of the earth unsuited to man's permanent settlement because of adverse physical controls.

Anthropogeography. A term first used by Ratzel, the German geographer, for the study of the distribution of mankind in relation to distinct environments. The word has been assumed synonymous with 'Human Geography' but it is no longer in current use.

Ard. A digging stick or primitive plough.

Assart. The process of converting land from woodland into arable.

Banlieue (Fr.). The area comprising the suburbs and outskirts of a city.

Baroque. A florid style of late Renaissance architecture prevalent in the late 17th and 18th centuries.

Bastide (Fr.). A defended settlement created with municipal privileges under royal authority.

Bocage (Fr.). Woodland. In France it is associated with a specific landscape of small, enclosed and wooded fields.

Burg. A fortified outpost which later became the nucleus of a municipal centre.

Cardo (latin). A main street in a Roman town.

Cartogram. A diagrammatic map.

Carucate. As much land as could be tilled by a plough (and eight oxen) in a year.

Centuriation. A Roman land system of dividing large square blocks of land into 100 smaller units.

Chorography. The art of describing a particular region.

Conurbation. An urban concentration of population as the result of two or more towns coalescing into one continuous built-up area. Sir P. Geddes who coined the term used it with specific reference to cities having over one million inhabitants.

Decumanus (Latin). A street in a Roman town at right angles to the *cardo* or main thoroughfare, providing the framework for a grid plan.

Demography. The statistical study of population data, such as age and sex composition, birth fertility and mortality rates, migration, etc.

Density of population. The average number of inhabitants living within a specified unit of area, usually in terms of a square mile or square kilometre.

Determinism. The doctrine that human action is not free but necessarily determined by physical forces. Modern views towards determinism in geography are now changing.

Ecology. The science of relationships of organisms to environment—coined by Haeckel (1866).

Economic geography. The branch of geography dealing with the production, distribution, trade and consumption of wealth. It is also the study of economic factors affecting the areal differentiation of the earth's surface.

Economy. The economic structure and functions of a state, area or society.

Enceinte (Fr.). An enclosure, usually referred to the fortified area of a town.

Entrepôt. A place acting as an exchange centre, an intermediary for trade between other countries.

Ergograph. A diagrammatic graph depicting the measure of work expended by a society or social unit within a specific time, usually a year.

Eschflur (Ger.). The irregular field system associated with the scattered holdings and settlements of lands cleared in woodland or heath.

Fermtoun. A small Scottish farming community or hamlet which before enclosure comprised a unit of ploughing, consisting of four to ten families.

Gavelkind. A land-tenure system by which property at the death of an owner was divided equally among his sons.

Geographical momentum. The tendency for places once established with services and installations to maintain or increase their importance after the conditions which originally influenced their establishment have altered.

Geometric progression. A series in which the ratio between the successive quantities is constant as in $1 : 3 : 9 : 27$, etc.

Geopolitics. The study of geographical factors in politics. As in the case of Nazi geopolitics, it can be only too readily subversive propaganda.

Gewannflur (Ger.). The orderly arrangement of strip-holdings associated with the open-field system of agriculture.

Haufendorf (Ger.). A type of irregular, agglomerated settlement.

Head-dike. A stone wall or ditch in Scotland, associated with the upper limit of former cultivation.

Hierarchical principle. The arrangement of unit groupings according to their size or importance.

Hinterland. The area behind a coast, referring usually to the area of trade served by a seaport.

Historical geography. The geography, both physical and human, of historical periods.

Historiography. The art of writing and studying history.

History of geography. The history of geographical knowledge and ideas.

Holism. The study of wholes from the ordered grouping of units in nature, after the philosophy of J. C. Smuts.

Huerta (Span.). An irrigated area or garden in Spain.

Human ecology. The study of man's adaptations and relations to his physical environment. As used by Barrows it is a philosophy rather than an objective study.

Human geography. As the complement of *physical geography*, it is the study of those features and phenomena on the earth's surface which relate directly to man and his activities.

Isarithmic line. A line joining places of equal arithmetic value.

Isohyet. A line of equal rainfall.

Isopleth. A line of equal value, showing the geographical distribution of an element.

Isotherm. A line of equal temperature when reduced to sea-level.

Kampfsaum (Ger.). A zone of conflict. Used by Ratzel to refer to the zone between permanent and temporary settlement on mountain slopes where conditions are marginal to human occupance.

Kolonialstadt (Ger.). A colonial town, usually referring to those towns founded in the expansion of the Germanic peoples in Eastern Germany and Central Europe.

Lake-dwelling. Prehistoric human shelter, raised on piles above the surface of a lake such as Neolithic settlements of Switzerland and N. Italy.

Latifundia (Latin). Large estates associated with great feudal systems of land tenure such as still occur in Southern Spain and Italy.

Limes (Latin). Roman frontiers of the Empire.

Logarithmic scale. A scale whose value is obtained by logarithm tables in abridged calculations.

Loess. Windborne loam deposit. Mixed with humus it forms fertile soil belts such as the 'Black Earth' of the U.S.S.R.

Man-land ratio. The ratio between the numbers of population and the natural resources of the land in a given area.

Marginal land. Land whose average returns are no more than sufficient to cover costs of production.

Megalopolis. Term coined by Lewis Mumford for an overgrown city.

Monoculture. Cultivation in which one crop predominates over all others in the region.

Morphology. The science of form and structures, and developments that influence their form. Thus *urban morphology* is the science of the plan and physical development of towns.

Neotechnic. With reference to cities developed according to principles of town planning (Lewis Mumford).

Nodality. A site or area having an important position in relation to its location and communications.

Normality. The character or state pertaining to a norm or average.

Oecumene (Gr.). The habitable world for human settlement.

Oleiculture. Cultivation of the olive.

Optimum population. The population estimated to be desirable for the full utilisation of the natural resources at an adequate standard of living.

Overpopulation. The condition of rural population when the redundancy of agricultural labour and therefore avoidable poverty indicates a population excessive to the existing standard of living, the economy practised and the natural resources.

Palaeotechnic. A type of industrial city (Lewis Mumford).

Parcellation. The fragmentation and division of holdings into scattered strips.

Peneplane. A tract of land, undulating or almost level as a result of long-continued processes of erosion.

Physiocrat. One of a French school founded by Quernay in the 18th century, who maintained that society should be governed according to a natural order.

Podzol. Soil of light colour, beneath a thin humus layer, usually leached and acidic, associated primarily with the coniferous forest belts of the world.

Polder. A low-lying land reclaimed from sea, lake or river, and protected by dikes, as in Holland.

Possibilism. The doctrine held by some geographers, chiefly the French school, which minimises the determining controls of the physical environment upon man.

Primary industry. Activity concerned with collecting or making available the resources of nature, such as mining, agriculture, forestry, fishing, hunting, etc.

Primary settlement. Colonisation of new lands associated with the first formative phase of occupation and settlement.

Primate city. The chief city of a country whose 'primacy' is measured by the percentage number of inhabitants which the next most important cities represent, when the primate city represents 100 per cent. (M. Jefferson).

Primogeniture. The system by which the inheritance descends to the eldest son (or child).

Procrustean analogy. Enforced similitude or association. Procrustes was an Attican robber who forced his victims to fit to the size of his bed by stretching or mutilitating their limbs.

Purpresture. Illegal encroachment or enclosure, as on royal forests, or common lands.

Repartimiento (Span.). Survey of property and land resources during the Reconquest of the Iberian Peninsula for purposes of allotting lands to the Christian settlers.

Retrodiction. The establishment on the basis of present evidence of what the past must have been like (Walsh).

Rodundszeit (Ger.). The process of forest clearance during the Middle Ages.

Rundorf-Rundling (Ger.). The Slavonic and E. German village, circular in shape.

Rundplatzdorfer (Ger.). The planned villages of the E. German marshlands which were built with a circular plan.

Run-rig. The system of land cultivation prevalent in Scotland and Ireland before enclosure.

Secondary industry. Industry which transforms the raw materials provided by nature into commodities more directly used for man, such as manufacture, construction, and power generation.

Secondary settlement. The infilling of an area by population, subsequent to the first and major phase of colonisation.

Snow-line. The lowest level at which snow lies permanently all the year round.

Stow. A site or place.

Strassendorf (Ger.). A street village, common to Eastern Germany and Central Europe.

Symbiosis. The association of two organisms living together. Hence the idea of biological association and inter-relationship.

Synoecism. The union of several towns or settlements under one capital city.

Teleology. The outlook of final causes, seeing design and purpose in nature.

Terp (Dutch). A settlement built on an artificial conical mound to avoid floods. Such round settlements are common to Holland and Lower Saxony dating from the early Middle Ages.

Terra mara. Prehistoric grid settlement associated with lake dwellings in the N. Italian Plain. Some consider this type of plan to be the origin of the grid but it is uncertain.

Terrier. A register of landed property, or rent roll.

Tertiary industry. Work performed for economic gain other than that associated with primary or secondary industry, e.g. transport, finance, the professions, personal and other services, etc.

Troglodyte. A cave-dweller.

Ubac (Fr.). Valley mountain slope in the shade, facing more or less poleward. The German term *Schattenseite* and the Italian *Opacco* are comparable.

Vill. A territorial unit of lands and buildings having a common social organisation.

Zone du voisinage. The suburban area of a city and surrounding country which is dominated by the city services.

REFERENCES QUOTED IN THE TEXT

ABBREVIATIONS USED

A.A.   American Anthropologist, Menosha, Wis.
Ann. Arch.   Annales Archéologiques, Paris.
A.A.G.S.   Annals of the Association of American Geographers.
A. de G.   Annales de Géographie, Paris.
A.H.E.S.   Annales d'Histoire Economique et Sociale, Paris.
Adv. of Sci.   British Association for the Advancement of Science, London.
A.J.S.   American Journal of Sociology, New York.
Ant.   Antiquity, London.
Austral. Geog.   Australian Geographer, Sydney.
B.R.S.G.   Boletín de la Real Sociedad Geográphica, Madrid.
B.A.G.F.   Bulletin de l'Association Géographique Français, Paris.
B.S.B.E.G.   Bulletin de la Societé Belge d'Études Géographie, Brussels.
B.S.G.Q.   Bulletin de la Societé Géographique de Quebec.
B.S.L.G.   Bulletin de la Societé Languedocienne de Géographie, Montpellier.
C.G.P.C.   Chronique Géographique des Pays—Celtes, Rennes.
C.R.C.I.G.   Compte Rendu du Congrés International de Géographie.
E.G.   Economic Geography, Worcester, Mass.
E.H.R.   English Historical Review, London.
Geog.   Geography, Sheffield (formerly Geographical Teacher, Manchester).
G.J.   Geographical Journal, London.
G.R.   Geographical Review, New York.
I.J.A.A.   International Journal of Agrarian Affairs, Geneva.
J.G.   Journal of Geography, New York.
J.H.S.   Journal of Hellenic Studies, London.
J.R.I.B.A.   Journal of the Royal Institute of British Architects, London.
J.S.S.   Journal of Soil Science, London.
La Géog.   La Géographie, Paris.
Man.   Man, a monthly record of the Royal Anthropological Institute, London.
Pet. Geog. Mitt.   Dr. A. Petermann's Mitteilungen aus Justus Perthes' Geographischer Anstalt, Gotha.
Proc. Ant. Scot.   Proceedings of the Antiquarian Society of Scotland, Edinburgh.
Pub. Admin.   Public Administration, London.
Pub. Soc. Géog. Lille.   Publication de la Societé Géographique, Lille.
Riv. Geog. Ital.   Rivista Geografica Italiana, Florence.
Rep. Br. Assoc.   Report of the British Association.
Rev. de Géog. Alpine.   Revue de Géographie Alpine, published by l'Institut de Géographie Alpine, University of Grenoble.
S.G.M.   Scottish Geographical Magazine, Edinburgh.
Trans. I.B.G.   Transactions of the Institute of British Geographers.
U.G.I., C.R.C.I.G.   Union Géographique Internationale. Comptes Rendu du Congres International de Géographie.
V.C.H.   Victoria County History.

CHAPTER ONE

1. Varenius, B., Geographia Generalis in qua effectiones generales telluris explicantur. Cambridge, 1650.
2. Davis, W. M., 'The Physical Factor in General Geography,' Educational Bi-monthly, Dec., 1906, p. 112.
3. Humboldt, A. von, *Cosmos, A Sketch of a Physical Description of the Universe*, Transl. by E. C. Otté. London, 1849, vol. 1, p. IX.

4. Bruhns and Lassell, Life of Humboldt—letter to Blumenbach, quoted on p. 197.

5. Quoted by Dickinson, R. E., and Howarth, O. R., *The Making of Geography*. Oxford, 1933, p. 152.

6. Quoted by Hartshorne, R., *The Nature of Geography*. Lancaster, Pa., 1939, p. 67.

7. Davis, W. M., 'The Relations of the Earth Sciences in view of their Progress in the Nineteenth Century,' Journ. of Geol., XII, 1904, p. 675.

8. Herbertson, Dorothy, *Life and Work of F. Leplay*. 1950.

9. Brigham, A. P., 'A Quarter Century in Geography,' Journ. of Geog., 1922, p. 13.

10. Vidal de la Blache, P., *Principles de Géographie Humaine*, Paris, 1918, p. 4.

11. This view had previously been considered by G. G. Chisholm. See his article, 'On the Relativity of Geographical Advantages,' S.G.M., 1897, p. 475.

12. Brunhes, J., *Géographie Humaine*. edit., p. 593.

13. See for example Sauer, C. O., *The Morphology of Landscape*. Chicago, 1925.

14. Barrows, H. H., 'Geography as Human Ecology,' A.A.A.G., 13. 1923, pp. 1-14.

15. Huntingdon, E., 'Geography and Natural Selections,' A.A.A.G., XIV, 1924, p. 1.

16. 'The Pioneer Fringe,' Foreign Affairs, Vol. 6, 1927-28, p. 49.

17. Roxby, P. M., 'The Scope and Aims of Human Geography,' S.G.M., 46, 1930, pp. 276-289.

18. Gilbert, E. W., and Steel, R. W., 'Social Geography and Its Place in Colonial Studies,' G.J. CVI, 1945, pp. 118-31.

19. Vidal de la Blache, P., 'Les Grands Agglomérations Humaines,' A. de G. XXVII, 1918, pp. 92-101, 174-187.

20. Finch, V. C., 'Training for Research in Economic Geography,' A.A.A.G., XXIV, 1944, p. 207.

21. Stamp, J., 'Geography and Economic Theory,' Geog., XXII, 1937, pp. 1-14.

22. Fisher, C. A., 'Economic Geography in a Changing World,' Trans. I.B.G., 1948, pp. 71-85.

23. See Kiss, G., 'Political Geography into Geopolitics,' G.R. 32, 1942, pp. 632-45, and Bowman, I., 'Geography as Geopolitics,' G.R. 32, 1942, pp. 646-58.

CHAPTER TWO

1. Barrows, op. cit.

2. Brunhes, Jean, 'Du caractère propre et du caractère complexe des faits de géographie humaine,' A. de G., XXII, 1913, p. 40.

3. Sion, Jules, 'Géographie et Ethnologie,' A. de G., XLVI, 1937, p. 461.

4. Evans-Pritchard, E., *Social Anthropology*. London, 1951, p. 5.

5. For example see Elliot-Smith, G., *The Ancient Egyptians*. London, 1925.

6. Vidal de la Blache, P., 'Les Genres de vie dans la géographie humaine,' A. de G., XX, 1911, p. 304.

7. Daryll Forde, C., *Habitat, Economy and Society—a Geographical Introduction to Ethnology*. London, 1942, p. 461.

8. Sion, op. cit., p. 459.

9. Wooldridge, S. W., and East, W. G., *The Spirit and Purpose of Geography*. London, 1951, p. 28.

10. Daryll Forde, C., 'Values in Human Geography,' Geog., XIII, 1925, p. 221.

11. Hart, C. W. M., *Essays in Sociology*. 1940, p. 51.

12. Bews, J. B., *Human Ecology*. London, 1935, p. 300.

13. Le Lannou, M., *La Géographie Humaine*. Paris, 1949, pp. 28-9.

14. Fleure, H. J., 'Geography and the Scientific Movement,' Geog., XXII, 1937, pp. 179-180.

15. Chevalier, Louis, 'Demographie et Géographie,' A. de G., LVI, 1947, pp. 201-2.

16. George, Pierre, 'Géographie de Population et Demographie.' Population, V, 1950, p. 299.

17. Taylor, Griffith, 'Racial Geography,' in *Geography in the Twentieth Century*. London, 1951, pp. 433-62.

CHAPTER THREE

1. Hettner, A., *Die Geographie—ihre Geschichte, ihr Wesen, und ihre Methoden*. Breslau, 1927.

2. Hartshorne, R., *The Nature of Geography*, op. cit., pp. 144-6.

3. Croce, Benedetto, *Theory of the Aesthetic*, translated by D. Ainslie. London, 1909, p. 67.

4. Febvre, Lucien, *La terre et l'évolution humaine,* Paris, 1924. Translated as *A Geographical Introduction to History*. London, 1932, p. 16.

5. Trevelyan, G. M., *Clio—a Muse*. London, 1913, pp. 144-7.

6. Kroeber, A. L., 'History and Science in Anthropology,' American Anthropologist, 37, 1935, pp. 539-569.

7. Evans-Pritchard, E., 'Social Anthropology: Past and Present,' Man, 1950, pp. 118-124.

8. Evans-Pritchard, E., *Social Anthropology*. London, 1951.

9. Kant, Immanuel, *Physiche Geographie*, edited by F. T. Rink. Königsberg, 1802. Quoted by Hartshorne, op. cit., p. 134.

10. See Buchan, J., *The Causal and the Casual in History*. Cambridge, 1929.

11. Consult Professor A. G. Ogilvie's article on this point, 'Relations of Geology and Geography,' Geog., 23, 1938, pp. 75-82.

12. Wooldridge and East, op. cit., p. 30.

13. Ackerman, E. A., 'Geographic Training, Wartime Research, and Immediate Professional Objectives,' A.A.A.G., 35, 1945, pp. 121-43.

14. Kimble, G. H. T. 'The Inadequacy of the Regional Concept,' in *London Essays in Geography*, edited by L. D. Stamp and S. W. Wooldridge. London, 1951, pp. 151-174.

15. Jones, S. B., 'The Enjoyment of Geography,' G.R., XLII, 1952, p. 547.

16. Hettner, op. cit., p. 131.

17. Darby, H. C. (Edit.), *An Historical Geography of England before 1800*. Cambridge, 1936.

18. Ogilvie, A. G., 'The Time Element in Geography,' Trans. I.B.G., No. 18, 1952.

19. Fleure, H. J., *Some Problems of Society and Environment*. I.B.G., 1947, p. 31.

20. Joseph, H. W. B., *The Concept of Evolution*, Herbert Spencer Lecture. Oxford, 1924.

21. Oman, Sir Charles, *Memoirs of Victorian Oxford*. London, 1941, p. 161.

22. Gilbert, E. W., 'What is Historical Geography?' S.G.M., XLVIII, 1932, p. 133.

23. Lebon, J. H. G., *An Introduction to Human Geography*. London, 1952, p. ix.

CHAPTER FOUR

1. Frödin, J., 'Plans cadastraux et répartition du sol en Suède,' A.H.E.S., 1934, pp. 51-61.

2. Vahl, I., 'The Distribution of Population in Denmark,' Second Report C.T.R.H., 1930, p. 13.
Thorpe, H., 'The Influence of Inclosure on the Form and Pattern of Rural Settlement in Denmark,' Trans. I.B.G., 1951, No. 17, pp. 111-130.

3. Hoskins, W. G., *The Heritage of Leicestershire*. 1949, p. 17.

4. Gray, H. L. *English Field Systems*. Cambridge, Mass., 1915, pp. 109-38.

5. Geddes, A., 'The Changing Landscape of the Lothians,' S.G.M., 54, 1938, pp. 129-142.

6. Lebon, J. H. G., 'The Face of the Countryside in Central Ayrshire,' S.G.M., 62, 1946, pp. 7-15.

7. Houston, J. M., 'The Rural Settlements of the Solway Firth Plain,' I.G.U., C.R.C.I.G., 1949, pp. 421-26.

8. Sinclair, Sir John, *General Report of the Agriculture of Scotland*. 1814, vol. I., pp. 259-300.

9. From data kindly supplied by Mr. A. R. Muir in a regional description on Arran, 1952

10. Curwen, E. C., *Air-Photography and Economic History*. London, 1938, p. 11.

11. Ibid., pp. 13-14.

12. Seebohm, F., *The Tribal System in Wales*. London, 1904, p. 46.

13. Estyn Evans, E., 'Some Survivals of the Irish Openfield System,' Geog., vol. XXIV, 1939, pp. 24-36.

14. Eck, A., *Le Moyen Age Russe*. Paris, 1933, p. 59.

15. Saltmarsh, J., and Darby, H. C., 'The Infield-Outfield System on a Norfolk Manor,' Econ. Hist., vol. III, 1935.

16. Grant, I. F., 'The Highland Open-field System,' Geog. Teacher, vol. XIII, 1926, pp. 480-88.

17. Quoted by Professor E. Estyn Evans, op. cit., p. 34.

18. Le Lannou, M., *Pâtres et Paysans de la Sardaigne*. Tours, 1941, pp. 113-137.

19. See Seebohm, H. E., *Customary Acres and their Historical Importance*, London, 1914, for a detailed description of types of open-field rigs.

20. Aakjaer, Svend, 'Villages, cadastres et plans parcillaires au Danemark,' A.H.E.S., vol. I, 1929, pp. 562-75.

21. Homans, G. C., 'Terroirs ordannés et champs orientés: une hypothèse sur le village anglais,' A.H.E.S., vol. 8, 1936, pp. 438-48.

22. Orwin, C. S. and C. S., *The Open Fields*. Oxford, 1938, pp. 1-14.

23. Flach, J., *L'Origine Historique de l'Habitation et des Lieux Habités en France*. Paris, 1899, p. 41.

24. Bloch, M., *Les Caractères Originaux de l'Histoire Rurale Francaise.*

25. Curwen, op. cit., pp. 15-17.

26. Eck, op. cit., p. 59.

27. Delisle, L., *Études sur . . . l'Agriculture en Normandie*. Paris, 1851, p. 297.

28. Lipson, E., *The Economic History of England*, London, 1947, p. 68.

29. Nicod, J., 'Problems de structure agraire en Lorraine,' A. de G., vol. LX, 1951, pp. 337-48.

30. On Spanish field systems see Costa, J., *Colectivismo Agrario en España*, Madrid, 1915, pp. 340-353.

31. Smith, W., *An Economic Geography of Great Britain*. London, 1949, pp. 7-8.

32. Juillard, Et., 'L'Assolement biennal dans l'agriculture septentrionale, le cas particular de la Basse—Alsace,' A. de G., LXI, 1952, pp. 34-45.

33. Dion, R., *Essai sur la formation du paysage rural français*. Tours, 1934.

34. Bloch, M., 'Les Paysages Agraires,' A.H.E.S., 1936, pp. 256-77.

35. Sion, J., 'Sur le structure agraire de la France Méditerranéenne,' Bull. Soc. Lang. Geor., vol. VIII, 1937, pp. 109-31, and 'Sur la civilization agraire Méditerranéenne,' op. cit., vol. X, 1939, pp. 16-41.

36. Demangeon, A., 'Paysages Ruraux,' A. de G., vol. XLIV, 1935, pp. 535-40.

37. Ridgeway, W., 'The Homeric Land System,' Journ. Hell. Studies, Vol. VI, 1885, pp. 319-39.

38. Jardé, A., *Les Céréals dans l'Antiquité Grecque*, 1925, p. 190.

39. Harris, S., 'Some Notes on Field Systems in Mediterranean Lands.' Rept. C.T.R.S., 1928, p. 88.

40. Bradford, J., 'A Technique for the Study of Centuriation,' Ant., vol. XXI, 1947, pp. 197-204.

41. See a poetic description of this change in 'Land and People' by J. C. Hawkes, in *The Character of England*, edited by E. Barker. Oxford, 1947.

42. Fox, C., *The Personality of Britain*, 4th Edition. Cardiff, 1943.

43. Wooldridge, S. W., 'The Anglo-Saxon Settlement,' in *An Historical Geography of England*, edited by H. C. Darby.

44. Holleyman, G. A., 'A Survey of the Celtic Field System of South Britain,' Ant., vol. IX, 1935, pp. 443-54.

45. Tansley, A. G., *The British Isles and their Vegetation*. Cambridge, 1949, vol. 1, pp. 173-4.

46. Gover, J. E. B., Mawer, A., Stenton, F. M., *The Place-Names of Middlesex*. 1942, p. xv.

47. Darby, H. C., 'Clearing the English Woodland,' Geog., vol., XXXVI, 1951, p. 75.

48. Darby, H. C., *The Medieval Fenland*. Cambridge, 1940, pp. 3-5.

49. Gray, H. L., *English Field Systems*. Cambridge, Mass., 1915.

50. Smith, W., op. cit., p. 9.

51. Bishop, T. A. M., 'Assarting and Growth of the Open Fields.' Econ. Hist. Rev., vol. VI, 1935, p. 17.

52. Douglas, D. C., *The Social and Economic Structure of Medieval East Anglia*. Oxford, 1933.

53. Joliffe, J. E. A., *Pre-Feudal England: the Jutes*. Oxford, 1933.

54. In the thirteenth century, groups of *heredes* cultivated their lands jointly, though the practice declined later. Joliffe, op. cit., p. 24.

55. Tawney, R. H., *The Agrarian Problem in the Sixteenth Century*. 1912, p. 172.

56. Jolliffe, J. E. A., 'Northumbrian Institutions,' Eng. Hist. Rev., vol. XLI, 1926, p. 12.

57. Quoted by Tawney, op. cit., p. 262.

58. Flatrès, M. P., 'Types de structure agraire du Comté de Cornwall,' B.A.G.F., 1939, p. 25.

59. Flatrès, M. P., 'La structure agraire ancienne du Devon et du Cornwall et les enclotures des XIII et XIV siecles,' Chron. Geog. des Pays Celtes, 1949, pp. 4-14.

60. Gover, J. E. B., Mawer, A., and Stenton, F. M., *The Place Names of Devon*. 1931, p. XIX.

61. See map in Flatrès, M. P., 'Aperçu de la structure agraire du Pays de Galles occidental,' Chron. Geog. des Pays Celtes, 1949, p. 16.

62. Jones, E., 'Settlement Patterns in the Middle Teify Valley,' Geog., vol. XXX, 1945, p. 106.

63. Slater, G., 'The Inclosure of Common Fields Geographically Considered,' Geog. Journ., vol. XXIX, 1907, p. 54.

64. Slater, G., *English Peasantry and the Enclosure of Common Fields*. London, 1907, p. 73.

65. Beresford, M. W., 'The Lost Villages of Medieval England,' G.J., vol. CXVIII, 1951, p. 146.

66. Slater, G. J., op. cit.

67. See plan in L.U.S., Cheshire.

68. Tawney, op. cit., p. 223.

69. Orwin, op. cit., pp. 113-14.

70. Ibid., p. 192.

71. V.C.H., *A History of Cambridge and the Island of Ely*. 1948, p. 58.

72. Darby, H. C., *The Medieval Fens*. 1940.

73. Ibid. Also Darby, H. C., *The Draining of the Fens*. 1940.

74. Gray, op. cit., pp. 313, 314.

75. Joliffe, op. cit.

76. Margary, I. D., *Roman Ways in the Weald*. London, 1948, pp. 204-7.

77. Flatrès, P., 'Aperçu de la structure agraire du Pays de Galles occidental,' Chron. Géog. des Pays Celtes, 1949, pp. 15-23.

78. For a general account of the fundamental division into Englishry and Welshry see Rees, Wm., *South Wales and the March, 1284-1415*. 1924.

79. See for example, Jones, E., 'Settlement Patterns in the Middle Teify Valley,' Geog., XXX, 1945, pp. 103-111.

80. For the whole island Miss D. Sylvester has mapped five types of field patterns. See her article, 'Rural Settlement in Anglesey,' Trans. Anglesey Antiq. Soc. and Field Club, 1949, pp. 1-24.

CHAPTER FIVE

1. Lefèvre, M. A., *L'Habitat Rural en Belgique*, Liége, 1926.
2. Keuning, H. J., 'L'Habitat Rural aux Pays-Bas,' Tydschr. Kon. Ned. Aardrs. Gen., vol. 55, pp. 644-5.
3. Martiny, R., 'Grundrissgestaltung der deutschen Siedlungen,' Petermans Mitt., 197, 1928.
4. Biermann, Ch., 'L'Habitat Rural en Suisse,' U.G.I., C.R.C.I.G. de Paris, t.III, sect. IV, pp. 17-32.
5. Biasutti, R., 'Richerche suit tifi degli insediamenti rurali in Italia,' op. cit., t.III, sect. III, pp. 7-16.
6. Cvijic, *La Géographie Humaine des Balkaniques*.
7. Mihaelescu, V., 'Une carte de l'Habitat rural en Roumanie,' C.R.C.I.G. de Paris, t.III, pp. 33-35.
8. Zaborski, B., 'Sur le forme des villages en Pologne et leur repartition.' Bol. Soc. Geog. de Quebec, vol. 22, 1928, pp. 65-76.
9. Demangeon, A., 'Une Carte de l'Habitat,' A. de G., XLII, 1933, pp. 225-232.
10. Allix, A., 'Examen critique de la methode de representation . . . de l'habitat rural . . . par A. Demangeon,' U.G.I., C.R.C.I.G. de Varsovie, 1934, t.III, sect. III, pp. 452-8.
11. Meynier, A., 'L'Habitat Rural dans les Ségalas,' C.R.C.I.G. de Paris, 1931, t.III, pp. 99-102.
12. Zierhoffer, A., 'Sur une formula servant á exprimer la dispersion et la concentration absolue de l'habitat rural,' U.G.I., C.R.C.I.G. de Varsovie, tome III, sect. III, pp. 410-415.
13. Bernard, J., 'Une formule pour la cartographie de l'habitat rural avec application au department de l'Yonne,' U.G.I., C.R.C.I.G. de Paris, 1931, t.III, pp. 108-117.
14. Debouverie, A. H., 'Une Methode à base numerique pour la cartographie de l'Habitat, spécialement applicable à la Belgique,' B.S.B.E.G., 1943, vol. 13, pp. 146-196.
15. Colas, M. R., 'Repartition de l'habitat rural,' B.A.G.F., 1945, pp. 51-6.
16. Meitzen, A., *Siedelung und Agrarwesen der Westgermanen und Ostgermanen*, vol. I., p. 518.
17. Ibid., p. 520.
18. Flach, J., *L'Origine Historique de l'Habitation et les Lieux Habités en France*, Paris, 1899, pp. 10, 19, 36, 37.
19. Schlüter, O., *Die Formen der Ländlichen Siedelungen*, p. 248.
20. Lefèvre, op., cit., pp. 39-46.
21. Harris, S., Village Settlements in the Channel Islands,' Rep. Br. Assoc. Leeds, 1927, p. 343.
22. Dion, R., 'La Part de la Géographie et celle de l'Histoire dans l'explication de l'habitat rural du Bassin Parisien,' Pub. Soc. de Géog. Lille, 1946, pp. 43-47.
23. Seebohm, F., *The English Village Community*, Cambridge, 1883, p. xv.
24. De Jubainville, D'Arbois, *Recherches sur les origines de la proprietés et les noms de lieux en France*. Paris, 1890.
25. Curwen, E. C., *Air-Photography and Economic History*. London, 1938.
26. Gradmann, R., *Die Arbeitsweise der Siedelungs Geographie*. Berlin, 1928.
27. See criticism by Lefèvre, M. A., 'La Géographie des formes de l'habitat,' B.S.B.E.G., Vol, 3, pp. 186-208.
28. Clark, G., 'Farmers and Forests in Neolithic Europe,' Ant., vol. XIX, 1945, p. 62.
29. Garnett, A., 'The Loess Regions of Central Europe in Prehistoric Times.' G.J., vol. CVI, 1945, p. 138.
30. Curwen, E. C., 'Early Agriculture in Denmark,' Ant., vol. XII, 1938, p. 153.
31. Grenier, A., 'Aux Origines de l'économie rurale: la conquête du sol francais,' A.H.E.S., 1930, p. 41.
32. Grundy, G. B., Saxon Land Charters, 'Wiltshire,' Archaeol. Jour., LXXVII, 1920, 'Hampshire,' ditto, LXXVIII, 1921.

33. Olsen, op. cit., p. 257.
34. Bloch, M., 'Les Plans Parcellaires,' A.H.E.S., vol. 1, 1929, pp. 60-69, 390-98.
35. Aakjaet, S., 'Villages, cadastres et plans parcellaires au Danemark,' A.H.E.S., op. cit., pp. 562-75.
36. Lebon, 'The Process of Enclosure in the Western Lowlands,' S.G.M., 62, 1946, pp. 100-110.
37. Albitreccia, A., *Le Plan Terrier de la Corse au XVIIIe Siècle*. Paris, 1942.
38. Des Marez, G., *Le Probleme de la Colonization Franque . . . en Belgique*. Brussels, 1926.
39. Wooldridge, S. W., 'Anglo-Saxon Settlement,' in *Historical Geography of England before 1800*, edit. by H. C. Darby, 1936, pp. 88-132.
40. Houston, J. M., 'The Rural Settlements of the Solway Firth Plain,' I.G.U., C.R.C.I.G., Lisbon, 1949, tome III, pp. 421-26.
41. Demangeon. A., *Les Pays Bas*, Géographie Universelle, tome II.
42. Gradmann, R., *Das ländliche Siedlungswesen der Konigreichs*. 1926, pp. 90-91.
43. Cambridge Economic History, vol. 1. *Agrarian Life in the Middle Ages*. Cambridge, 1941, pp. 278-283.
44. Joshua 17.15.
45. Musset, R., *Le Bas-Maine*, Paris, 1917.
46. Perroy, Edward, *The Hundred Years' War*. London, 1951, p. 41.
47. Ibid., p. 51.
48. Zaborski, op. cit., p. 76.
49. Eck, A., *Le Moyen Age Russe*. Paris, 1933, pp. 56, 275.
50. Beaver, S. G., *L.U.S. Northamptonshire*, pp. 364-5.
51. Dion, R., op. cit., p. 16.
52. Demangeon, A., 'La Géographie de l'Habitat Rural,' A. de. G., vol. XXXVI, 1927, p. 13.
53. Vidal de la Blache, P., *Principles of Human Geography*, pp. 188-9.
54. Garnett, A., *Insolation and Relief*, I.B.G., 1937.
55. Dion, op. cit., p. 33.
56. Grimes, W. F., 'Early Man and Soils of Anglesey.' Ant., vol. XIX, 1945, pp. 169-73.
57. Dion, op. cit.
58. Wooldridge, S. W., Journ. Soil Sci., vol. 1, 1949, p. 31.
59. Brutails, A., *Etude sur la condition des populations rurales du Roussillon au moyen âge*, Paris, 1891, pp. 38-39, 43.
60. Le Lannou, M., Note in B.A.G.F. 1940, p. 59.
61. Marinelli, O., Geog. Teacher, 1925, p. 202.
62. Houston, J. M., 'Village Development in Scotland, 1745-1845,' Ad. Sci., 1947, pp. 129-32.
63. Seebohm, op. cit., p. 187.
64. Lefèvre, op. cit., p. 49.
65. Marinelli, op. cit., p. 203.
66. Woeikof, A., 'Le Groupement de la population rurale en Russie,' A. de G., XVIII, 1909, p. 20.
67. Demangeon, op. cit. p. 20.
68. Cvijic, op. cit., p. 222.
69. Keuning, op. cit., p. 644.
70. Dickinson, op. cit., p. 263.

CHAPTER SIX

1. Blanchard, *Les Alpes Français*. Grenoble, 1939, 3 vols.
2. Deffontaines, P., *Les Hommes et leur travaux dans le pays de Moyenne Garonne*.
3. Demangeon, A., *La Plaine Picarde*. Paris, 1905.
4. Lefèvre, M. A., *L'Habitat Rural en Belgique*. Liége, 1926.

5. Pessler, W., *Der Niedersachsische Kulturkreis*. Hanover, 1925.
6. Biasutti, G., 'Richerche sui tipi di insediamenti,' Memorie della Soc. Geog. Ital., XVII, Rome, 1932.
7. Cvijic, J., *La Péninsula Balkanique*. Paris, 1918.
8. Cordingley, R. A., *Rural House Types*. Adv. of Sci., vol. VI, No. 22, p. 123.
9. Ling, A. G., 'Peasant Architecture in the Northern Provinces of Spain.' Journ. Roy. Inst. Brit. Arch., 1936, p. 845.
10. Tacitus., *Germania*, 16.
11. Brooks, C. E., *Climate in Everyday Life*. London, 1950, p. 61.
12. Davie, W. G., and Dawber, E. G., *Old Cottages and Farmhouses in the Cotswold District*. London, 1905, p. 10.
13. Brooks, *op. cit.*, p. 74.
14. Ter Linden, A. J., *Das Sommerklima in Geräuden Gesundshting*, 1936, vol. 60, p. 522.
15. Urabayen, L., *La Casa Navarra*. Madrid, 1929.
16. Caro Baroja, J., *Los Pueblos de España*. Madrid, 1946.
17. The importance of reed as a thatch material is indicated by the French word 'to thatch'—'Chaume,' derived from the Latin 'calamus,' a reed.
18. Mitrany, D., *The Land and the Peasant in Rumania*, London, 1930, p. 484.
19. Seebohm, F., *The English Village Community*. Cambridge, 1926, pp. 240, 241.
20. Addy, S. O., *The Evolution of the English House*. London, 1933, pp. 195-215.
21. Brunhes, J., *Human Geography*. London, 1952, p. 51.
22. *Atlas de Finlande*, trsl. 1910, vol. 2, pp. 33, 34.
23. Boyd, L. A., *Polish Countryside*. New York, 1937, pp. 106-8.
24. Mitrany, op. cit., p. 484.
25. Walker, W. G., *Sardinian Studies*. Leplay Society. London, 1938, pp. 21, 25.
26. Capt. Thomas, Proc. Ant. of Scot., vol. 3, 1859, p. 139.
27. Bertaux, E., 'Etude d'un type d'habitation primitive—Trulli, caselle et specchia des pouilles.' A. de G., 1899, pp. 207-30.
28. Slazman, L. F., *Building in England down to 1540*. Oxford, 1952, p. 119.
29. Arkell, W. J., *Oxford Stone*. Oxford, 1950 (see map on p. 35).
30. Turner, T. H., *Some Account of Domestic Architecture in England*. London, 1851, vol. 2, p. 349.
31. Davie, G., and Dawber, E. G., *Old Cottages and Farmhouses in Kent and Sussex*. London, 1900, p. 26.
32. Parkinson, J., and Ould, E. A., *Old Cottages and Farmhouses and Other Half-timbered Buildings in Shropshire, Herefordshire and Cheshire*. London, 1904, p. 12.
33. Jones, S. R., *English Village Houses*. London, 1936.
34. Davie and Dawber, *Old Cottages . . . in the Cotswolds*. Op. cit., p. 5.
35. Howe, J. A., *Geology of Building Stones*, p. 3.
36. Oliver, B., *The Cottages of England*. London, 1929.
37. Peate, J. C., *The Welsh House*. London, 1940, p. 28.
38. Lefèvre, M. A., 'La Zadruga,' A. de G., XXXIX, 1930, pp. 316-20.
39. Henning, R., *Das Dautsche Haus in seiner historischen Entwickelung*, 1882.
40. Demangeon, A., 'Essai d'une classification des maisons rurales,' Paris, 1942. Reprinted in Problèmes de Géographie Humaine, pp. 230-235.
41. Brunhes, op. cit., p. 61.
42. Lefèvre, M. A., *Principles et Problèmes de Géographie Humaine*. Brussels, 1945, pp. 136-144.
43. Edwards, K. C., *Sweden, Dalarna Studies*. Le Play Society. London, 1940, pp. 29-30.
44. L. of N., E.C.R.L., *Rural Housing and Planning*. Geneva, 1939, p. 53.
45. For Polish house-types, see Smolenski, J., *Excursion A3 Cracovie*, C.I.G., 1934, pp. 17, 46, 68.
46. Krebs, N. (edit.), *Landeskunde von Deutschland*, 11. Berlin, 1931, p. 75.
47. Addy, op. cit. p. 99.
48. Schrepfer, H., *Landeskunde von Deutschland*, band. 1. Berlin, 1935, pp. 70-78.
49. Addy, op. cit., p. 95.
50. Harrison's *England*, edit. by Furnivall, vol. 1. p. 238.

51. Seebohm, M. E., *The Evolution of the English Farm*, London, 1927.
52. Seebohm, M. E., op. cit., p. 77.
53. Lefèvre, M. A., *L'Habitat Rurale en Belgique*. Liége, 1926, pp. 244, 247.
54. Faucher, A., 'Evolution des types de maisons rurales,' A. de G., 1945, p. 252.
55. Vidal de la Blache, P., *Principles of Human Geography*. London, 1926, pp. 238-70.

CHAPTER SEVEN

1. Ratzel, 'Die geographische lage der grossen Stadte,' in *Die Grosstadt, Vortrage und Aufsätze zur Stadteausstellung Gehe Steftung zu Dresden*. Dresden, 1903.
2. Christaller, W., *Die Zentralen Orte in Suddeutschland*. Jena, 1933.
Christaller, W., 'Rapports Fonctionnels entre les agglomérations urbaines et les Campagnes,' U.G.I., C.R.C.I.G., Amsterdam, 1938, tome 2, IIIa, pp. 123-37.
Christaller, W., *Das Grundgerust der räumlichen Ordnung in Europa*. Frankfurt, 1950.
3. Kant, E., 'Umland Studies and Sector Analysis,' in *Studies in Rural-Urban Interaction*, Lund, 1951, pp. 1-13.
4. Christaller, W., Das Grundgerust, op. cit., p. 12.
5. Ministry of Town and Country Planning, *The Redevelopment of Central Areas*. London, 1947, p. 4.
6. Christaller, W., op. cit., p. 9.
7. See Smailes, A. E., 'The Urban Mesh of England and Wales,' Trans. I.B.G., 1946, pp. 85-101.
8. Aristotle, *Politics*, ii, 5.2.
9. Thucydides, I.5.
10. On Greek cities the most authoritative works are: Von Gerkan, A., *Griechische Stadteanlangen*, Berlin, 1924. Wycherley, R. E., *How the Greeks built Cities*, London, 1949.
11. Frotheringham, A. L., *Roman Cities in Northern Italy and Dalmatia*. London, 1910.
12. Blanchet, A., *Les Enceintes romaines de la Goule, Étude sur l'origine d'un grand nombre de villes françaises*. Paris, 1907.
13. Lavedan, P., *Histoire de l'Urbanisme, Antiquité—Moyen Age*. Paris, 1926.
14. For example, the French *villeneuve*, *villefranche*, *sauvetat*, the Italian *villanova*, *Castelfranco* and the Spanish *villanueva*, *villafranca* and *salvatierra*.
15. Annales Archeologiques, vol. X, p. 270.
16. Curie, *Seibres, Essai sur les villes fondees dans le S.O. de la France du XIII et XIV siecles*. 1880.
17. Dickinson, R. E., 'The Morphology of the Medieval German Town,' G.R., 35, 1945, pp. 74-97.
18. Tout, T. F., *Medieval Town Planning*. Manchester, 1934.
19. Woodbine, G. E. (edit.) Bracton's *De Legibis et Consuetinibus Anglia*, New Haven, 1915-22.
20. Hernandez, F., 'Los Reyes y la colonización interior de España, B.R.S.G., vol. 8. 1880, p. 193.
21. Ibid.
22. Dickinson, R. E., *City Region and Regionalism*. London, 1947.
23. Dickinson, R. E., *The West European City*. London, 1951, p. 291.
24. Ibid.
25. Stenton, Lady, *English Society in the Middle Ages*. London, 1951, p. 171.
26. Braudel, F., *La Méditerranée et le Monde mediterraneén à l'époque de Philippe II*. Paris, 1949, p. 269.
27. Olbricht, K., 'Die Vergrosstädterung des Abendlandes zu beginn des Dreissigjahrigen Krieges,' Pet. Geog. Mitt., 1939, pp. 349-53.
28. Stow, J., A *Survey of London*. London, 1598. Edit. by W. J. Thomas, 1876, p. 205.

29. Baker, J. N. L., 'England in the Seventeenth Century,' in *An Historical Geography of England before 1800*, edit. by H. C. Darby, 1936, p. 442.

30. Meuriot, P., *Des Agglomerations Urbaines dans l'Europe*. Paris, 1897, pp. 30-31.

31. Weber, A. F., *The Growth of Cities*. London, 1899, p. 57.

32. Mumford, L., *The Culture of Cities*. London, 1938, p. 171.

33. Jefferson, M., 'The Distribution of British Cities, and the Empire,' G.R., IV, 1917, p. 392.

34. Gilbert, E. W., 'English Conurbations in the 1951 Census,' G.J., CXVIII, 1952, pp. 64-68.

35. Weber, op. cit., pp. 80-93.

36. Soulas, J.; 'Les Conurbations Françaises,' A. de G., XLVIII, 1939, pp. 466-71.

37. Jefferson, M., 'The Law of the Primate City,' G.R., XXIX, 1939, pp. 224-31.

38. Kirk, D., *Europe's Population in the Inter-war Years*. Princeton, 1946.

CHAPTER EIGHT

1. Grimes, W. F., 'The Jurassic Way,' in *Aspects of Archaeology* . . . *Essays presented to O. G. S. Crawford*. London, 1951, pp. 144-171.

2. See Musset, L., 'Les Villes du Danemark, origines ét evolution,' A. de G., vol. LVII, 1948, pp. 308-321.

3. Leighley, J., *The Towns of Mälardalen in Sweden. A study in Urban Morphology*. Univ. of California Publications in Geography, 3, No. 1, 1928, pp. 1-134.

4. Wycherley, R. E., *How the Greeks built Cities*. London, 1949, pp. 5-7.

5. Guinard, P., and Mobeig, P., 'Madrid,' A. de G., XLI, 1932, pp. 481-99.

6. Mears, F. C., 'Primitive Edinburgh,' S.G.M., 35, 1919, pp. 298-315.

7. Tout, T. F., *Medieval Town Planning*. Manchester, 1934 pp. 16-18.

8. Frotheringham, A. L., *Roman Cities*. op. cit.

9. Bruun, D., *Danmark: Land og Folk*, bund II, Copenhagen, 1919, pp. 90-118.

10. Data derived chiefly from Ganshof, F. L., *Étude sur le dévelopement des villes entre Loire et Rhin au Moyen Age*. Paris, 1943; and Gilbert, E. W., 'Roman Britain,' in Darby, H. C., *An Historical Geography of England before 1800*. Cambridge, 1936.

11. Frotheringham, op. cit.

12. Marinelli, O., 'La carta topográfica e lo sviluppo di Firenze,' Rev. Geog. Ital., XXVIII, 1921, pp. 18-38.

13. On the towns in northern Spain see Lacarra, J., 'El Desarrollo Urbano de las Ciudades de Navarra y Aragón en la Edad Media,' Pirineos, No. 15, 1950, pp. 5-34.

14. See for other examples Blanchet, A., *Les Enceintes romaines de la Gaule. Étude sur l'origines d'un grand nombre de villes françaises*. Paris, 1907.

15. Dickinson, R. E., *The West European City*. London, 1952, p. 379.

16. Ibid., p. 389.

17. On East Prussian towns see Conzen, G., 'East Prussia,' Geog., XXX, 1945, pp. 1-10.

18. The Morería was well represented in Burgos and Murcia and the Judería in Seville and Toledo. See Lamperez y Romeo, V., *Las Ciudades Españolas* . . . *Finalizar de Edad Media*. Madrid, 1917, p. 21.

19. Smith, L. T., *The Itinerary of John Leyland, c. 1535-43*, part VIII. London, 1909, p. 113.

20. 'Montpazier,' Annales Archéologiques, VI, 1847, p. 74.

21. Lavedan, P., *Histoire de l'Urbanisme: Antiquité—Moyen Age*. Paris, 1926, pp. 312-13.

22. Tout, op. cit.

23. On Italian towns see, Giovannoni, G. and others, *L'Urbanistica Dall' Antichità ad Oggi*. Florence, 1943.

24. Mumford, L., *The Culture of Cities*. London, 1938, p. 77.

25. Unwin, R., *Town Planning in Practice*. London, 1909, pp. 69-70.

26. Van der Meulen, J. J., and Reijs, W. W., *Nederland vanuit de lucht*, Baarn, 1948, p. 131.

27. Ganshof, op. cit.

28. Cowan, W., and Inglis, H. R. G., 'Early Views of Edinburgh,' S.G.M., 35, 1919, pp. 315-27.

29. Ministry of Town and Country Planning, *The Redevelopment of Central Areas*. London, 1947, pp. 2-3.

30. Langbein, O., 'Grande Vienne,' A. de G., XLVIII, 1939, pp. 513-517.

31. See Bartholomew, H., *Urban Land Uses . . . an Aid to Scientific Zoning Practice*. Cambridge (Mass.), 1932.

32. Colby, C. C., 'Centrifugal and Centripetal Forces in Urban Geography,' A.A.A.G., XXIII, 1933, pp. 1-20.

33. Halbwachs, M., 'Gross Berlin; Grande Agglomeration ou Grande Ville,' A.H.E.S., Vol. 6, 1934, p. 551.

34. Stamp, D. L., 'Replanning London,' G.R., XXXV, 1945, p. 665.

35. Quoted by Dickinson, R. E., *The West European City*. London, 1951, p. 173.

36. Beynon, E. D., 'Budapest: An Ecological Study,' G.R., XXXIII, 1943, pp. 256-75. See also Houghton, J. P., 'The Social Geography of Dublin,' G.R., XXXIX, 1949, pp. 257-77.

37. William-Olsson, W., 'Stockholm: its Structure and Development,' G.R., XXX, 1940, pp. 420-38.

38. De Geer, Sten, 'Greater Stockholm, A Geographical Interpretation,' G.R., XIII, 1923, pp. 497-506.

39. Moscheles, J., 'The Demographic, Social, and Economic Regions of Greater Prague: A Contribution to Urban Geography,' G.R., XXVII, 1937, pp. 414-429.

40. Chambers, W. T., 'Geographic Areas of Cities,' Econ. Geog., 7, 1931, pp. 177-88.

CHAPTER NINE

1. Gilbert, E. W., 'The Industrialization of Oxford,' G.J., CIX, 1947, pp. 1-22.

2. Biermann, G., 'Les Villes de Cure,' C.R.C.I.G., Warsaw, 1934, pp. 212-18.

3. See the account by H. Belloc, *Paris*, London, 1900, also the authoritative history of Paris, M. Poëte's *Une Vie de Cité, Paris de sa naissance à nos jours*, 3 vols., Paris, 1924-31.

4. The density of St. Gervais was 441 persons per acre in 1931.

5. See Target, F., 'The Drainage of Paris,' Proc. Inst. Civil Engineers, III, 1877-8, pp. 257-82, for a study of the development of its sewerage system.

6. Demangeon, A., *France Économique et Humaine*, Paris, 1948, Tome II, p. 785-840.

7. Crone, G. R., 'The Site and Development of Paris,' G.J., XCVIII, 1941, pp. 33-47.

8. Dupuy, P., 'Le Sol et la Croissance de Paris,' A. de G., IX, 1900, p. 340-358.

9. Gallois, P., 'Origin and Growth of Paris,' G.R., 13, 1923, pp. 345-67.

10. Demangeon, op. cit., p. 788.

11. Belloc, op. cit.,

12. Ganshof, F. L., *Étude sur le developpement des villes*, Paris, 1943.

13. Target, op. cit., p. 258.

14. Demangeon, A., *Paris, La ville et sa banlieue*, Paris, 1933.

15. Demangeon, *France Économique*, op. cit., p. 809.

16. George, P., Agulhon, L., Lavandayra, A., Elhai, D., and Schaeffer-Espindola, R., *Études sur la banlieue de Paris*, 1950.

17. See also George, P., *La Ville*, Paris, 1952, pp. 117-146.

18. Houston, J. M., 'Urban Geography of Valencia—the regional development of a Huerta City,' Trans. I.B.G., 15, 1950, pp. 19-35.

19. Primatiu, N., 'D'Arqueologia Excavacions de Valencia,' Anales del Centro de Cultura Valenciana, 1932-33, Vol. II, pp. 8, 9.

20. Jurgens, O., *Spanischen Städte*, Hamburg, 1926, p. 40.
21. Escalapes de Guillo, P., *Resumen Historial . . . de la Ciudad de Valencia*, Valencia, 1805, p. 15.
22. Rodrigo y Pertegas, J., 'La Urbe Valenciana en el siglo, XIV,' III, Congreso de Historia de la Corona de Aragon, 1923, Vol. I, p. 273.
23. Bofarull, edit., *Llivre del Repartiment*.
24. Valentín-Gamazo y García-Noblejas, G., *Plan de Ordenación de Valencia*, Madrid, 1946.
25. West Midland Group, *Conurbation*, London, 1948.
26. Gill, C., *History of Birmingham, Vol. I, Manor and Borough to 1865*, Birmingham, 1952.
27. Wise, M. J., and Johnson, B. L. L., 'The Changing Regional Pattern during the 18th century,' in *Birmingham and its regional setting*, 1950.
28. See Wise, M. J., 'Some Factors Influencing the Growth of Birmingham,' Geog., 33, 1948, p. 185.
29. Wise, M. J., 'On the Evolution of the Gun and Jewellery Quarters in Birmingham,' Trans. I.B.G., Vol. 15, 1950.
30. Gill, op. cit., p. 367.
31. Briggs, A., *History of Birmingham, Vol. II, Borough and City, 1865-1938*, Birmingham, 1952.
32. Bournville Village Trust, *When We Build Again*, Birmingham, 1941.
33. *Conurbation*, op. cit., p. 172.
34. Gilbert, E. W., 'The Growth of Inland and Seaside Health Resorts in England,' S.G.M., 55, 1939, pp. 16-34.
35. Früh, J., *Géographie de la Suisse*, 1939, Tome II, p. 371.
36. Gilbert, E. W., 'The Growth of Brighton,' G.J., CXIV, 1949, p. 34.
37. Ibid., p. 49.
38. Gilbert, 'The Growth of Inland and Seaside Health Resorts,' op. cit., p. 19.
39. Dale, A., *Brighton, its History and Architecture*, London, 1950, p. 57.
40. Sitwell, O., and Barton, M., *Brighton*, London, 1935.
41. See Dale, A., *Fashionable Brighton, 1820-1860*, London, 1947.
42. Gilbert, Brighton, op. cit., p. 51.

CHAPTER TEN

1. Fawcett, C. B., 'Population Maps,' G.J., LXXV, 1935, pp. 142-159.
2. De Geer, Sten, *Karte över Befolkningens Fordelning i Sverige*, Stockholm, 1917.
3. Granö, J. G., *Die Geographischen Gebiete Finnlands*, Helsinki, 1930.
4. Söderlung, A., 'The Population Map of Norway and other Maps,' U.G.I., C.R.C.I.G., Warsaw, 1934, tome 1, pp. 274-8.
5. Tammekann, A., *Outlines of the Distribution of Population in Estonia*, Tartu, 1929.
6. Badley, L., 'Buffon, Precurseur de la science demographique,' A. de G., 38, 1929, pp. 206-20.
7. De Martonne, E., *Recherches sur la Distribution Géographique de la Population en Valachie*, Paris, 1903.
8. Wallis, B. C., '*Distribution of Nationalities in Hungary*,' Geog. Journ., XLVII, 1916, pp. 177-88.
9. Romer, E., *La Population Polonaise dans les Pays Limitrophes Baltiques*, Lwow, 1919, pp. 248-9.
10. Barnes, J. A., and Robinson, A. H., 'A New Method for the Representation of Dispersed Rural Population,' Geog. Review, 30, 1940, pp. 134-7.
11. Kant, E., *Quelques Problèms concernant la représéntation de la densité des habitations rurales, Lund*, 1950.
12. Peattie, R., 'Limits of Mountain Economies,' Geog. Rev., 21, 1931, p. 426.

13. Flückiger, O., *Zeitschrift f. schweiz. Statistik*, 1906.

14. Krebs, N., *Die Ostalpen und das heutige Österreich*, Stuttgart, 1928, 2 vols.

15. Walser, H., *Karte der Hohenregionen der Siedlungen der Schweiz*, Berne, 1918. See also Früh, J., *Geographie de la Suisse*, tome II, pp. 416-27.

16. Allix, A., 'La limite supérieure de l'habitat permanent dans les Alpes,' Rev. de Geog. Alp., XI, 1923, p. 296.

17. Peattie, R., *Mountain Geography*, Cambridge, Mass., 1936.

18. Albix, A., *L'Oisans*, Paris, 1929.

19. Flückiger, op. cit.

20. Früh, op. cit.

21. Garnett, A., *Insolation and Relief*, I.B.G., London, 1937.

22. European Conference on Rural Life, 1939. *Population and Agriculture, with Special Reference to Agricultural Overpopulation*, by C. J. Robertson, p. 18.

23. Anfossi, M. G., 'Recherches sur la distribution de la Population en Corse,' Rev. de Géog. Alpine, VI, 1918, pp. 72-135.

24. Almagia, R., 'La distribuzione della populacione in Sicilia,' Rev. Geog. Ital., XIV, 1907, pp. 1-15. See also Mori, A., Ibid. Rev. Geog. Ital. supplement IV, 1920.

25. Robert, J., 'La Densité de Population des Alpes Françaises,' Rev. Géog. Alpine, VIII, 1920, pp. 5-124, see also Blanchard, R., 'Altitude moyenne des régions naturelles des Alpes Françaises,' Rev. Geog. Alp., VII, 1919, pp. 245-308.

26. Stevens, A., 'The Distribution of Rural Population in Great Britain,' Trans. I.B.G., 1946, pp. 23-53.

27. For discussion on the coefficient of productivity see Moore, W., *Economic Demography of Eastern and Southern Europe*, Geneva, 1945, ch II.

28. George, P., *Introduction à l'Étude Géographique de la Population du Monde*, Paris, 1951, p. 133.

29. Harris, C. D., 'The Ruhr Coal-Mining District,' Geog. Rev., XXXVI, 1946, pp. 194-221.

30. O'Dell, A. C., and Houston, J. M., 'Central Scotland,' in *Studies in Regional Planning*, edit. by G. H. J. Daysh, London, 1949.

31. For a comparable study see Smailes, A. E., 'Population changes in the colliery districts of Northumberland and Durham,' G.J., XCI, 1938, pp. 220-32.

32. Vahl, M., 'The Distribution of the Population of Denmark,' U.G.I., Second Rept. C.T.R.S., 1930.

33. See also Snodgrass, C. P., 'The Density of Agricultural Population in Scotland with English and European Comparisons,' Geog. Journ., XCVII, 1941, pp. 236-45.

34. Houston, J. M., 'Irrigation as a Solution to Agrarian Problems in Spain,' Geog. Journ., CXVI, 1950, pp. 55-63.

35. Almagia, op. cit.

36. Anfossi, op. cit.

37. Houston, Valencia, op. cit., p. 19.

38. Kant, E., 'L'Estonie: Principaux Aspects Géographiques,' A. de G., XLI, 1932, pp. 460-79, also pp. 600-17.

39. Jonasson, O., 'The Relation Between the Distribution of Population and of Cultivated Land in the Scandinavian Countries, Especially Sweden,' Econ. Geog., I, 1925, pp. 107-23.

40. Freeman, T. W., 'The Congested Districts of Western Ireland,' Geog. Rev., XXXIII, 1943, pp. 1-14.

41. Dobby, E. H. G., 'Galicia: a little-known corner of Spain,' Geog. Rev., XXVI, 1936, pp. 555-80.

42. Laûtensach, H., *Portugal, II. Teil: Die portugiesischen Landschaftern*, Peterm. Mitt., 1937.

43. Comitato Nazionale per la Geografia and Istituto Nazionale di Economia Agraria, *Lo Spopolamento Montano in Italia*, 1932-8, 5 vols. See also Toniolo, A. R., 'Studies of Depopulation in the Mountains of Italy,' Geog. Rev., XXVII, 1937, pp. 473-77.

44. See especially, Chardonnet, J., *Géographie Economique de l'Europe Danubienne et de la Pologne*, Paris, 1949. Moore, W., op. cit., Robertson, C. J., *Population and*

Agriculture with Special Reference to Agricultural Overpopulation, European Conference on Rural Life, Geneva, 1939. Warriner, D., *Economics of Peasant Farming*, London, 1939, ch. 3.

45. Bićanić, Rudolf, 'Agricultural Over-Population in Eastern Europe,' Adv. of Sci., 2, 1942, pp. 141-45.

46. Elik, P., 'La densité de la population agricole en Hongrie,' Magyor Stat., Szemle, 1938.

47. See Gorzhowski, S., 'Some Aspects of Rural Poland,' in *Polish Countrysides*, Amer. Geog. Spec. Publ., 20, 1937, pp. 90-113. Jalowiecki, A., 'La question clímographique et l'agriculture en Pologne,' Rev. Intern. Agric., 1938, pp. 370-80.

48. Milojević, B. Z., 'Le peuplement de la région dinarique montagneuse,' Bull. Soc. belge d'Etudes géogr., V, 1935, pp. 124-9.

49. Ogilvie, A. G. 'Population Density in Greece,' G.J., CI, 1943, pp. 250-8.

50. Ancel, J., 'Les Migrations de Peuples dans la Grèce actuelle,' A. de G., XXXIV, 1925, pp. 277-80. See also Schultze, J. H., 'Greek Frontier Colonisation in Thrace and Macedonia,' S.G.M., LIII, 1937, pp. 81-89.

51. Institut National de la Statistique et des Études Economíques, *Les Transfers Internationaux de Populations*, Paris, 1946, p. 24.

52. For definition of term, see Fairchild, H. P., 'Optimum Population,' Proc. World Pop. Conference, London, 1927, pp. 72-85.

INDEX